Comments about

NEPAL'S QUEST FOR HEALTH - 3rd Ed.

1. *Mr. P.N.K. in The Rising Nepal of 7th October, 2005*

The need is not only for the medical students but for medical practitioners in general to get a clear picture of the development of modern medical services in the country. It is an effort that materialised in the form of Nepal's Quest for Health spanning many years. Going through the book, there are ample evidences that a lot of effort and time had been spent by the writer in the course of getting the picture clear. This effort is successful in the sense that the information and data provided add to the understanding of health scenario of the country both past and present together with the projections for the future.

The comprehensible and concise form of the presentation makes the book not only very useful but also handy. There is no doubt that medical students will benefit besides the medical practitioners but the planners too can get something to moot over.

2. *Dr. Arun Neopane in Kathmandu University Medical Journal, Vol 3(3), Issue No. 11*

As a whole the book is extremely well written; the content flows without problem by being well organised. Attention to categorization of ideas is obvious; the writer exhibits a sophisticated control of language and tone. The writing is exceptionally engaging, clear, and focussed.

The book is a 'must read' for all those who want to know about the status of health in Nepal. It would be an effective tool not just for doctors but also for research by other persons, who need reliable information about the health status of Nepal. The book has provided opportune and comprehensive information on the above subject.

3. *Ms Renu Kshetri in The Himalayan Times of 27th November 2005*

Nepal's Quest for Health by Dr. Hemang Dixit, published by the Educational Publishing House is a book meant for all readers who want to know the medical history of the country.

He has mentioned that Development of Health Services – the expansion of the health services both in the government and the private sector is little compared to the increase of the population, which is apt.

4. **Book Information. Nepali Weekly (Nepali) 4th December 2005. Vol. 6. No. 7**

The 3rd edition of the book Nepal's Quest for Health, covering the past and present of Nepal's health services is now available in the market. To say that this book, the result of intensive study will be useful to students and to all interested in the health services will not be an overstatement.

5. **Mr. Atul Mishra in the Kaintipur Daily (Nepali) of 24th December, 2005**

Nepal's Quest for Health covers all past, present and future aspects of health in Nepal.

The population of Nepal is expected to reach five crores in the next three decades. The book whilst laying stress on population control draws attention to developing facilities for other service aspects. To bring about changes, the efforts of the government alone are not enough.

6. **Prof. Pushpa Raj Sharma in Journal of the Institute of Medicine, Vol. 27, Issue 3, 2005**

The third edition of the book which originally came with the title of "Quest for Health" is probably the most widely readable book on Nepal's health development. The beauty of this book is the author's personal experience as a service provider, health educator and health administrator. ......I will end by writing: this is the book which should be owned by every health worker.

7. **Prof. Damber B. Karki in The Himalayan Health, Vol. 6, Issue 23**

Prof. Dixit deserves high appreciation for producing such a useful book not only for medical personnel but also for all those interested to know about the health related national events of the past.

8. **Prof. Ramesh Kant Adhikari in Journal of the Nepal Medical Association, Oct – Dec. 2005, Vol. 44**

The latest volume of "Quest for Health" has appeared with a revised title "Nepal's Quest for Health" and the author's reason for this revision in the title is that the previous title was "too vague and broad". The assumption of the title is that the type of health services available to the people determines the health as the book has exclusively dealt with the health services, health policies and plans and development of human resources for health in Nepal.

.........., this book is a "must read" for anybody who is interested in the development of health services, health status and its determinants in Nepal. I am certain that the students of health sciences, practitioners of health services, researchers, health administrators and policy makers will find this book very useful in their day-to-day work.

NEPAL'S QUEST FOR HEALTH

(The Health Services of Nepal)

Dr. Hemang Dixit

MBBS (U. Lond), LRCP (Lond), MRCS (Eng), DTM&H (Lond), DCH (Lond)

Professor in Paediatrics and Head, Department of Medical Education

Kathmandu Medical College

Educational Publishing House

Kathmandu, Nepal

Published by:
Educational Publishing House
P.O. Box: 5178
Jamal, Kathmandu, Nepal
Tel: 4241255

First Edition - 1995
Second Edition - 1998
Reprinted - 2000
Third Edition - 2005, as Nepal's Quest for Health
Reprinted - 2009
Fourth Edition - 2014 (Revised & Updated)

Price: Rs. 425.00

Printed at:
Modern Printing Press
Kantipath, Kathmandu, Nepal.
Tel: 4253195

ISBN: 978-9937-551-57-1

PREFACE

The last edition of this book which appeared as Nepal's Quest for Health, some eight years ago, attempted to give a concise account of the health services of Nepal. There have been over the course of the last twenty years, following the formulation of the National Health Policy in 1991, a large number of changes in the health sector. The guidelines of a New National Policy on Health, in the context of the constitution guaranteed Health Rights for the people have been brought out. About three years ago, my publisher had broached the subject of bringing out a new edition of this book. I hesitated then and remember stating that our country was going through a state of reorganisation of the state apparatus and whatever was brought out would be soon out of date. There are various opinions on the number of provinces and districts. This has not been finalised yet and what the final form will be is anyone's guess. The stance of the parties taking part in mid-November 2013 elections shows no clear cut opinions nor decisions. On consultation with my publisher I have now tried to update this book although there will be some changes in the administrative responsibilities in future years.

The health coverage has increased, mainly because of the increase in the number of care providers and the greater number of health care institutions. This is mostly due to the vast participation of the private sector in the form of Medical Colleges or Nursing Homes. There are also numerous privately run hospitals. Last but not least are the various community hospitals and other health institutions developed on the initiative of the community in various parts of the country. The mushrooming of the Community Hospitals, like the "Nursing Homes / Hospitals and Research Centres" of the past is mainly due for availing of the maximum facilities and tax rebates from the government. No wonder that these institutions come and close down on a regular basis. This is the private / public mix at work in the health sector and there are indications that all this is for the good. Thus whilst there is general despondency all around, there have been quiet changes in the health sector. There is enough ground for optimism. What must be noted is that a number of political changes have occurred during this period. As from 18th May 2006 all references to 'HMGN' have been replaced by the 'Government of Nepal' (GON). This is the form of reference now. It must also be noted that all relevant legislation will have to be revised, updated and enacted. A start was made with the Health Act.

Coming back to reality however, one sees at the end of 2013 that even district hospitals in various parts of the country do not have the appointed number of personnel on duty. This is in spite of the fact that a number of doctors who had received medical education on government scholarships have started manning hospitals out in the districts. The shortage of staff or more correctly, the absence of those that have been posted to different parts of the country seems to be an almost permanent or endemic feature of our health services!

I would like to thank Mr. Mahendra B Shah of BNMT for drawing my attention to the fact that Health Service Governance, based on the Local - Self Governance Act - 2055 BS (LSGA-1999) was lacking in this book. I have tried to correct that. I would like to thank Prof. Indur Dudani, Prof. Dr. Ramesh Adhikari and Dr. Bhim Acharya for suggestions and also for giving time to answer my queries. I would also like to thank Sanjay Mani Dixit, Bishop Joshi and Nirmal Bista also for helping me to collect information although my task this time has been made easier because of the websites of various organisations. I feel that more improvements can still be made in this book. The website: www.moh.gov.np of the Ministry of Health and Population, which has still been referred in this book as MoH is a case in point. As far as this edition is concerned I would like to thank Prof. Ishwar B Shrestha who has helped me immensely in the course of bringing out all the editions of this book. The suggestions and the work that he has put in to bring out this new revised and updated one has gone beyond that and has been tremendous. Though I have tried my best in this regard and have revised the book, there are still, I feel a lot of lacunae. One example of this would be particulars of the private nursing homes and hospitals that are mentioned in Chapter 6. Any reader who feels that certain information should be included should send the same to me by e-mail as given below and I will try to oblige. This will help me to make quick corrections.

E- mail: h2dixit@gmail.com; h2dixit@hotmail.com

Website: http://www.hdixit.org.np

Dr. Hemang Dixit

1st March 2014.

Introduction to the Second Edition

"Only a fool learns from experience, the trick is to learn from the experience of others."

Bismarck.

The idea of writing this book has been with me for a number of years. Its start may be said to have been as far back as 1965 when together with my father, the late Dr. Siddhimani, I did manage a history of sorts of modern medicine in Nepal. Subsequently during the following years I updated the information on two occasions, first in 1974 and then in 1987. The first edition of this book, printed in 1995, was an attempt to recount the development or otherwise of medicine over the years. It was also an effort to try to forecast what may happen in the years to come, at least till the year 2000 AD.

After the starting of the MBBS course in Nepal in 1978 it was very imperative that a concise and comprehensive work be prepared for the sake of the medical students of this country so that they would be aware of the medical conditions of the past, the existing health services and the contemplated health services for the future. Following the establishment of a half dozen more medical colleges it became more urgent to bring out such a work.

Some of the initial research for this work was done during the time that I visited the India Office Library, at London in 1981. Later work was done at Kathmandu during 1994 when I took sabbatical leave for this purpose. My thanks are to many people who have encouraged and helped me in this work over the course of many years. However whilst acknowledging their help I must state that any mistakes that exist are due to my misunderstanding or wrong interpretation. My personal feeling that this book has some shortcomings and is thus incomplete. There is also a certain amount of repetition, which was unavoidable because of the necessity of making that particular aspect of health discussion clear without having to refer back to other parts of the book. My intention being to make this book more comprehensive, correct and up-to-date, I will be grateful for any corrections and suggestions to be sent to me at the under mentioned address. To make the flow and understanding easier, a list of acronyms plus operational definitions of service centres and personnel has been included at the very start. In the matter of dates the references to Bikram Sambat, when used, are denoted by BS.

Feb 1, 1999
18th Magh, 2055 BS

Dr. Hemang Dixit,
GPO Box 2730,
Kathmandu

CONTENTS

ABBREVIATIONS & ACRONYMS

AIIMS	All India Institute of Medical Sciences
AMS	Aide Medicals et Sanitaire
BMHN	Basic Minimum Health Needs
BPKIHS	BP Koirala Institute of Health Sciences
CBS	Central Bureau of Statistics
CDO	Chief District Officer
CDPS	Central Department of Population Studies
CHL	Community Health Leader
CHRP	Country Health Resources & Priorities
CHV	Community Health Volunteer
CIDA	Canadian International Development Agency
CPR	Contraceptive Prevalence Rate
CTEVT	Council for Technical Education & Vocational Training
DDA	Department of Drug Administration
DDC	District Development Committee
DHO	District Health Office
DHS	Department of Health Services
DPHO	District Public Health Office
EDP	External Development Partner
EHCS	Essential Health Care Services
FCHV	Female Community Health Volunteer
FP/MCH	Family Planning/Maternal Child Health
FPAN	Family Planning Association of Nepal
GDP	Gross Domestic Product
GNP	Gross National Product
GENETUP	German Nepal Tuberculosis Project
GoN	Government of Nepal
HFA 2000	Health For All by year 2000
HRH	Human Resources for Health
HSS	Health Sector Strategy

IBHS	Integrated Basic Health Services
ICHP	Integrated Community Health Programme
ICHSDP	Integrated Community Health Services Development Project
IEC	Information, Education & Communication
INF	International Nepal Fellowship
INGO	International Non-Governmental Organisation
IPPF	International Planned Parenthood Federation
JICA	Japan International Cooperation Agency
JIPMER	Jawaharlal Institute of Postgraduate Medical Education & Research
JNSP	Joint Nutrition Support Programme
KU	Kathmandu University
LMP	Licensed Medical Practitioner
LMS	Licentiate in Medicine & Surgery
LTHP	Long Term Health Plan
MBHN	Minimum Basic Health Needs
MCHW	Maternal & Child Health Worker
MDG	Millennium Development Goals
MDT	Multiple Drug Therapy
MIS	Management Information System
MoEC	Ministry of Education & Culture
MoF	Ministry of Finance
MoHP	Ministry of Health & Population
NDAC	National Development Action Committee
NDC	National Development Council
NEB	Nepal Evangelical Board
NEFAS	Nepal Foundation for Advanced Studies
NESP	New Education Systems Plan
NHSP	National Health Sector Programme
NMC	Nepal Medical Council
NMEO	Nepal Malaria Eradication Organisation
NPC	National Planning Commission
NTP	Nepal Tuberculosis Programme
PBHW	Panchayat Based Health Worker
PFAD	Planning & Foreign Aid Division
PPFA&MD	Policy, Planning, Foreign Aid & Monitoring Division
PPM&SD	Policy, Planning, Monitoring & Supervision Division

RHSD	Regional Health Services Directorate
RTC	Regional Training Centre
SAARC	South Asia Association for Regional Co-operation
SATA	Swiss Association for Technical Assistance
SCC	Short Course Chemotherapy
SSNCC	Social Services National Coordination Council
SWAp	Sector Wide Approach
SWC	Social Welfare Council
TA/DA	Travel Allowance/Daily Allowance
TB	Tuberculosis
TBA	Traditional Birth Attendant
TBCP	Tuberculosis Control Project
TEAM	The Evangelical Alliance Mission
TFR	Total Fertility Rate
TUTH	Tribhuvan University Teaching Hospital
U5MR	Under Five Mortality Rate
VDC	Village Development Committee
VP	Village Panchayat
VHW	Village Health Worker

Operational Definitions of some terms used

AHW Programme - A programme for auxiliary health workers. Initially a 2 year programme with students who had done eight years of schooling it was subsequently changed. The new programme after ten years of schooling did a one year course and was designated as a Community Medicine Auxiliary (CMA), a basic level Auxiliary Health Worker (AHW).

Alma-Ata - Capital of the former Soviet republic of Kazakhstan where the WHO international conference on Primary Health Care was held. Now renamed Almaty.

Anchal - A zone. There are fourteen such in the country.

ANM Programme - A programme for auxiliary nurse midwife, a basic level health worker. This programme was previously run by the IoM but is now run by the CTEVT.

Aushadhalaya - Dispensaries for the selling or distribution of traditional or ayurvedic medicine.

Awal - Local term for malaria.

Baidya / Vaidya - Local term for a practitioner of the ayurvedic system of medicine.

BS - Stands for Bikram Sambat, an era started by King Vikramaditya. This started 57 years before the Gregorian Calendar. Whilst most of the dates are given as per the Gregorian Calendar the denotation of **AD** has not been written down in all such instances. Nepali months start from Baishakh which lies between mid Apr-mid May and the last month is Chaitra which is mid-March to mid April.

Dharmashala - A lodging house, generally established by social organisations or individuals, where such facilities are provided free or at very nominal prices for travellers or visitors to the place.

Dressers - Term used for those health workers whose job was to "dress" wounds. Term originated from the days of the British in India when, local personnel were used to help in the running of health care posts.

Health Assistant - A category of middle level health worker who is in charge of the health post.

Health Centre - A health institution in-charge of a doctor which over the course of years was due to be done away with. The aim was to either upgrade these into hospitals or downgrade them into health posts.

Health Posts - There are supposed to be nine or one in each ward or ilaka of the district. There will be a total of 675 or 9 in each of the 75 districts of the kingdom.

Ilaka - In the process of administration during the Panchayat days each of the 75 districts of the country was divided into ilakas or wards.

Janch Bujh Kendra - Literally "Investigation Centre" or office. This authority was had been specially established and had the authority to look into and investigate complaints against government offices.

Kaviraj - Local term for a category of ayurvedic practitioner.

Lac (kh) - A number equivalent to 100,000. 10 lacs = 1 million.

Lal Mohur- Red seal, signifying the fact that the Act, passed or proposed has been given the seal of approval by the reigning monarch or the de facto ruler.

Panchayat Days - The time (Dec. 1960 - April 1990) when the country was ruled with the concept of a Panchayat system of government.

Primary Health Care Centre - A health institution with a medical officer and with three beds as inpatient facilities, in each electoral constituency. There are 240 electoral constitutes.

Seimei-kyo - One Meishusama started the origin of jorei or 'soul cleansing' in Japan. One Bhikshu Sumangal who had previously been to Japan to study this method of healing started this in Nepal in 1979. The diseased are said to be cured by rays with healing powers emanating from the palm of the healer.

Shumsher - Jung Bahadur together with his brothers Bam Bahadur and Ranoddip Singh were the first three of the Rana prime ministers. Bir Shumsher and the subsequent prime ministers, also added "Shumsher" as a common name preceding their Rana surname. Hence some prime ministers have been referred to as Shumsher in historical records and thus also in this book.

Singha Durbar - Literally "Lion Palace" or the former official residence of the Rana prime minister. After the political changes of 1951 it became the Government secretariat or the seat of the government.

Unani - This is the "Greco-Arab" medicine based on the four-humour theory of Hippocrates but developed further by the Arab world. It assesses the patient's needs in terms of temperature and taking into consideration the body's natural powers of self preservation and adjustment, it aims to maintain a proper balance between the body and spiritual functions.

VDC - Village Development Community, the lowest level of administrative unit. There are about 4,000 VDCs.

1.

MEDICINE IN THE BEGINNING

The history of medicine in Nepal may be considered to be fairly long. From the *Ramayana* one learns that Hanuman[1] was told to bring the *Sanjeebini*[2] from the mountains in the Himalayas. Without arguing whether the actual mountain transported to Lanka was from India or Nepal one can say that many herbal medicines were in use then in these lands. The fact is that most of the medicinal plants used in Sri Lanka are similar to the ones used in India and for that matter in Nepal. Perhaps it is this sameness which "may have given rise to the popular legend that certain forested hills, (of Sri Lanka) e.g. Doluwakanda and Rumassalankanda, from which drug plants are often collected, are only fragments of a part of the Himalayas that was carried over to Ceylon by the mythical monkey-king Hanuman, to provide drugs for the wounded in the Rama-Ravana battle." (1) It is these same magical herbs with their healing properties, which sustained the people of Nepal in the past.

Lord Buddha (563-477 BC) is said to have attended regularly to all the sick disciples in his camps. His teachings which said "to be born is to suffer, to die is to suffer, and to fall sick is to suffer" motivated his followers to look after the sick. Buddhist hospitals in India existed before the invasion of Alexander the Great. "It is to Gautama and his followers that we owe, apparently the hospital idea." (2) The same authority states "Lord Buddha in his day enunciated the *vinaya* or disciplinary rules for the monks. These rules touched all aspects of their life and included guidelines on healthy living." (1) Buddha laid down five essential qualities that a person

1. The Monkey God who in mythology is said to have carried Sanjeebini the magic cure from the Himalayas to Sri Lanka where a war was being fought between Ram and Ravana. As Hanuman could not identify the herb, he is depicted in the illustrations as carrying a whole hill on his palm.

2. The magical herbal cure for all ills.

attending to the sick, should :

i. be able to prescribe,
ii. know what is good from what is not good for the patient,
iii. attend to the sick out of love and not greed,
iv. not revolt at removing excreta, saliva or vomit,
v. administer religious consolation to the patient from time to time. (3)

One of Buddha's disciples, King Ashok is credited to having established charitable hospitals for both men and animals (4).

It is the Ayurved, or "the science of life" system of medicine that is found in this part of the world. A WHO publication (5) has described it as one of the oldest formulated system of medicine, based on doctrines which takes into account the physical, chemical, biological and spiritual dimensions of life. Its various faculties include internal medicine, paediatrics, psychosocial medicine, otorhinolaryngology, ophthalmology, surgery, toxicology, geriatrics and eugenics.

It has been recorded that *Arogyashala* or ayurvedic hospital existed in Nepal during the reign of Amshu Verma (605-620 AD) of the Lichchhavi period (6). These facilities were extended in the reigns of subsequent rulers.

Mention of these health institutions is not found again till the time of Pratap Malla (1641-1674 AD) who established an ayurvedic dispensary in the Hanuman Dhoka Complex, which then was the residence of the ruler. It is believed that the Singha Durbar Vaidyakhana[3] was established during this period. (Ibid)

Nepal being a multi-ethnic society, it is no surprise that the various groups have their own concepts of disease, various methods of warding it off and also for dealing with illnesses.

As is done all over the world, the Nepalese too pray to various deities for protection, not only at times of stress but for comfort and well being in future years. There are even specific deities to whom special offerings and prayers can be made. Thus in the valley, or in the greater Kathmandu area, there are specific temples where worship can be done for a particular purpose.

3. A place where ayurvedic medicines are made and sold.

Sital Mai	In the Pashupati area to protect against smallpox.
Kandeutathan	At Kupondole for ear ailments.
Bhatbhatini	For children when frightened by spirits.
Way Sya Dyo	At Bangemuda for toothache.
Swayambu Ajima Sarati Maya	For wellbeing of children.
Santaneswar Mahadev	For infertility.
Gyaneshwar Mahadev	For infertility.
Kumbeshwar	The Water Pot God of Lalitpur has an accompanying *Naag* and the spring water coming out is said to cure several skin diseases including leprosy.

There are also existing in Nepal the various forms of traditional healing by such practitioners of the art such as *Dhamis, Jhankris, and Jharphuks*. Accepting the fact that *dhami-jhankris* exert a lot of influence regarding health matters, some research work has been done in using them for health education, family planning and treatment of diarrhoeal diseases.

Prof. Macdonald in the introduction that he has written for CJ Miller's book (7) states, "the *jhankri* is a caste and social free-wheeler. ...the *jhankri* is, to some extent, prior to the official arrival of Hinduism, the creator and the maintainer of certain forms of religious centralisation in the Nepalese hills."

Lediard, co-author of another work goes on to state in the introduction, "the specialists who can best care for Nepal's major ailment are those who are administering daily to most of the health needs in the village: the faith healers - the *dhamis* and *jhankris* of Nepal." (8) Other investigators have mentioned traditional healers such as *amchis* who have the background of Tibetan medicine and bring in concepts of the body becoming hot or cold as a result of eating hot or cold food. In the same system of medicine other practitioners such as *lamas* gave the concept of *lu,* said to be inhabiting watercourses and when offended then leading on to afflictions such as skin eruptions or even insanity. This investigator felt that modern medicine rather than displacing the traditional healing practices tended instead to be integrated in into a network thus creating a pluralistic form of health care being practised in the country (9). Clifford states that 'the medicines practised by the *amchi* emphasises the relationship of the mind to the body, which is seen as a whole, and the body to the universe' (10).

Though Judith Justice mentions also *jharnes* and *fuknes* she found in her investigations that the ill generally "waited in the house to get well." The next recourse was to use herbal and dietary remedies (11). Lediard and Shrestha estimated in 1978/79 that there were then between four to eight hundred thousand faith healers in rural Nepal. This by all accounts is a fantastic statement and is perhaps dependent on what is one's definition for the term. Other workers have quoted this and whilst looking at the types of practices conducted in and around Kathmandu, have noted interesting points. There are what the authors have termed as "popular healers" and one criterion for their classification was that patients had to wait a long time to see them! The brief consultation, routine and quick treatment by an unknown practitioner in a new locality were the other features (12). These "popular healers" could be a *jhankri* or spirit-medium, a *tantrik* or healer practising tantrism or even a *deuta* i.e. healer possessed by a mother goddess. This investigator Skultans commented on the fact that some of these traditional healers made, "somewhat eccentric use of a stethoscope" in their practices.

The Nepalese in the rural areas first seek treatment from the system/ form near at hand. Shrestha in listing these, stated that the Sherpas of the Everest region usually applied the paste from the *Sharma guru,* whilst the Jyapoos of Kathmandu valley used a preparation from the *Ghod Tapre* to heal their cuts and wounds (13). In the first instance this means the use of herbs by the herbalists. This has existed since time immemorial and traditional healers such as *dhamis* and *jhankris* also use plants as their means of cure. Then there are the other healers such as *gubaju, jhar phuke* and *sudeni*. Besides the ones enumerated above, there are also the ayurvedic practitioners and of late, the Tibetan medicine men referred to as *amchis*.

C.J. Miller SJ did research on the *jhankris* of Dolakha and in the introduction to his book feels that the role of this traditional healer is complementary to both priest and doctor (7). He goes on to write, "I believe that a closer look would reveal to him (doctor) that, at least according to the world-view of his villager patients, he the doctor is treating symptoms while the *jhankri* is getting at causes. There is room, and need, for both. The doctor will certainly realise that a shared world-view between patient and physician can be a powerful factor leading to a cure; he should also realise that his modern medical education, based on a secular view of the world, has deprived him of this advantage which the *jhankri* continues to possess."

The practitioners of the different traditional systems of medicines being practised in Nepal can be called the "barefoot doctors" of the country. With the increase in education, new knowledge and technology it is time for new research in these areas.

INTRODUCTION TO MODERN WESTERN MEDICINE

One is prompted to presume, with some confidence, that the Western system of medicine has been practised from about 1740 AD (1797 BS). Records show that one de Recanti had received permission from Raja Ranjit Malla to preach, teach and convert to their religion, the people "without violence and of a free will". Raja Jayaprakash of Kathmandu also issued a *sanad*[4] in 1742 AD and renewed it in 1754 AD allowing the missionaries to enter Kathmandu.

One of the earliest visitors to Nepal was Father Greuber, an Austrian Capuchin monk who on his return journey from China to Europe, passed through Nepal. In 1624 both he and a Father Dorville met Pratap Malla at Kantipur and were allowed by the king to preach and teach plus also to run health and education services in Kathmandu. Around this period various other Fathers of the religious order were expelled from Tibet and consequently they all came and congregated in Kathmandu. (6).

Grueber must have been greatly disturbed by what he saw for he went on to write:

"There is another custom in this country of monstrous cruelty. If a sick man is near to death and no further hope of his living is entertained, they take him outside away from his house into the fields, and there throw him into a ditch already full of dying men. He there remains exposed to the inclemencies of the weather, without consolations of religion nor pity they leave him to die; afterwards his corpse is given to birds of prey, wolves, dogs, and other similar beasts to eat. They are convinced that the only monument of a glorious death is to find a resting place in the belly of living animals (14)."

4. Edict / Royal directive.

Whilst Nepal's quest for health has been going on for a long time, the first reference to the modern system of medicine or to their practitioners in this country occurs in an account of the siege of Kirtipur by King Prithvi Narayan Shah in 1766/67. Chaudhari (15) mentions that it was Swarup Ratna, the King's brother, who had been cured of a wound by one Michael Angelo, a Capuchin monk. Other sources identify the one wounded as Prince Pratap Shah of Gorkha. Landon too, mentions this and states that the health care provider was Michelangelo of Tabiago.

Later however, following the conquest of the Kathmandu Valley by King Prithvi Narayan Shah, the Capuchin fathers withdrew in 1770 from the valley and proceeded to the mission home in Bettiah. The missionaries were perhaps prompted to take this step because of the atmosphere then in existence. It is aptly summed by a saying then current in Nepal, viz. *"With the Bible comes the Bayonet, and with the Missionaries comes the Musket".* However the missionaries were supposed to have returned to Kathmandu at the request of King Pratap Singh Malla when he suffered from and ultimately died from smallpox in 1777 (6). Thus ended the first chapter of the Western or modern system of medicine in Nepal. The practice of this form of medicine by the missionaries was not to be resumed till the 20th Century.

The first reference to diseases occurs in the account of Father Georgian Estonian, a monk who passed by Makwanpur in the middle of the 18th Century. He had noted the dangers of *awal* or malaria and says that windows must be closed at night, and that the only chance of escaping the curse is to climb high enough upon the mountains to avoid the miasma that bathed their feet. He writes, however, that whatever precautions are taken and however quickly a man may seek a kindlier climate, he often carries with him the seeds of the *awal*, which will not fail to attack him at a later date. Kirkpatrick, who toured Nepal in 1793 and has written an account, has stated that "*owl*" or malaria, as we know it, was present in the lowest valleys and the Terai. The prevalence of this disease is also confirmed by the fact that no less a person than the Senior Queen died in 1841 from malaria contracted in the Terai. Kirkpatrick had also noted the presence of "guttural tumours" (? goitre) being present at Deopatan and Kaurigaon, within a few miles of Kathmandu. This tumour, he mentions was thought by the natives to be "produced by a certain insect generated in the water usually drunk by the inhabitants of goitrous places" (16).

The first medical doctor of the modern system of medicine to set foot in Nepal was Francis Buchanan (later called Hamilton) who had come with Captain W.D. Knox, the East India Company's 1st Resident, as the Mission's first doctor in 1802. (17)

The next reference to disease in Nepal occurs in the Papers of Brian Hodgson (18), published in 1857 (1914 BS). He mentions that the epidemics of the plains hardly ever reached the Himalayas. He instances the case of cholera, which though prevalent in India most of the time, had only occurred twice in Nepal. Hodgson goes on to mention that the Terai region of Nepal was notorious as a malarious region.

After this, the next reference to the modern system of medicine in Nepal occurs in Dr. H.A. Oldfield's book "Sketches in Nipal" (19). Dr. Oldfield had initially served as a surgeon in the Bengal Army and was transferred to the British Residence in 1850. He stayed in Nepal till 1863 and as his duties were mainly medical, he gives some accounts of diseases seen in Kathmandu, and the treatments practised. He mentions that parts of Kathmandu were dirty and because of the common custom of throwing garbage in the central courtyard, it was likely for one to get various fevers and diseases:

"There is an utter absence in all the cities of any system of drainage; nearly stagnant gutters on each side of the street, running immediately below the house-fronts, do the duty of sewers, and into them most of the filth and refuse of the adjacent buildings find their way."

Oldfield was allowed to go to different parts of the country. He not only wrote of what he saw, but also pencilled drawings of various places. The doctor states that the air and water of Kirtipore was very healthy and pure and that goitre was not seen in the inhabitants of Kirtipore.

Writing about malaria, he states, "The Nipalese profess that *awal* sets in Nayakot at the same time as it does in the Terai, viz 15th March. It probably commences about a month later. The great festival in honour of Devi at Devi Ghat does not take place till the middle of April (beginning of Baisakh), and at it thousands of persons from Nipal are always present with impunity. The Nipalese account for this by saying that through the intervention of the deity, the *awal* is "suspended" to all who go to worship her during the time the festival lasts. But that it sets in again as soon as the festival is over.'....." They say that the day after the festival closes the goddess lets out the spirit of the savage and destroying monarch of the forest, who disguised as the "*awal*" fever seizes and feeds upon all those whom he finds trespassing upon his domain, the jungles."

Oldfield had noted too that some tribes of Nuwakot, such as Darris, Kumhals, Manjhis, Bramus and Denwar, enjoyed some sort of immunity and did not suffer from malaria. This finding of Dr. Oldfield is confirmed by Sir Richard Temple (20) who in the account of his tour through Nepal in May 1876, states, "The feverish jungles of the Terai again, are inhabited in Nepal, as elsewhere by the primitive tribes, called there generically as Awalias whose position is peculiar, in that they dwell with impunity in places where the terrible Awal or malarial fever is sure to destroy the rest of their kind and that quickly."

Oldfield in his journals gave other information about Nepal. His estimate of the population of the country was four millions or an average of about 66 inhabitants per square mile. The valley was sparsely populated too, having barely a quarter of a million people but still the conditions of living were terrible as has already been stated.

As the Residency doctor acted as a family physician to Maharaja Jung Bahadur, Dr. Oldfield was required to make weekly visits to Thapathali Durbar. The first reference to these visits is in 1850. Jung Bahadur was apparently a great believer in vaccination and had the children of the Royal Household, his nephews and nieces and all his own children vaccinated. When Jung Bahadur was in England, Oldfield vaccinated his eldest boy in 1850 and received for his services the sum of Rs. 500. Oldfield also gives an account of the vaccination of the Mahila Sahib's (king's brother's) daughter in 1851 (1908 BS).

Though Jung Bahadur accepted being treated as per the modern system of medicine he did not forsake the use of traditional remedies. This is confirmed by Jung Bahadur's action in 1850 when he took along Kaviraj Chakrapani Vaidya as his personal physician during his visit to England. Jung's feeling was that it was an opportunity for him to learn. He came back with new ideas, one of which was to sell opium to the Chinese and make quick money. He had seen the trade of the British viz. opium for teas and silks from China (21). However his visions of a shrewd investment and quick returns for his money did not succeed as he had hoped.

In November 1851 Oldfield mentions his being summoned to see the youngest wife of Bam Bahadur, who happened to be the younger brother of Jung Bahadur. She had recently given birth to a child, but her own condition was serious. Jung Bahadur wanted Oldfield to treat her but the patient felt that she would much rather die than allow an European to see and treat her. She died 8 days later.

Dr. Oldfield is the first author to mention about a hospital in Nepal. He states that an enclosure for deer, built by Jung Bahadur in 1852 AD, was very near the Residency.

In November 1852 on one of these weekly visits, Dr. Oldfield was asked to see a "lady of rank", who later turned out to be Jung Bahadur's sister. She was married to the Raja of Jumla and had been ill for eight months. She had lost weight, and had a bad cough with lots of expectoration. After examining her, Dr. Oldfield felt that she was a case of consumption in a poor state of health and that she was a hopeless case. Oldfield told Jung Bahadur the bad prognosis and was advised by the latter not to treat her, lest the blame fall on him. She died four months later of this tubercular infection.

In August 1854, Dr. Oldfield lanced an abscess on one of Jung Bahadur's wives — a daughter of the ex-Raja of Coorg, a principality in India. Jung Bahadur apparently had great faith in European surgical skill but as far as medical cases were concerned, he told Oldfield that the Nepalese doctors (baidyas) understood this treatment much better than the Europeans. That he patronised ayurvedic medicine is proved by the fact that the *Vaidyakhana*[5] set up at Hanuman Dhoka during Malla times was shifted to Thapathali (22).

Oldfield records the excision of a small fatty tumour on a man's neck by Jung Bahadur. On various other occasions he also gave treatment for slight injuries. Jung Bahadur's enthusiasm to do surgery probably started after his visit to England and France. During his visit to England, Jung Bahadur had been taken to Edinburgh to see the castle, Holyrood Palace, the University and the College of Surgeons (23). Jung Bahadur probably brought along some surgical instruments for we come across a statement by Oldfield to the effect, "I have found it exceedingly convenient to be able to borrow some of his instruments when our hospital was deficient in them (19)."

5. A place where ayurvedic medicines are made and sold.

Writing about another occasion in 1854 when he treated a wife of Jung Bahadur, Oldfield states, "I opened a large abscess on her right side, much to Jang's delight and the astonishment of his own two native doctors, who were present. On her being a little faint, I told them to give her a little water; while she drank it, I had to stand looking into the court so that my feet might not touch the drugget, or any part of the furniture directly or indirectly connected with her bed, although two minutes before there was no objection to my feeling her pulse, and etc examining and lancing her side – a regular case of swallowing the camel and straining at the gnat." Such an attitude was usual not only in those days but even up to the middle of the twentieth century as it was based on the caste system and foreigners were after all *malekshas*[6] !

Jung Bahadur apparently dispensed medicines too, for Oldfield writes, "He has a sort of laboratory in his garden where he prepares constantly a large quantity of a particular sort of medicine in which he has great faith. Its composition is a profound secret; he says it contains the precious metals, even diamonds and pearls. He considers it very valuable, and, I suspect derives a profitable trade by selling it in small quantities to his brethren and family and others when sick. As a compliment to him, and to please him, they will willingly take it, and pay well for it too, whatever faith they may have in its real efficacy."

From various sources, Landon (24) also confirms this, for writing about Jang Bahadur, he states, and "He had an inveterate liking for medical treatment. The medicines he used were Nepalese, not European, but he occasionally called in the professional services of Dr. Wright".

During the time that he was in power Jung Bahadur tried to dissuade the people from practising *sati*[7] or the burning of widows on the funeral pyre of their dead husband. Oldfield records this as, "He says, and probably truly, that when the common people get accustomed to see that men of rank die and their bodies are burnt without *sati*, they will of their own accord, gradually give up such an inhuman and unreasonable practice." Ironically however, two or three of Jang Bahadur's wives insisted and commited *sati*.

---

6. Usual term for foreigners from across the seas.
7. The act by which a living wife burnt herself on the funeral pyre of her dead husband as per the prevailing custom.

It also needs to be noted that the first health institution to be set locally by Nepali authorities was the Khokna Leprosy Asylum in 1857. It must be noted that it functioned more as a detention centre for those with leprosy rather than one for providing treatment (25).

At this time, just before and during the 1857 uprisings in India, considerable correspondence seems to have taken place between the officials at Fort William in India to Major Ramsey, Resident at Nepal (26).

Thus one sees that there has been some influence of British military medicine on the medical system that developed in Nepal.

Following Jung Bahadur's death in 1877 one finds a certain amount of scarcity regarding medical information. During 1883 (1940 BS), the army Commander-in-Chief Dhir Shumsher was unwell. One Bengali doctor Adar Nath treated him. However during the time that this treatment was being followed, a course of treatment by one Raj Baidya accompanied it. This consisted of *mantra,* which was to be pressed on different parts of the body wherever there was pain. Similarly the mantra written paper was to be waved over the painful part. Needless to say, after a little while the pain lessened over that area but passed to a different site. In course of time the pain shifted to the neck. Doctors said that a fish bone was lodged there, and the mantras did not afford relief. Ultimately Dhir Shumsher died.

The following year 1884 we find Dr. Adar Nath treating the then General Bhim Shumsher, successfully for colic. However Dr. Adar Nath must have had some difficulty practising medicine for we find that lay treatment for testicular swelling at that time was to wear scrotal support of tobacco leaves. How it worked was not known but its side effects, which appeared within half an hour, included bouts of dizziness and vomiting.

In 1886 (1943 BS) there is reference to vaccination of children by Raj Baidya. At that time they were probably vaccinated with non-attenuated strains and we find references stating that death occurred following vaccination in children.

Whilst gathering material it is interesting to note that Jai Prithivi Bahadur Singh of Bajhang had the foresight to establish in the early years of the 20th Century the Satyvadi School, an iron industry and a dispensary. This "Khaga dispensary" had doctors on deputation from Calcutta Medical College, working there (27).

In conclusion it may be noted that the military doctors posted at the British Residency at Kathmandu have contributed much to our knowledge by their writings which they generally published on their return to the home country. (15). They were:

a. Dr. Francis Buchanan (later Hamilton) in 1801 and 1819.
b. Dr. A Cambess regarding the earthquake of 1833.
c. Dr. Henry A Oldfield, Surgeon in Nepal from 1850-1863.
d. Dr. Daniel Wright - Surgeon Major in Nepal from 1863-1877.
e. Dr. GHD Gimlette – Surgeon from 1883-1888.

HEALTH CARE DEVELOPMENT DURING THE RANA DAYS

From the time of Jung Bahadur, the country was dependent on the largesse of the rulers and what the commoners got was what the defacto rulers, the prime ministers felt should be given. As soon as a new Rana became prime minister, he with all the trappings of power, had to start thinking immediately of his next step so that history would remember him for his good deeds.

Health facilities during the rule of the Ranas were instituted as a form of charity for the poor. The range of services was limited and very much dependent on the finances at hand. This finance in turn was from the income of the land, which had been set aside as *guthi*[8]. The sum, so identified was very nominal and over the years its actual value decreased relatively. Over the course of years coupled with the non-payment of the actual dues by the people utilising the land, the process of financing the *guthi* became more complex.

Bir Shumsher, after he became Prime Minister in 1885 (1942 BS), was the first person to think of building and providing other supporting logistics in terms of a health institution. He probably felt that the small hospital established within the British Residency compound would no longer be able to cope with the increased demand for services. A number of health institutions, including hospitals came into being over the course of the century of Rana rule.

The first and the most important was the Prithvi Bir Hospital built in 1890 (1947 BS) at Kathmandu. The naming was so because the reigning

8. The local term for trusts which were set up by benefactors with the aim that money or other resources so obtained would be utilised for the upkeep of the earmarked institution e.g. temple, hospital or for certain acts e.g. special worships or giving scholarships.

monarch was King Prithvi Bir Bikram Shah Dev and the Prime Minister Bir Shumsher. Initially started at the North-Western corner of the Ranipokhari, at the present Rastriya Naachghar (National Theatre) site, it had both the male and female sections. The total number of beds was however only 30. The hospital was later shifted to its present site at the South-Western corner of the Ranipokhari.

The first document regarding this institution is one from the *Nijamati Kitab Khana* dated 15th Asar, 1947 BS. In this document one finds budgetary provision made to pay from the next financial year starting in a fortnight's time, for the services of a Dr. Ganguly from India (28). During his period of prime ministership, Bir Shumsher also invited to Nepal, for short periods of time a number of other well known doctors.

These years being the heyday of Rana rule, what was seen elsewhere was soon copied at Kathmandu. Thus it came about that buildings built in Nepal following the visit of Jung Bahadur to England, reflected the trends of Victorian architecture. Thus white massive columnar structures were not only the prototypes for official palaces or residences but some of the designs were also incorporated in the Bir Hospital of those days.

Besides this central hospital in the capital, a number of other hospitals were opened in administrative headquarters of a number of districts. These other health institutions, to be called Prithvi Bir Hospitals were set up at Birgunj, Jaleshwar, Hanumanagar (Rajbiraj), Nepalgunj and Taulihawa.

The Leprosarium at Khokana was also further built at that time with a capacity for 200 inmates. The British, who as always were monitoring events in Nepal, were not convinced that this institution was functioning properly (21). The Cholera Hospital, which became in succession the Infectious Diseases Unit of Bir Hospital, then the Infectious Diseases Hospital and finally the Sukra Raj Tropical and Infectious Disease Hospital was also initially built in 1890 (1947 BS). It was shifted to its present site at Teku in 1950 (2007 BS).

Browsing over old health records we find that Bir Shumsher, tried other forms of treatment besides modern medicine. During the year 1899 he apparently vomited up 2 to 3 pints of blood and for this one Kacha Baba, a jogi from Benaras treated him with good effect. This vomiting of blood recurred from time to time and Bir Shumsher died on 5th March 1901 as a result of the bursting of an aneurysm (24).

Dr. Raj Krishna Mukerjee, more than likely came to Kathmandu during Bir Shumsher's time. Later, during Dev Shumsher's short premiership of 114 days, Dr. Mukerjee was appointed as lecturer at the Nepal Medical School. A news item in the then weekly issue of the *Gorkhapatra* dated 11th Jestha, 1985 BS reported that Dr. Mukerjee had dissected dead bodies and showed the various internal organs to the then prime minister Dev Shumsher and to a group of *vaidyas* or local practitioners. In retrospect such an event was no less than the dissection demonstration of a cadaver by Andreas Vesalius at Padua in 1537 AD. We in Nepal were just a few centuries behind!

During King Prithvi Bir Bikram Shah Dev's reign from 1880-1913 (1937-1979 BS), Chandra Shumsher followed Bir Shumsher as Prime Minister in 1901 (1958 BS). One of the initial hospitals to be built was the Chandra Loka Hospital at Bhaktapur, which opened its doors in 1904. Chandra Shumsher experienced real contact with diseases during his trip to Simara in 1904. Arrangements had been made for a *Shikar,* when there was an outbreak of cholera. Some form of disinfection was tried by handling or smelling camphor. Some advocated "pill made of opium and camphor" as treatment for cholera. From all accounts this outbreak of cholera took epidemic form. Because of his personal experiences it is likely that Chandra was prompted to provide health facilities in different parts of the country. Another less kinder view suggests that these facilities came to be set up at places such as Dhankuta, Palpa, Doti and other places where ex-Prime Ministers, Commander-in-Chiefs and ambitious Generals were periodically banished during the course of the 104 years of Rana rule in Nepal. As such persons could not leave the district without permission, a hospital with a doctor or compounder and rudimentary health facilities was generally established at the administrative headquarters (21). It was more therefore to look after the health of the ruler's relatives rather than that of the people, which led to increase in health care institutions.

During Chandra Shumsher's time we find Dr. Raj Krishna Mukerjee, LMS became the Inspector of Hospitals in Nepal. It was this same Dr. Mukerjee who brought out a Textbook of Anatomy (*Shareer Tattwa*) in Parbatia (Nepali) in 1909 for use perhaps by health workers in service or for informal training (29).

Landon's opinion was that Chandra Shumsher was no less energetic than the preceding Prime Minister Bir Shumsher in spreading medical facilities in the country. The additional hospitals that he built made it easier to deal with epidemics. One of the greatest difficulties that advocates of modern medicine had encountered even in India was the natural preference of the inhabitants for their own Ayurvedic system of medicine. This view was also prevalent in Nepal and so facilities at an Ayurvedic School were improved. The preventive aspects were not neglected, for though vaccination was not compulsory, it was free to those who chose to avail themselves of this protection against a disease that, though never attaining the gravity of an epidemic was rarely absent from Nepal.

King Prithvi Bir Bikram Shah Dev was succeeded by King Tribhuvan (1913-1955). Following this, Chandra Shumsher opened hospitals, which were named Tri-Chandra Hospitals at Palpa and Palhi (Parasi). Others followed at Jhapa (Bhadrapur), Sarlahi, Dhankuta, Doti, Bardia, Ilam, and Rangeli. To make medicines more freely available, the Chandra Sale Dispensary was set up at Bir Hospital in 1917 (30). Addition was made to the female wing of the Bir Female Hospital. Two new sections of Pathology/ Bacteriology plus also an X-ray department were started in the hospital. Whilst a number of health personnel were recruited from India, the specimens of signatures of medical practitioners were registered and kept at the Chandra Sale Dispensary so that there was no misuse of drugs. There were said to be a total of eighteen hospitals and fourteen dispensaries in various parts of the country (31). Dr. Siddhimani Acharya who graduated with the M.B. (Cal) in April 1921 was probably the first person to qualify with a degree in modern medicine, which declared him, to quote "competent and authorised to practise medicine, surgery and midwifery."

The major hospital with which Chandra Shumsher set up was the sixty-four bedded Military Hospital completed in 1926. It was rightly reported in the press that this hospital was built as a memorial to Nepali soldiers who had lost their lives in World War I (32). This was a major event with active participation of the people. The opening on Thursday, the 9th of September 1926 was a day of rejoicing. PM Chandra Shumsher arrived first with the British Envoy Wilkinson. The actual inauguration started after the arrival of the King. In his speech on the occasion, the engineer went on to say, "The bronze statue of a Gurkha warrior which adorns the top of this building is the work of a local artist Ratna Bahadur and gives a graphic reproduction of the men in whose memory this monument is dedicated. I might also say that there is every reason for our gratification as this is the first attempt of its kind in Nepal" (33). The building was shaped as two "E"s, back to back. At the end of his speech Col. Kishore Narsingh Rana, went on to state, "With paternal solicitude Your Highness has not only established several allopathic dispensaries at the more important and populous towns and villages in the hills and Terai, but has arranged to start many Ayurvedic pharmacies in the far-off interior where up to now the nostrum from village quacks was all the medical help available to the people. To provide trained men for those pharmacies, Your Highness has opened Ayurvedic schools under our own *kavirajas* who have come back after completing their full course of study and training in good and reputable Ayurvedic institutions in India..."

Subsequently, Chandra Shumsher in his speech stated that this hospital had been built with the aid of the friendly states in gratefulness to the Nepalese who had laid down their lives. PM Chandra went on to state that a sum of Rupees seven hundred thousand (or 7 *lakhs*) had been set aside to build a modern sanatorium for the treatment of tuberculous patients. Unlocking the padlock of gold by King Tribhuvan did the formal "opening" of the hospital. Provision had been made by way of an endowment fund of Rupees Twelve lakhs worth of Indian Government Promissory Notes. For the proper running of the hospital a board of trustees was formed with the Commander-in-Chief as head. The monthly rate of pay for a Nepalese doctor then was Rupees sixty. In the evening there was *deepavali* or illuminations with especially fixed lights. As was the custom then, *juwa* or gambling with miniature conch shells or *kaudi* was allowed for a period of sixty hours. The following day, the army was given the day off and all the *addakhana* or civil offices were closed. In his efforts to be humane, Chandra had done away with slavery. He also abolished *sati* in 1920.

The population of the country stood at 5.5 millions in 1925. A malaria survey was done at that time.

During this period was built also the Lalitpur Hospital in 1924 (1981 BS), Leprosy Department and Khokana Leprosarium in 1927 and the Ramghat

Dispensary in 1929. Rumour had it that Prime Minister Chandra Shumsher was keen to have the TB Sanatorium built at Tokha as he himself suffered from the disease. After the starting of construction, Chandra Shumsher suddenly died. Thus 1929 saw Gen. Bhim Shumsher assuming the mantle of prime minister.

The hospitals built subsequently were at Bhairahawa, Butwal and Shivraj. Dispensaries like the one at Ramghat were opened at Sindulimadi, Ramechhap, Okhaldhunga and Pashupatinagar. (NB. These have all been converted in the subsequent years into Health Centres or hospitals. The Butwal Hospital was also upgraded and was made into a 50-bedded hospital in 1966).

A report in the Times of 25th July 1931 mentions about the 68th birthday celebrations of Prime Minister Bhim Shumsher. It goes on to mention that the PM had, "done much to deserve the gratitude of the people... The question of hygiene is also receiving his attention, the latest evidence of which is the new hospital opened near the shrine of Pashupati, for the benefit of the poor people of the locality. The hospitals already existing in Khatmandu have also been greatly expanded." Some sources have said that PM Bhim Shumsher suffered from phthisis, the name then in vogue for tuberculosis (34).

Bhim Shumsher has been portrayed as a rather weak prime minister in that Chandra Shumsher his predecessor has overshadowed him. In fact giving justice where due, Bhim went to the extent of decreeing the tentative abolition of capital punishment in the country, except in cases falling under military law and high treason, for a period of five years. Such a bold step prompted Mr. Morley of the British Residency to remark, "This experiment will be watched with great interest by Western countries which have not yet ventured to take the plunge." The fact that some Nepali nationalists were subsequently hanged during the prime ministership of Juddha that followed is another matter. Bhim Shumsher fell ill following an infected gallbladder. The surgeon at the British legation had recommended immediate surgical treatment. There was delay in agreeing to the operation. During the course of that night of 1st September 1932 (1989 BS) Prime Minister Bhim Shumsher died.

Then in 1932 Juddha Shumsher became Prime Minister and had a hand in the opening of the Dharan Hospital. The Tokha Sanatorium was however built in 1931 with a personal endowment left by Chandra Shumsher. Following the inauguration of the new Tokha Sanatorium, an English doctor was appointed as the first Superintendent at the princely sum of Rs. 700/- per month. New Prime Minister Juddha was also keen that personnel working in Nepal should be well trained for we find a letter dated 28th Oct. 1932 stating:

"In order that the benefit of the latest improved surgical technique might be made available to the general public here, we are thinking of sending to Calcutta, Doctor Suresh Chandra Dass Gupta LMS to learn at the premier institution at that place. The doctor is the Chief Medical Officer of the Bir Hospital, Kathmandu, and is also known to the British Legation Surgeon as a good hand in surgery."

The bed number of Bir Hospital was increased from 30 to 60 during the course of Gen. Juddha Shumsher tenure as prime minister. Lalitpur Hospital was upgraded. In the course of time the Lunatic Asylum at Kathmandu and the Mulanga Lunatic Asylum were opened. So also was the hospital at Makwanpur.

In 1933 the Department of Health Services (DoHS) was established. Its responsibilities were for the promotion, regulation and management of facilities provided by the government. Between this period and 1951 when the new government was installed, the facilities under the DoHS were:

Thirty three HMG hospitals
Several Ayurvedic dispensaries
Nepal *Rajakiya*[9] Ayurved Vidyalaya established in 1990 BS (35)
Singha Durbar Vaidyakhana
Civil Medical School established in 1934 (1990 BS).

In August 1942, King Tribhuvan had his first heart attack and was treated by Col. Denham White, a British physician who subsequently returned to India via Birgunj in a Puss Moth, which was the first airplane to land in Nepal (21).

Though there were hospital facilities existing, it was not always possible to have the necessary investigations done. Even as late as 1945 it was not really possible to have good quality X-rays done to diagnose peptic

9. That related to the king or royalty - that under royal patronage.

ulceration and patients had to go to one of the Indian city hospitals (6).

After World War II, in the later years of Rana rule there were rumblings for change. It was in this context that the then Prime Minister Padma Shumsher decided in 1947 to introduce some reforms. These reforms were classified in five categories viz. social, agricultural, commercial, judicial and local self-government (36).

Under the local self government reforms the municipalities of Kathmandu, Patan, Bhatgaon (Bhaktapur), and Biratnagar were directed to do certain specific functions. These tasks for which they were responsible were to install water taps, record births and deaths, plus to popularise inoculation and vaccinations especially at the time of epidemics. Thus what this meant was that measures directed toward prevention of diseases were under local self government. As a result of this precedence, the minister who had charge of this ministry was thus responsible for health matters in the subsequent years.

After Mohan Shumsher became the PM two eye camps, of which the first was at Butwal, were conducted. It is conjectured that because the PM also had some eye trouble that he was keen to do this. Some doctors came from the Eye Hospital at Sitamarhi in India, for this specific purpose.

During the course of 1949 a new Health Centre was opened at Sankhu. Later, a new building for Ramghat Dispensary and the Homeopathic Hospital was built. This was in fact a new site for the homeopathic dispensary which had been previously located near the Dharahara or Bhimsen's Stambha. Mr. Lila Nath Adhlkarl, then a fairly junior administrator at the health ministry, inaugurated both the Sankhu Health Post and the Ramghat Dispensary. The reason was that the higher up officials of the ministry were hesitant to do these functions because of the people's wrath against the Rana administration. This was later upgraded to a hospital in 1952.

Up to this time most of the health service personnel had been expatriates from Bengal. Facilities for investigations prior to treatment of disease were very limited. The training of Nepalese personnel in the far away England of those days was a radical concept. The fact that the new Prime Minister Mohan Shumsher had committed to give support to this from his personal funds was another matter but the upshot of all this was that Nepalese doctors were sent abroad for Diploma level studies in Pathology, Radiography and Chest Diseases. His personal physician Dr. Siddhimani is credited to having persuaded the Prime Minister in this regard. All of the three physicians so trained viz. Dr. D. N. Baidya, Dr. Raghubar Vaidya and Dr. Yagya Raj Joshi went on to become Director Generals of Health in course of time.

Though the Tokha Sanatorium had been opened nineteen years previously, 1950 saw a new chapter started in the history of the control of tuberculosis in Nepal. It was in the reign of King Tribhuvan and during Mohan Shumsher's premiership that the first Chest Clinic at the Bir Hospital was opened in 1951. As tuberculosis was and still is a major problem in Nepal, this was an attempt to control the disease in a cheap and effective manner. It was the start of the domiciliary form of treatment for tuberculosis in Nepal. With the advent of democracy in the country, greater efforts were made and stronger measures taken to provide basic health facilities to the people. Subsequent years saw the opening of more health centres in different parts of the country.

POINTS TO PONDER

It was customary for many Nepalese to do social service e.g. helping the ill to recover, aiding the needy etc from time immemorial. This was done usually on an individual basis. In course of time it became an enlarged undertaking, inclusive of ayurvedic and modern medicines when the Rana rulers took over the running of the country from the Shah kings.

References

1. History of Medicine in Sri Lanka. CG Uragoda, 1987, Sri Lanka Medical Association, Colombo.
2. Editorial in BMJ, 1928, 2, 541.
3. TW Rhys Davids & Hermann Oldenburg, The Mahavagga, 41-145.
4. Medical Heritage of India. NH Keswani in The Science of Medicine & Physiological Concepts in Ancient & Medieval India, 1974. AIIMS, New Delhi.
5. Traditional Medicine and Health Care Coverage, 1983, WHO, Geneva.
6. Marasini, BR. Health and Hospital Development in Nepal: Past and Present, JNMA, 2003, 42, 306- 311.
7. Miller, CJ. Faith-Healers in the Himalayas. CNAS, Kathmandu.
8. Shrestha, RM and Lediard, M. Faith Healers: A Force for Change. 1980, UNICEF, Kathmandu.

9. Parker B, Ritual Coordination of Medical Pluralism in Highland Nepal: Implications for Policy. Soc Sci Med 1988; 27(9): 919-925.
10. Mountain Medicine & International Aid. Susan Hayden. 2009. Orient Black Swan, India.
11. Justice, Judith. Policies, Plan, & People. 1985. UCLA, Berkeley.
12. Skultans V, Letter, The Lancet, 1986; **1**(8488): 1025-26.
13. Shrestha, TB. Traditional Medicines and Native Plant of Nepal. J Nep Pharm Assoc 7, 45-48.
14. Grotesque Lands: What Earlier Visitors Saw. 1990 HIMAL, 3(1); 10.
15. Chaudhari, KC. Anglo-Nepalese Relations. 1960, Modern Book Agency, Calcutta.
16. Kirkpatrick, W. An Account of the Kingdom of Nepaul (being the substance of observations made during a mission to the country in the year 1793). 1811, William Miller, London.
17. Jordon, RR. From Missionaries to Mountaineers – Early Encounters with Nepal. 2010. Kathmandu.
18. Papers of Brain H Hodgson, 1857, John Gray, Calcutta.
19. Oldfield, H. A. Sketches in Nipal. 1880 .: W. H. Allen and Co.,London. 2 Vols.
20. Journals Kept in Hyderabad, Kashmir, Sikkim & Nepal, Vol II 1887. Sir Richard Temple, WH Allen & Co, London.
21. Stiller, Ludwig F. Nepal: Growth of a Nation. 1993, HRD Research Center, Kathmandu.
22. Dahal, BM. The Rising Nepal, Friday Supplement, 3rd March, 1995.
23. Sanwal, BD. Nepal and the East India Company. 1965. Asia Publishing House, Bombay.
24. Landon, Perceval. Nepal. 1928. London: Constable & Co., 2 Vols.
25. Mali, IB. Leprosy Services in Nepal. JNMA, 1966, **3**, 3, 225-229.
26. Various letters from Fort William to the British Resident at Kathmandu, in possession of the India Office Library.
27. Humanism and Jai Prithivi Bahadur Singh. Padma B. Singh. The Kathmandu Post, 23rd August, 1998.
28. Bir Hospital of Yesteryears. Paudel N.N., Dixit H. Souvenir, Bir Hospital Centenary, 1989-90.
29. Mukerjee, Raj Krishna. Textbook of Anatomy (*Shareer-Tatwa*).1909. Prabhakar Printing Works, Benaras.
30. Drug Legislation & Regulatory Procedures, 1993. Drug Bulletin of Nepal. Vol.**3** Nos. 1 & 2.
31. Yadhav, Pitamber L. Political History of Nepal. 1990.
32. Report in Times of India of 23rd Oct. 1926 from India Office Library, London.

33. Shrestha KB, Rajbhandari BB: The Establishment of Tribhuvan Chandra Military Hospital. 2043 B.S. Ramjham, 22. 34-47.
34. Adhikari B. in The New Spotlight, June, 2013.
35. Shrestha I.B. Health Personnel Training in Nepal, 1979, J Inst Med 1, 155-172.
36. Shrestha, Kusum. Monarchy in Nepal-Tribhuvan Era. 1984, Sangma Books, London.

2.

DISEASES AND CONTROL ATTEMPTS

Nepal being a developing country has many health problems, which escalate in intensity at different times of the year or take epidemic form. Most of the records of diseases in the early days have been gleaned from the records kept by the Britishers in the residency at Kathmandu. Dr. Oldfield was one such early person and had been promoted as Surgeon to the British Residency from a previous appointment of Assistant Surgeon in the Bengal Army (1). Writing about conditions in 1849 he states, "On the 3rd of November Dr. Login left Nipal for the plains; he reached Sigauli in thirty hours, having gone partly on pony, mostly on foot; he escaped the **awal**, but died, after a few hours' illness, of cholera at Dinapore."

Brian Hodgson, a prolific record keeper however had different views (2). In his papers published in 1857 he stated that "The fearful epidemics of the plains seldom penetrate the Himalayas… for forty years, cholera has ravaged the plains continuously almost. But in all that period, Nepal has been visited only twice."

In the past there had been outbreaks of diseases such as cholera, smallpox and plague. Later attempts were at notifications and collection of data on various diseases and their effects. Nepal being one of the least developed countries it is but natural that infectious diseases played an important role in the disease pattern seen in the country. Regarding the diseases of importance one can categorise these by their origins as given below:

a. Viruses

b. Spores

c. Bacteria

d. Parasites

e. Others

a. Due to Viruses

Smallpox: The Nepalese had been inflicted over the years with this disease. The death of the son of King Pratap Malla, (1641-1674) by smallpox led to profound sorrow in his Rani. In an attempt to cheer her up, and also to show that she was not the only one so bereaved, the custom of *Gaijatra* in memory of all who had died in the previous year was started as an annual event.

In later years no less a person than King Girvan Yuddha Bikram Shah died of smallpox in 1816 (3).

Oldfield (1) also mentioned about the practice of vaccination against smallpox during the time of Jung Bahadur. "I received five hundred rupees for vaccinating his eldest boy in 1850, when he was in England."

Public awareness about the necessity of preventive measures against smallpox increased over the years. It was however not until after the ushering of democracy in 1951 that greater efforts were made regarding mass vaccinations. The last big epidemic was that in the winter of 1963. Many in the urban areas were affected and even some of the porters of the American Everest Expedition contacted it and subsequently were the cause of spreading it to their respective villages. After supply of the dry vaccine to a total of 700,000 doses, the epidemic was contained by May, 1964 (4,5). Once the concept of eradication was accepted then extra efforts were made in the areas of expanded vaccinations and disease containment.

After ten years of worldwide efforts in which WHO played a major role, the last case of naturally occurring smallpox was reported at Merka in Somalia on 26th October, 1977. Then the global eradication of smallpox was officially announced two years later. This success should not be a harbinger of complacency.

Measles: This was a major cause of childhood morbidity and mortality in Nepal due to then prevalent custom of not treating measles until the child was at death's door. A number of children went on to have diarrhoea, much malnutrition and some even blindness as a result of accompanying Vitamin A deficiency. A study at Sarlahi showed that Vitamin A had the most protective effect against measles (6). With the possibility of polio eradication soon, the focus has shifted to measles.

Measles surveillance was integrated with Acute Flaccid Paralysis (AFP) surveillance in March 2003. Starting in Sept 2004, all children above 1 year but lower than 15 years of age were given the second dose of measles vaccine all over the country in an attempt to protect the child further. It is hoped that measles will be controlled by 2015.

Rubella: In the olden days any rash on a baby was labelled as measles by the mother. With the elimination of measles, rubella has come to the forefront and because of the possibility of Congenital Rubella Syndrome occurring, the government started immunisation against the disease from mid July 2013.

Hepatitis: Cases of acute hepatitis have occurred sporadically at Kathmandu during last forty years. Three epidemics of non-A and non-B were seen in Kathmandu Valley in 1973, 1981/82 and in 1987 (7). A study in 1985 had reported that following blood antibody levels studies at Kathmandu it was estimated that as much as 87% of the cases occurring were due to non-A and non-B hepatitis virus (8). Hepatitis in its various forms was a regular occurrence in the capital and other parts of Nepal in the 1980s. Quite a lot of the treatment for it is by ayurvedic practitioners. Though a study at the Bir Hospital over a 8-year period ending 1987, showed a total of 100 cases only, the author in his conclusion felt that hepatitis B virus infection is one of the important causes of liver cancer in Nepal (9). Amongst the 1878 units of blood collected by the Western Regional Blood Transfusion Centre run by the Nepal Red Cross at Pokhara during the financial year ending mid July 1996 (i.e. 2052-53 BS) a total of 192 were infected. The breakdown of this was 177 Hepatitis B +ve, 15 HIV +ve and 10 VDRL reactive. Shrestha and Gaffney have estimated that there were then more than 15,000 drug abusers in Nepal and that the majority of them are hepatitis C virus carriers. Research was conducted at Kathmandu with support of the Macfarlane Burnet Centre of Australia on Hepatitis E (former non A, non B enteral). A study of 293 samples from acute viral hepatitis cases at Kathmandu in 1997 showed it to be prevalent throughout the year with Hepatitis E virus and then Hepatitis B being the causal agents. It is estimated that there have been epidemic spread of this in the past. Incidence of acute hepatitis is high in Nepal (10). Another study done in 1997 showed that 56% of acute hepatitis in Kathmandu valley was caused by hepatitis E and that hepatitis A, hepatitis B and hepatitis C accounted for 3% each only (11). Sero-prevalence of hepatitis C virus was seen in intravenous drug users (IDU) of Kathmandu (12).

Rabies: Most of the injections for the prevention of rabies used to be given at the Infectious Diseases Hospital at Teku. That facility continues to this day except that newer vaccines are being used. A lot of injections are being given for bites or scratches by suspected animals such as stray monkeys and cats. In rural areas jackals may be involved. Noting the reality of dogs in urban centres a review of 1983 recommended the killing of stray dogs as a possible strategy to reduce human deaths due to hydrophobia (13).

Another epidemiological review of rabies cases seen at Kathmandu valley over a 3-year period showed that more than 75% of the total anti rabies vaccine consumed in Nepal was used to treat the victims of dog assault. The authors of the study suggested that elimination of stray dogs and compulsory vaccination of all pet dogs should be an integral part of the control programme.

According to the Epidemiology & Disease Control Division (EDCD) 1,692 people lost their lives to dog and fox bites between 2000 and 2009 June. Although the GoN had formulated a 20-year National Strategic Plan in 2007 the document has still to see the light of day. Vasectomy of the males and 'bucket' operation for the bitches was being carried out in 2010. This same year various suggestions were again made stating that the government should formulate a proper strategy to deal with rabies because of the increasing number of stray dogs in urban centres.

Now there is much more awareness in urban dwellers of the necessity of giving vaccines to dogs also for protection from the disease. The vaccines currently available and in use in Kathmandu are:

a. Purified Chick Embryo Vaccine
b. Purified Verocell Vaccine
c. Human Diploid Vaccine
d. Purified Duck Embryo Vaccine.

All four vaccines are freeze dried and are to be given on days 0-3-7-14-28 or 30 days. The Human Diploid vaccine should be given preference, but it is expensive and not always available (14).

Encephalitis: Japanese encephalitis (JE) was recognised for the first time in Nepal in 1978 (15). Though **Culicine** mosquitoes have been identified as the vectors on the Asian subcontinent, no particular species has been shown to be responsible in Nepal. Confirmation of previous infection has been shown by the fact that one third of both human and pig sera from the Terai areas such as Itahari and Chitwan showed presence of JE antibody (16). Cases peak during the rainy season.

The reporting of cases had shown that the incidence is highest in the mid-West region of Nepal. There had been a total of 27,584 cases of which 5382 had died over the years 1978 to 2004. During the course of these years the highest incidence of cases was in 1997 (2953) and second highest in 1999 (2924). Insecticide spraying has not been found to be effective for controlling the disease. Vaccination campaigns have been done in recent years and have been found to be effective in reducing the morbidity and mortality due to JE. (17).

It is thought that discontinuation of spraying insecticides during the last decade has resulted in the increased number of not only mosquitoes but even sand flies. It is this increase of vectors, which is said to be the cause of the increased incidence of encephalitis and also leishmaniasis.

AIDS: Screening for HIV infection was started in the country in April, 1986 and the first case of HIV/AIDS was diagnosed in Nepal in July 1988 and was in a non-Nepalese. At that time the infection in the very young or the very old was limited. Since then Nepal's classification has changed from 'low prevalence' country to one with so-called 'concentrated epidemic in certain sub-groups of the population (18). The increased movement of many Nepalese to the major cities of South Asia for work or as traders plus also the luring of many young Nepalese girls to brothels both in and out of the country as sex workers is assumed to have tremendous social, cultural and economic consequences in the country. Certain areas e.g. Sindhupalchowk, Nuwakot were first identified as places from where girls were procured. The thought now is that the activity of those involved in the flesh trade has shifted to other districts of Nepal. Increased mobility of migrant workers to many other areas of the world is expected to fuel this rise. HIV/AIDS has been reported in all the 75 districts of Nepal. As of July 2012, the national estimate was that approximately 48,600 adults and children are affected by the HIV virus in Nepal (18).

High Risk Group

1. Injecting Drug Users (IDUs)
2. Men who have sex with men (MSM)

3. Female Sex Workers (FSWs)
4. Clients of female sex workers
5. Seasonal male labour migrants.

NB. i. Heterosexual transmission is dominant.
ii. HIV prevalence in general population is 0.3%.

A total of 48,600 cases of HIV were registered as of July 2012. The breakdown of HIV infection amongst different age group is as follows:

Children (0-14 years)	4,000
Adults (15-49 years)	41,000
Adults (50+ years)	3,600

The adult prevalence rate (15-49 years) is 0.28% and overall prevalence rate of HIV in the country is 1%.

The national antiretroviral treatment program had been started in Nepal from Feb. 2004. Three or more ARV drugs are recommended for the treatment of individuals with HIV infection and are being given out at 44 places in the country in 2013.

Dengue Fever

During the two years 1980/81 it was suspected that there was an outbreak of dengue fever in a district, which was endemic for Japanese encephalitis. **Aedes** mosquito was thought to be the major vector of the viral infection dengue fever. In 2004 it was proved that 2 Japanese tourists who had visited areas in the Terai had been infected with Dengue Type 2 virus. In 2006 there was a total of 32 laboratory confirmed cases. An initial outbreaks of 27 cases of Dengue fever in 2007 was followed by 10 and 30 in the next two years. However in 2010 there were cases of Dengue Fever / Dengue Haemorrhagic Fever (DF/DHF) in both hilly and lowland districts of Nepal. In that year there were 4529 cases of which 917 were serologically confirmed. There were five deaths. (19).

Avian Influenza (Bird Flu)

This has now spread in many countries after its emergence in 2003. Poultry affected by H5N1 strain of the virus, prevalent in Asia can be transmitted to humans and had till end of Dec. 2007 infected 351 humans of which 143 were in the South East Asia Region (20). In Europe the H7N7 strain of the virus is involved.

The H5N1 virus is now prevalent in Nepal. There has been over the years a gradual increase in the number of cases reaching a peak in August 2013 when over a million chickens were culled. It must be noted also that Pandemic Influenza A (H1N1) or swine flu has occurred from time to time in Nepal and has been transmitted to humans.

b. Due to Spores

Tetanus: A number of studies on tetanus have been done in hospitals in the Terai. Studies as late as the seventies and eighties of admissions at the Bheri Zonal Hospital in Nepalgunj had shown a high incidence of tetanus neonatorum. A common cause in children and adults was injury. For a couple of years now there have been campaigns for the elimination of neonatal tetanus by the strategy of giving tetanus toxoid to pregnant women.

c. Due to Bacteria

Tuberculosis: Though the early medical records have shown that tuberculosis or consumption as Western doctors knew it previously also, was present in Nepal, the attempt to control and prevent the disease from spreading started much later. The fight against tuberculosis may be said to have started with the building of the 50-bedded Tokha Sanatorium, on the Northern hill surrounding Kathmandu in 1934. Subsequent work showed also that many in the army and police, being from the rural areas, were very likely to get the disease.

Towards the end of the 104 years old Rana rule, the Chest Clinic at Kathmandu was started in 1951 at the Bir Hospital with Dr. Y. R. Joshi as the first TB specialist and the domiciliary treatment of tuberculosis was started on a limited scale. After 10 years of its establishment the Chest Clinic became a separate institution (National Tuberculosis Centre) and no longer part of Bir Hospital.

In 1966 there was an attempt to introduce direct vaccination of the Bacillus Calmette Guerin (BCG) vaccine, both in the schools and by house-to-house visits in the Kathmandu valley. In 1968 the BNMT started anti-tuberculosis activities in Koshi and Mechi zones in Eastern Nepal. During the course of the years other NGOs such as UMN, Dooley Foundation and JICA have been involved in the fight against tuberculosis. Later it was another NGO viz. INF that too became involved in the fight against tuberculosis in Western Nepal.

The Japanese Medical Cooperation Team which started work in 1973 led subsequently to the formation of the Western Region Tuberculosis Centre at Pokhara and also the relocation of the Central Chest Clinic at Sano Thimi in Bhaktapur district. The importance of TB as a major killer has been recognised not only in Nepal but in the SAARC region. After a number of meetings it was only at the 5th Summit held at Male in 1990 that the decision was made to establish such a TB Centre at Thimi, Bhaktapur in Nepal. The 1994 Regional Centre of SAARC is now the SAARC Tuberculosis and HIV / AIDS Centre (STAC).

The "STOP TB Strategy" was adopted in 2006. The overall goal of the National Tuberculosis Programme (NTP) is to reduce mortality, morbidity and transmission of tuberculosis to a level, which is not a public hazard. This is the objective of the Directly Observed Treatment Short Course (DOTS) programme that has now been implemented by the government in all of the 75 districts of Nepal. Stress has been laid in having urban DOTS programme in the major towns with the help of the private sector too, there is now total coverage in the country (21). However it must be noted that drug resistant tuberculosis is considered a potential threat to TB control programmes even with the new DOTS.

More recently because of the fact that there are a number of medical colleges in the country, the policy has been to have DOTS Centres in them. This ensures that whilst providing service to the community, the medical students or the future doctors of this country are aware of the problem of TB in Nepal.

Whilst major work has been done about the human type tuberculosis bacillus, some work has been done in the past on the bovine type too. Joshi (22) has identified factors existing in Nepal, which leads on to the continuation of the bovine TB cycle in slaughtered or milking animals. Some provision was made in 1998 by the enactment of an Animal Slaughterhouse and Meat Examination Act 1998. It was hoped that there would also be at the district level, the provision of diagnostic facilities for tuberculosis in animals.

Leprosy: Leprosy has been a disease that has affected the world community for centuries. Patients with the disease were outcasts of society and so the tendency was to hide and not come for treatment. Institutions such as leprosarium were the last resort and treatment for the disease was long and very limited.

It is estimated that the Khokana Leprosarium was established round about 1857 and the one at Malunga in 1939. As elsewhere the patients with this disease went to such institutions when there was no other option. The main treatment in those early days was Chaulmoogra Oil. Later, with the setting up of a leprosarium at Pokhara in 1957 patients with leprosy started receiving modern care at the Green Pastures Hospital. In 1958 the Leprosy Mission International also started a dispensary at Chapagaun in Lalitpur District. The establishment of the Anandaban Leprosy Hospital followed this. This 100-bedded referral hospital had also a 10-bedded section which provides primary health care to the community of that locality (23).

The prevalence rate of leprosy was estimated in 1961 as one per thousand. The control of this disease may be stated to have started with the formation of the leprosy-tuberculosis control project, started with the initiative of WHO in 1965. In 1966 a health survey done by Shah and Worth (24) found that there were more cases in the Western and Far Western regions of the country and that the disease was prevalent in all the three belts viz mountains, hills and Terai of Nepal. There were some small-congregated pockets as with the Tharu community in Nawalparasi. Reorganisation of services provided for leprosy made it into the Expanded Leprosy Project in 1967 but surprisingly its main area of functioning was restricted to two small areas in Bagmati and Narayani Zones.

Before the Fifth Five Year plan, agreement was reached between the Leprosy Control Project and the INF for the establishment of the Green Pastures Leprosy Hospital with inpatient facilities. INF was responsible for the provision of services for leprosy cases in the Western and mid Western regions of Nepal.

Work by expatriates such as Pedley in Tansen showed that leprosy bacilli seldom ever emerge from intact lepromatous skin. He had earlier shown that leprosy bacilli could be transmitted as a result of strong sneezing by patients with lepromatous leprosy (25). Other workers at Anandaban did research into cultivation procedures on mice regarding resistance of Mycobacterium lepra to dapsone and rifampicin (26). Work on leprosy has been done by a number of INGOs or NGOs such as the Netherlands Leprosy Association, TEAM, Sasakawa Memorial Health

Foundation, NELRA, and Nepra E.V. etc. More than a dozen surveys have been done since 1985.

The WHO recommended MDT in 1982 (27). It had long been advocated that the treatment of leprosy should be integrated into the general health services. The leprosy control programme was integrated into general health services in 1987 to provide wider coverage. The hope was that there would be improvement in the attitude towards the disease. A study in 2000 in Eastern Nepal showed that there was still negative community behaviour (28). However, an effective campaign on TV and cinema using popular cine stars about MDT is thought to have had a positive impact on the operational and epidemiological solution. In mid July 2003, Nepal had as many as 7,549 registered cases. There is also a defaulter rate even with the MDT campaign well underway. In January 2010 the government announced officially the elimination of leprosy from the country as there were only 0.89 cases per 10,000 persons. There were just 2,445 cases under treatment and 80% of these were in the Terai region. This same situation exists in 2013 but 14 districts in the Terai still had a population ratio of over 1 in 10,000 population in 2067/68 BS. To arouse more awareness Leprosy day is being observed annually on 29th January every year (29).

Diarrhoeal Diseases: These are important being one of the major causes of childhood mortality in Nepal. It must however be noted that the causes of such states is not restricted to bacterial origins but could also be due to viral causes. A survey on Control of Diarrhoeal Disease (CDD) in 1991 revealed that on average, each child suffered from 3.3 episodes of diarrhoea per year. The number of deaths due to diarrhoea was estimated to be 45,000 per year. It has now decreased.

Typhoid: A study of admissions at the Infectious Diseases Hospital showed that in 1983, enteric fever cases constituted about 5% of total admissions. The cases were treated with chloramphenicol alone or a combination of chloramphenicol with another drug such as ampicillin. The reality however is that salmonellosis is almost endemic in the capital and many other urban centres of Nepal. The work at Patan Hospital has shown that typhoid fever has a regular yearly cycle with the least number of cases occurring during the last quarter of the Nepalese year i.e. from Magh to Chaitra. As typhoid is a regular occurrence in Kathmandu valley, the government is in the process of introducing vaccination against typhoid as a regular Public Health measure in the Kathmandu Valley. The annual report of 2011-12 of DoHS states that typhoid and paratyphoid fevers constitute now 3% of all hospital admissions within the country.

Cholera: A particularly severe outbreak of the disease occurred in 1818 in parts of Northern India and subsequently extended to Nepal (30). Some sources claim that the first recorded epidemic was in 1823. That the disease was present in Nepal is shown by the fact that Queen Tripurasundari, who as Regent Mother looked after the kingdom of King Rajendra Bikram Shah from 1806 till 6th April 1832, died as a result of cholera. The most severe outbreak was said to have been in 1856 when the mortality rate in Kathmandu was "for some weeks, 200-250 daily."

Cholera was very much prevalent as shown by the death of Chandra Shumsher's Maharani in 1905. This seemed rather ironic for the lady in question had been involved in the fight against cholera. Tuker's recording the event goes on to state that there was great grief and sorrow in many homes of the Valley, "in Patan particularly which owed to her and to her determination to wipe out cholera with the provision of its water supply."(31).

In 1958 there was a cholera outbreak in the Kathmandu valley. The Kathmandu City Municipality launched a "Kill the flies" campaign to try to contain the epidemic. A **mana**[1] of dead flies was priced at two and half rupees and a man collecting the largest number was to be given a medal (32) !

Since the last twenty years, cholera cases have tended to occur annually in Kathmandu. The fact that laboratory facilities were not easily available in other areas may be the reason for its non-identification more frequently. An analysis of the cases of diarrhoea at Kanti Children's Hospital showed Vibrio Cholerae being isolated from 285 out of 683 children with watery diarrhoea. It was suggested by the investigators that the spread pattern suggested it to be due to contaminated river water (33). Things seemed to get out of hand during July 1995 when cholera not only occurred at a number of sites of Kathmandu and Bhaktapur in Kathmandu valley but also in different parts of Nepal, including the Far Western Region.

An incident of international importance took place in Oct/Nov of 2010.

1. A measure of volume equivalent to sixteen ounces formerly used to measure liquid or even grain.

A Nepali contingent of the UN Peace Keeping force was based at Haiti - a country in the Caribbean that had not had an outbreak of cholera for over half a century. Then on 21st October an epidemic originated in the Artibonite Valley in Central Haiti where the Nepali contingent was based. It was said to originate at a camp near the central town of Mirebalais where many of the Nepali soldiers had been stationed. Though there had been no outbreak of cholera in the camp, the Nepali troops were accused of being the originators. The UN authorities vehemently refuted this. The type was said to be closely related to a South Asian strain of Cholera. As the epidemic spread to the capital and other parts of the country a total of about 5,500 Haitians died during the course of this epidemic. The UN, has stated that the report "does not give conclusive evidence of linking the outbreak to the UN Peacekeepers."

Meningococcal Meningitis: A major outbreak of meningococcal meningitis with 1475 cases occurred in the Kathmandu valley over a twenty-five month period starting April 1982. This led to an extensive vaccination campaign, which in turn resulted in a decrease of cases then. After this, a certain base line of cases has been seen over the course of years. Some form of vaccination has been kept up over the years and so perhaps the expected recurring cycle is not apparent. Subsequent outbreak in 1990-92 was controlled with drugs (34).

Brucellosis: This disease was an unconsidered entity till 1979 when it was first reported as a result of infection by **Brucella melitensis**, in shepherds of sheep rearing stations of Pokhara (35).

Plague: Outbreaks of plague have occurred in Nepal in the past (15). From 1960 to 1962 a total of 150 cases were reported in Rupandehi and Mahottari districts. As the programme to eliminate malaria also controlled the flea population, the incidence of plague declined sharply (36). In 1967/68 it was seen again in the villages of Naura and Pitholake in Bajhang district. It is suspected that in this second epidemic, the infection was first contracted from wild rodents or their fleas and subsequently went on to cause an outbreak of pneumonic plague.

The plague epidemic which occurred in India in August of 1994, created a stir in Nepal. The media had maintained that one case did occur but as it was cremated fairly soon after death, there is no convincing proof of this. Some doubt has been raised in India itself as to whether the original cases were in fact pneumonic plague.

Streptococcal Infections: These are important precursors of subsequent rheumatic heart disease (RHD) in the country. It is quite usual to see advanced cases even in children and is reminiscent of the conditions that existed in the developed countries in the first half of the twentieth century. A report by Pandey & Ghimire (37) had found the incidence of rheumatic heart disease to be declining. Hopefully, as economic conditions improve, the incidence of rheumatic heart disease and glomerular nephritis as a sequelae to streptococcal throat infections will also decrease. A seminar in 1987 made suggestions for effective prevention of RHD and rheumatic fever by pleading for these measures to be incorporated into existing primary health care procedures.

Sexually Transmitted Diseases: The earliest references to these diseases in Nepal is by Dr. Francis Buchanan (later Hamilton in 1801, when he wrote: "I have seen no country where the venereal disease is so common as in Nepal, nor so generally diffused among all classes of the people, who are indeed very dissolute.".

Whilst AIDS has been listed already in view of the world wide focus on it, the others such as gonorrhoea and syphilis have been of importance in the Nepalese scene in that a lot of Nepalese have always been on the move because of employment or trade.

Various studies indicate that the prevalence of STDs in Nepal is quite high and it is estimated that up to 3% of the population is infected by some or other STD (38). The major hospitals of the country report high prevalence of gonorrhoea followed by syphilis, chancroid and herpes genetalis.

d. Due to Parasites

Malaria: Malaria, as has been mentioned in the second chapter had been reported by Dr. Oldfield, who during the course of his thirteen years in the country had travelled widely and mentions "that **awal** sets in Nayakot at about the same time that it does in the Tarai, viz. 15th of March." Oldfield noted too about the immunity of the local tribes such as Darris, Khumbals, Manghis, and Bramus for he wrote, "These tribes inhabit with impunity the lowest and hottest valleys in Nipal, just as the Tharus do the Terai of Nipal."

It is therefore of no surprise that the malarious areas of the Terai and the inner Terai were often referred to as "Kalapani" in view of the dark coloured urine that those infected passed. Even some of the valleys of Nepal were affected by malaria. Cowper of USAID, writing about the Surkhet Valley recalled: "the first time we went through there, there was nobody living in the valley, only a few animal sheds and fields. The farmers lived up on the hillsides and would come down to farm the valley in the day, but went back up before nightfall. Although they didn't know the mechanics of malaria transmission, they did know that if they spent even one night in the Valley, they would fall sick within two weeks" (5).

USOM's anti-malaria programme started in Nov. 1952 with the setting up of a malaria control office. In August 1954 a joint GON/USOM project - the Insect Borne Disease Control Bureau (IBDCB) was started. This same year after becoming a member of WHO, Nepal became an ardent supporter of this organisation. When WHO declared in 1955 that malaria can be eradicated, then Nepal started its efforts. The amalgamation of the IBDCD and the WHO project in Dec. 1958 led to the founding of the program and the Nepal Malaria Eradication Organisation (NMEO). In a matter of twelve intervening years the number of people suffering from malaria had been brought down to 0.4 per thousand (1 per 2500). The "From the more than 2 million cases annually in the 1950's, malaria was reduced to an all time low of 2,468 in 1968." The goal became eradication of the disease by 1971 but this was extended to 1973. After 4 successive years, when there were less than 3,000 cases per year the Malaria Control Project was terminated in 1972. However after some years, perhaps because the mosquitoes had developed resistance to DDT, the number of cases went up to 2.2 per thousand i.e. 6 per 1500. As a consequence, WHO in 1976 made a call to change to a Malaria Control Programme instead (39). Respraying was started. Other causes for resurgence are thought to be chloroquine resistance cases and also the importation and reinfection of cases from across the Indian border.

In 1994 the malarious areas of the country had been stratified into five epidemiological regions. The Annual Parasite Incidence increased from 0.14 per 1,000 in 2009/10 to 0.16 per 1,000 in 2010/11. The proportion of P. falciparum has decreased by 5.0%. It has also been shown that cross border importation of cases is taking place. A review of the Nepal Malaria Control Program in 2010 concluded that the program has progressed from control to pre-elimination stage.

In 2012 malaria cases were seen in 65 of the 75 districts of Nepal, which meant that 73% of the population lived in malarial areas. Of this total tally of 65, 13 are high risk, 18 moderate and 34 low risk areas. The 10 mountainous districts have no malaria.

Three species of plasmodia viz. Plasmodium vivax, Plasmodium falciparum and Plasmodium malariae have been detected in Nepal. Some persons coming from Africa and infected with Plasmodium ovale have been detected (40). P. vivax is responsible for about 80-90% of cases of malaria. P. falciparum is about 10-20% though it is responsible for most epidemics.

Rapid detection tests (RDT) are now available for the detection of malaria. These may be of a general type for malaria or even specific for P. falciparum.

A National Malaria Treatment Protocol, 2009 now provides standard guidelines on detection and treatment of cases (41). The Government of Nepal (GoN) has developed a strategic plan of malaria elimination 2011-2016, to make the country malaria free by 2026. There has recently been news of an effective vaccine against malaria.

Kala-azar: It had been postulated in 1953 that Visceral Leishmaniasis (VL) or Kala-azar, was endemic in Southern Nepal. Kala- azar is a vector borne disease which was first seen in 1980 when cases were detected. It is caused by the parasite Leishmania donovani and transmitted by the sand fly Phebotomus argentipes and is prevalent in 12 of the 75 districts of Nepal. Following the spraying of malarious regions the vector of Kala-azar too was controlled. The subsequent increase of the sand fly population has led to spread of the disease by the female of these vectors. The first case cause is thought to be due to the inadequate spraying of insecticides. Since 1980 the cases have been on the increase though the numbers have varied over the years. Numbers of recorded infections were 25,842 with 515 deaths over the 23 years period from 1980 to 2003. However it is felt that there is gross under reporting. Analysis of district wise data showed that the highest incidence of Kala-azar was in Mahottari and the lowest in Rautahat. The case numbers are generally highest in June. A community study in Morang district showed that the most important factors affecting prevalence of leishmaniasis infection were socio-economic status, living conditions, environmental sanitation and the behaviour and practices of the population (42). Indoor residual spraying has been undertaken in the Terai to control the vectors and thus the disease. Ph.argentipes has been incriminated as a vector since 1992 but Ph.papatasi is probably involved too as a vector (43). Their diagnosis has been simplified by rK39 dipstick and the treatment is now effective with the oral drug Miltefosine.

Out of 12 districts in which Kala-azar is seen in now, five have an incidence of more than 1 and 7 have an incidence of less than 1 per 10,000 population (18).

During the World Health Assembly in 2005, Bangladesh, India and Nepal have signed a MoU to try for the elimination of the disease by 2015. In line with this the government carried out a preparatory phase from 2005-2008. The attack phase which started in 2008 is to last till 2015. The consolidation phase is from then onwards (43).

Lymphatic Filariasis (LF): This has been a problem in many parts of the country resulting in lymphedema of leg (**hathipaila** or elephantiasis), hydrocele and chyluria. This filarial infection is transmitted from one human to another by vector mosquitoes. It was only in 2003 that the government started Mass Drug Administration (MDA) first in Parsa and then gradually extended it to other districts with a view to eradicating the disease by 2020. The single dose of Diethylcarbamazine being given on the Filarial eradication day and has to be taken yearly for six years. There have been some complications following this MDA (18). A single dose of Albendazole is also being given at the same time to get rid of other worms that may be in the gut of the individual. Dhading is a district with heavy infestation.

Amoebiasis: This has been present for many years. Prof. Carl Taylor writing of the Nepal of the nineteen fifties had this to say:

"Amoebiasis is the greatest medical problem in the hills of Nepal... The reason for the high incidence of amoebiasis and other intestinal infections is quite obvious as one walks the trails of Nepal. The usual latrine areas are the places where paths cross streams. This means, of course, that practically all the lovely, sparkling mountain streams are heavily contaminated."

In a serological study of amoebiasis done among 280 subjects above 15 years of age at the Teaching Hospital Tribhuvan University (TUTH) in

Kathmandu, 25% were found to be positive for amoebic antibody, 10% were doubtful and 65% were negative (44).

Echinococcus: A total of 76 cases of hydatid disease were seen amongst the 27,188 cases operated upon for various reasons in three Kathmandu valley hospitals over the period 1979 to 1988. Diagnosis is being made more often because of the advent of ultrasonogram. It is also suggested that *E. granulosus* infection is controllable in the domestic animal cycle by applying strong rabies control and meat inspection (45).

Cysticercosis: Infestation with *T. solium* and *T. saginata* are seen quite frequently. Epilepsy due to cerebral cysticercosis is thought to be quite common in Nepal. It has also been seen and reported amongst Gurkha troops in Hong Kong. A histopathologic study of 62 cases over a 5-year period at Patan Hospital showed that as much as 82 percent presented as solitary skin nodules and most patients were younger than 30 years of age (46).

Other Worm Infestations: The major ones would be due to roundworm and hookworm infestations. Whilst roundworm would be very common and affect the growth and development of a lot of children, it is seen that hookworm is an important cause of anaemia in both children and adults. In past community reports, over 50% of infections were due to ascariasis - but in hospital records about 30-40% were seen. Government of Nepal has now a policy of deworming all children between 1 and 5 years at the time that Vitamin A is given. Pregnant women are given a tablet of Albendazole during the first trimester. Besides this, the School Health and Nutrition (SHN) program, gives deworming tablet twice a year to all the children in all the public and private schools in Nepal. The building of toilets and the subsequent declaring of 'Open defecation free districts' has brought down the incidence of worm infestations. Bhaktapur has been declared ODF districts in the valley very recently.

e. Others

Cor Pulmonale: An assignment report on cardiovascular diseases reviewed an epidemiological study of admissions at Bir Hospital, Kathmandu over the period 1970-75. This and another review at the Gandaki Zonal Hospital showed a high proportion of cor pulmonale. The conclusion was that domestic smoke in houses with open-fires and no chimneys was the major cause of this condition. An epidemiological study done over a four month period in 1979 revealed a fairly high prevalence of chronic obstructive lung disease (COPD) (47).

Cancers: Pathological specimens study at TUTH by Shrestha HG et al over a 5 year period 2048-2052 BS had shown that the commonest cancer seen was that of the stomach (16.0%). Others in order of frequency were: lung (11.5%), cervix (9.7%), skin (6.0%) and breast (5.7%). It was also noted that the change of lifestyle of Nepalese population, exposure of carcinogenic substances had changed the pattern of cancers seen e.g. cancer of lung increased in frequency from 7.3% in 2048 BS to 17.5% in 2052 BS (48).

A multi-institutional study involving data from seven institutions in Nepal was co-ordinated by the BP Koirala Cancer Hospital in Chitwan. The compiled results showed that: Overall the most common sites in males was the lung followed by the oral cavity and stomach. In females it was cervix uteri, breast and stomach. Age also had a role in the type of cancer. Leukaemia and lymphomas were seen in the young, lung, oral lesions and stomach in middle age and lung, stomach and larynx in the oldest males. In women it was breast in the young, cervix in middle age and lung in the very aged.

High Altitude Sickness: Because of the popularity of mountaineering and increased movements of people along the mountains and high altitudes this condition is being encountered more frequently. Local porters and mountaineers who have climbed at fast rates have been seen to suffer from it. Another aspect is the religious pilgrimage to shrines on the high Himalayas and the non divulgence of symptoms of high altitude sickness by the devotees in their quest for spiritual attainments. A study by Basnyat on pilgrims going to Gosaikunda (4154 m) showed that 4.4% appeared to have altitude sickness (49).

Iodine Deficiency Disorders (IDD)

Because of the mountainous terrain the iodine lyses out of the soil and the produce from such areas do not contain much of this micronutrient. Whilst far flung areas did not utilise iodised salts previously, this has changed over the years. It is more common in Western mountains and mid hills. Because of roads and modern modes of transportation foods containing iodine and also iodised salt are reaching such areas where cases of iodine deficiency disorders were seen. The month of February every year is being used to create country wide awareness of this problem.

Iron Deficiency Anaemia

The micronutrient status survey of 1998 has shown that this is a major problem. This is very much prevalent in Nepal and seen in young girls and also pregnant mothers. In the pursuit to reduce perinatal mortality efforts are being made to reduce the incidence of anaemia in prospective mothers. The government has a policy to give iron tablets from second semester to all pregnant mothers free of cost. This is also continued in the post-partum period.

Thalassemia / Thalassemia Trait

This is also a genetically determined hereditary blood haemoglobin disorder which results in varying grades of anaemia. Patients with this disorder should not be given iron for their anaemia. Though originally thought to be restricted to the Mediterranean region this genetically predisposed disorder was carried by the migration by boat of genetically affected people to Gujarat and the Western Ghats. Those who migrated by the North West Region of India brought it to those areas and also Nepal. Its incidence in the Mediterranean Region has been reduced by genetic counselling and advising persons with the gene/trait not to marry those with similar condition as the chances of having an offspring with the disease will be greater.

The common types are α and β thalassemia. Its symptoms vary from death at birth or soon after, in cases of α thalassemia, to cases of β thalassemia which have varying degrees of anaemia and splenomegaly (50).

Sickle Cell Disease / Sickle Cell Trait

This is also a genetically determined disorder. Though a large proportion of this disease is seen in persons of Central African descent, it is seen also in of the Mediterranean region and also India. Sickle cell anaemia is caused by homogeneity for the sickle gene and manifests as sickle cell disease. Heterozygous carriers of the sickle gene have the sickle cell trait (50).

Many doctors were aware of the fact that Tharus based mainly in the Western Region of Nepal were resistant to malaria. It has recently been realised that this is due to the fact that a substantial percentage of them have sickle cell anaemia.

Vitamin A Deficiency: This had at one time become a major cause of childhood blindness as a result of keratomalacia and damage to the eye. The importance of this vitamin was then highlighted for its protective effect against diarrhoea and chest infections. Research in Sarlahi in

1989/90 and in Humla (1992) showed the important role of Vitamin A in increasing child survival (6 & 51). The MoH launched a National Vitamin A Programme in 1993 with the support of USAID and UNICEF. Two major components of this programme were to:

1. give high dose 200.000 units vitamin A capsules supplementation.
2. motivate to increase production and regular consumption of vitamin A rich foods in preschool children and pregnant and lactating women.

The semi-annual Vitamin A capsule distribution was at first started in 32 priority districts and gradually expanded further into the remaining ones. Vitamin A campaigns, during the course of the Polio Pulse exercise on a country wide basis during the last six years have been very beneficial and manifestations of its deficiency are now rarely seen.

PRESENT STATUS

Table 2.1. Top Ten OPD Diseases- 2068/2069 (18)

Types of Disease	%
Gastritis (APD)	3.9
Headaches, Migraine	3.7
ARI (Lower Respiratory Tract Infection)	3.6
Upper Respiratory Tract Infection	3.6
Impetigo/Boils/Furunculosis	2.8
Intestinal Worms	2.8
Pyrexia of Unknown Origin	2.6
Presumed Non-infectious Diarrhoea	2.3
Amoebic Dysentery	2.2
Falls/Injuries/Fractures	2.0
Other Diseases	70.5
Total	100.0

This pattern of diseases as has been shown above is as per the attendance in the government health facilities. It has been changing over the years and whilst the incidence of ARI is up, that of skin diseases and diarrhoeas have come down. These figures may not however be wholly representative for a substantial percentage of the Nepali population now avails of services provided by the medical colleges and the private sector.

There are in August 2013, a total of nineteen medical colleges and many nursing homes which are now functioning and providing service to the Nepali people.

As one goes over the status of diseases seen in Nepal, one realises that the people are subjected to a relatively large number of afflictions, present almost all the time. Besides these **endemic** illnesses, a number of other diseases take **epidemic** proportions from time to time. The cholera epidemic during the time of Chandra Shumsher was but one of such episodes in the history of diseases in Nepal. In such situations it makes much more sense to try to work on the premise, **"Prevention is better than cure"**. This is the reason why health policies are made and it is obligatory to try to put into practice what has been delineated as policy. The post Rana period after 1950 is an example of this as a number of specific projects were started to deal with the various problems of the populace.

The major causes of morbidity and mortality vary tremendously according to which sources one has consulted. Examining these figures, one sees that the summer months are the time of the year when most people are ill. Such illnesses, generally due to gastrointestinal upset, occur because of faecal contamination of water or food by various offending organisms. A clean environment with a good water supply and proper sewage disposal will get rid of all the major illnesses associated with this.

PRIMARY HEALTH CARE IN NEPAL

Presently stress is being laid on the preventive aspects of health care. People are being made aware of the fact that they should be looking after their own health. As the media has a great role in creating public awareness, a special section dealing with the concept of Information, Education and Communication (IEC) has been set up.

The MoH, from the time of its inception in 1956, was aware of the necessity of controlling communicable diseases. The subsequent years saw the setting up of various projects.

Malaria Eradication Project -	1958
Leprosy Control Project -	1965
Tuberculosis Control Project -	1965
Smallpox Eradication Project -	1967
Family Planning and MCH Project -	1968

Following the official eradication of smallpox, this project was converted into the Expanded Programme of Immunisation (EPI) in 1977. Later attention has been given for the eradication of polio, neonatal tetanus and measles.

Malaria Control

The history of malaria, or **awal** as was known in the country has been recounted. The locals believed it to emanate from swamps, marshes and similar environment. Some people of Italy, having lived in such areas, believed that the condition was caused by bad air or **mala aria**. Thus originated the name for the symptoms, which later was shown to be caused, not by bad air, but by a parasite aided by its vector, the mosquito.

From 1955 Nepal attempted for four years to try to eradicate malaria. After a period of 12 years it was noted that there was a marked reduction in the number of malaria cases. However, a further five years the picture had changed, perhaps because the mosquitoes had developed resistance to DDT. Seeing that eradication now seemed an impossible task, WHO in 1976 advised to change to a Malaria Control Programme instead.

Integration

By the late sixties both USAID and WHO had come around to the thinking that the Nepalese health services needed to be integrated (5). This led naturally on to the proposal of trying the process in two districts viz. Kaski and Bara, which were dissimilar in terms of location, living styles etc. The administrative aspects were initially handled by Community Health and Integration Division (CHID). A Central Integration Board (CIB) was also formed. As time went on, 4 more districts were added. In 1980 however, both the CHID and CIB were disbanded and a new Integrated Community Health Services Development Project (ICHSDP) was formed as per the Development Boards Act of 1956 (52).

The various slogans of WHO starting from Basic Minimum Health Needs culminated ultimately in the Health For All 2000 (HFA 2000) strategy of 1978. This in course of time, following acceptance by the world at the Alma Ata Conference of 1978, became the "Health Call of the World".

By 1987 the MoH decided to integrate all the vertically run programmes. The Department of Health Services was done away with and the Ministry took over the overall functioning. The District Public Health Offices were established. By this time the ICHSDP had a total of 23 integrated districts under it. All these now came under the newly established Public Health Division, which also became the central focal point for the DPHOs.

In June 1996, during the time that the three party coalition government of NC, RPP and NSP was in power, the Malaria Research and Training Centre at Hetauda was converted into the Vector Borne Disease Training and Research Centre (VBDTRC) with the aid of USAID. This centre has been designated the focal point for the fight against vector borne diseases such as malaria, kala-azar and Japanese encephalitis.

Confronted with the problems stated above, Nepal though being a least developed country had to find a way out. It was with this hope that Nepal was in the forefront for the acceptance of the Primary Health Care concept. This became the new 'Mantra' for the health sector. With these new developments, Nepal is now planning to be accepted into the Developing Countries category by the year 2022.

PHC and HFA 2000

Nepal had sent an official delegation to the Alma Ata conference in 1978. From then onwards, like most of the countries of the world, Nepal committed itself to providing Primary Health Care to its citizens. Goals were set, and revised from time to time. Five of the targets then set to be attained by 2000 AD were as follows:-

1. IMR per 1000 live births: reduce from 107 to 45.
2. Population growth rate: reduce from 2.66 to less than 2 percent.
3. Life expectancy at birth: increase from 51 to 65 years both for men and women.
4. Drug supply locally: increase from 9 to 60 percent production.
5. Health Worker to Population ratio:
   a. One health worker (Trained Doctor, Kaviraj, Health Assistant, Vaidya, Auxiliary Health Worker) for every 3000 of the population.
   b. One trained nurse (Staff Nurse, Assistant Nurse Midwife) for every 600 population.
   c. One health volunteer for every 500 population.

Post Alma Ata

For the sake of practicality this package of PHC was broken down into eight components (53):

a. Education about existing health problems and how to prevent and control them.

b. Promotion of food supply and proper nutrition.
c. Adequate supply of safe water and basic sanitation.
d. MCH care including family planning.
e. Immunisation against major infectious diseases.
f. Prevention and control of locally endemic diseases.
g. Appropriate treatment of common diseases and injuries.
h. Provision of essential drugs.

The Situation in Nepal

At the time that the concept of Primary Health Care was getting acceptance world wide, the Institute of Medicine (IoM) at Kathmandu, was starting its community oriented medical course. As a prelude to this, a number of community oriented studies were done at three out of the seventy five districts of Nepal. The study in Tanahu showed that 70% of the need for care could possibly be prevented (54). There was also the unavailability of health personnel and that government health services were providing barely 10% of consultations and only 3% of the estimated needs of ill persons. Even in such a situation there was a preference for health services if available vis-à-vis the traditional methods.

Studies in Nuwakot showed that health institutions, which were within one hour or at utmost two hours walking distance, had a better chance of being utilised by the populace (55). It was also apparent that rural communities, by and large were unaware of basic health knowledge about sanitation and nutrition etc. It was confirmed also that the government health services met only a fraction of the health requirement of the rural population.

Studies by members of the British Nepal Medical Trust (BNMT) in Taplejung District has also stressed the need for more communication between the rural health service providers and the client population. This was very important in the case of infections which required a relatively long period of treatment e.g. leprosy and tuberculosis. The use of the services of traditional medical practitioners as referral agents has been found to work (56). This better communication about PHC facilities raised the confidence of the people in a setting where some of the health posts were at 3 to 4 hours walking distance.

Studies by IoM personnel in later years at Dhankuta also confirmed that health infrastructure in the rural areas, being minimal were not functioning properly. Important issues of over population and environment degradation plus the necessity of increased health education, and changing life styles were focused on. This study had major recommendations on status of women such as late marriage, increased literacy, income generation, increased breast feeding, birth spacing etc. (57).

It has been shown that 91% of the population which used the free health services provided by the government in 2068/69 BS did so at the health post and sub-health posts, 5% at hospitals and 4% at PHCCs.(18).

Thus whilst thinking about the health services to be provided to the people one would have to take into account the various documents that Nepal is signatory to:-

A. The Convention on the Rights of the Child. 1990: Part 1 Article 24 starts by stating, "State Parties recognize the Right of the Child to the enjoyment of the highest attainable standard of health and to facilities for the treatment of illness and rehabilitation of health. State Parties shall strive to ensure that no child is deprived of his or her right of access to such health care services. Children's Act was enacted in 1992 and its regulations in 1995 to make it in conformity with Nepali policy, laws and regulations on the rights and welfare of children. In 2012 Nepal Government brought out a National Policy on Children by which 10% of the budget (both National and local) is committed to children and their agenda.

B. Declaration of Alma Ata. 1978: Nepal is a signatory to this document by which we have accepted the concept of PHC as a practical approach to making essential health care universally accessible to individuals and families in the community in an acceptable and affordable way, and with their full participation.

C. Basic Minimum Health Needs: The goal stated in 1985 was that the country would achieve a standard of living as per "basic needs according to Asian standard". What this meant was not clear though the National Planning Commission (NPC) later produced a "Basic Needs" list.

Following the constitutional commitment (Interim Constitution) of 2007 an implementing policy of providing 'Free Health Care Services' to the people was put in place. The obligation is to provide PHC to every citizen with consideration for the poor, very poor, disabled, destitute and senior citizens. In 2009 a PHC Revitalisation Division was set up in the Department of Health Services to act with the under-mentioned concepts:

- National Free Health Care
- Social Heath Protection, and
- Urban and Environmental Health

Water supply, sanitation and sewage status

The sources of water used in the past in Kathmandu valley plus in other parts of the country were:

Stone water spouts	**dhunge dharas**
Springs, ponds	**pokharis**
Water holes	**kuwas**
Rivers	**nadi**
Wells	**inars**

Water Supply - The Beginning

Bir Shumsher, after becoming Prime Minister employed a British Engineer Mathew Lochard Sinclair in 1891 to introduce modern technology into Nepal as an act of expiation for the killings that had been engineered by the Shumshers. Water was first supplied to the palaces of the Ranas and the Phohara Durbar with its fountains was a prime example (58). Bir Shumsher also utilised the services of *Kau* or blacksmith i.e. the forerunners of plumbers to install piped water supply or provide *Kaldharas* both at Bhotahity in Kathmandu and at Bhaktapur.

Later the piped water supply system of Kathmandu was expanded on a very limited scale at Kathmandu and Bhaktapur by Prime Minister Bhim Shumsher. As a result of this the number of water borne diseases e.g. cholera etc decreased. The system was not overloaded and so that is why it functioned. This service was free and though the proposal was made that people using the facility should pay for it, it was turned down by the PM on the grounds that if he was instrumental in such a decision, he would never get to heaven! Pressure for more connections did not mount during the succeeding years because the prevailing system did not allow it. Those not fortunate enough to use this facility had to get their water from natural sources as stated already. In the immediate post 1950 period however, the sources of water at Sundarijal, Pharping and Panipokhari were not adequate and a larger supply reservoir was to be constructed at Mahankal in Chabahil. The designs of 1965/66 were said to have been prepared with a 22 years projection in mind but a reassessment even then suggested that the water supply would not even be adequate for a population that would inhabit Kathmandu in the year 1972 AD. In actual fact the days of water in plenty did not last long and limited supply came into vogue in three years time. In the Terai region it was the supply of tube wells that came to be accepted. The government established the Water Supply and Sanitation Board (WSSB) in 1974. This took a new form when the Nepal Water Supply Corporation (NWSC) came into being in 1989.

In the context of South East Asia the sanitary situation in most of the countries is at bursting point. Whilst it is true that industrial pollution is gradually becoming a problem, it is the magnitude of it that staggers planners. In the South East Asian countries, the provision of adequate sanitary facilities is going to cost more for the simple reason that most of the population live in the rural areas; 83% in the case of Nepal in 2011.

These problems exist in Nepal and are in fact highlighted by the prevailing situation in the urban centres. It is here that the supply of drinking water and sewage disposal seem to go hand in hand. This is borne out by the almost annual recurrence of cholera, typhoid and infective hepatitis in the population of urban areas especially Kathmandu.

As far as the capital was concerned, the government formulated a fifteen year plan to improve the quality of service as regards water supply and the waste water.

The situation in 1990-96 was that safe water supply was said to be present for 63% of the population and the breakdown was said to be 88% and 60% availability in the urban and rural areas respectively. Coverage for the year 2001 and the situation in 2010 is as given below.

Table 2.2. Water Supply Coverage

Water Supply Coverage	2001+-	2005*	2010*
Urban	90%	93%	93%
Rural	75%	82%	88%
Total Coverage	77%	84%	89%

+- State of World Children 2005

* State of World Children 2013 (59)

The recent news that is going around is that quite a large amount of water obtained from underground sources contains not only iron but also substantial amounts of arsenic. Report of a study by IDS-Nepal in 20 districts of the Terai has shown in May 2005 that as many as two million Nepalese may be drinking arsenic contaminated water. Prior to this arsenic had been found in Morang, Sunsari and Jhapa in 1998. Later samples found arsenic in Rautahat, Bara, Parsa, Nawalparasi, Rupendehi and Kapilbastu. The Red Cross Societies of Japan and Nepal also found arsenic in the water of mid-Terai.

In 1998 the government with the intention of involving the private sector formed the High Level Private Sector Participation Committee to try to get the private sector to manage Kathmandu's water supply. An organisation known as the Kathmandu Upatyaka Khanepani Limited (KUKL) came into being.

Currently different projects are going on at the local village levels, the reality is the development of a large number of firms supplying drinking mineral water in plastic bottles to the thirsty public. These vary from the tankers bringing so called drinking water from any nearby rivulet to various bottling plants producing mineral water in plastic bottles. There is a lot of controversy as to whether it is potable. Plans are afoot to privatise the process of water supply to the population. The prospect of getting water in plenty from Melamchi is still a mirage.

In 2005 some ordinances were passed with the objective of privatising the distribution of water supply in the urban areas.

Sewage Disposal

Surprising as it may seem, the Malla kings of Kathmandu valley had arranged to have built from bricks, arched underground drains for the use of the community of the particular area. Other covered drains built subsequently during the period of Rana rule helped towards the disposal of sewage for a period of almost two centuries in the urban areas of the valley. The increasing urbanisation of the capital led to difficulties regarding sewage disposal in the 1970's.

However though some drains for sewage disposal existed, these were not adequate for Wright in his description of Kathmandu of the 1870's gives a very vivid picture of the environment in those days (60).

"The streets of Kathmandu are very narrow, mere lanes in fact; and the whole town is very dirty. In every lane there is a stagnant ditch, full of putrid mud, and no attempt is ever made to clean these thoroughly. The streets, it is true, are swept in the centre, and part of the filth is carried off by the sellers of manure; but to clean the drains would now be impossible without knocking down the entire city, as the whole ground is saturated with filth. The houses are generally built in the form of hollow squares, opening off the streets by low doorways; and these central courtyards are too often only receptacles for rubbish of every sort. In short, from a sanitary point of view, Kathmandu may be said to be built on a dunghill in the middle of latrines" was what Daniel Wright said in his book 'History of Nipal' as long ago as 1877.

Regarding sewage disposal in Nepal, one can perhaps start with Kathmandu and compare with what is happening elsewhere. In the pre 1950 period, a sewerage system had been made for Kathmandu. It went from the New Road area and the Bir Hospital area, through the Tundikhel and discharged its effluence in the Tukucha, which in turn went into the Bagmati.

The rest of the inhabitants of Kathmandu, because the houses were fairly well dispersed then had to do with individual septic tanks and soak pits. The citizens of the capital city have not got a water sewerage system of sewage disposal. Other parts of the country have not really thought about it, so the future is anybody's guess. For the record however the existing situation is that on an overall basis the disposal of wastes and sewage is just 31%. The further breakdown of the figure shows that the disposal of the sewage and wastes is 48% and 27% in the urban and rural areas respectively. Past coverage for the year 2001 and the situation in 2010 are as follows:

Table 2.3. Sanitation Coverage

Sanitation Coverage	2001+-	2002+-	2010*
Urban	75%	68%	48%
Rural	25%	20%	27%
Total Coverage	31%	27%	31%

+- State of World Children 2005

* State of World Children 2013

The basic Guidelines of Sanitation Master Plan 2068 BS stresses the need to declare areas free of Open Defaecation. This is gradually being implemented all over the country as people become more aware. The 5th SAARC Sanitation Conclave held at Bhaktapur in Oct. 2013 came out with the Kathmandu Declaration to accelerate the momentum of sanitation in the region. A new target set at this Conclave for Nepal is to ensure total water and sanitation facility by 2017.

The problem of urban centres such as Kathmandu is the disposal of the garbage that is being generated daily in ever increasing amounts. Garbage disposal has become a political issue and reaches periodic impasses due to temporary short term agreements to dump it in specific rural areas. The rural dweller on the other hand is refusing to accept the trash of the urban inhabitant. More recently, small groups of workers have started in the urban areas to tackle the problem of garbage disposal on a locality to locality basis.

After a number of years of discussion, a new landfill for the waste disposal of the towns of Kathmandu and Lalitpur has been set up with the aid of JICA at Okhar Pauwa in the Nuwakot area. The space here will be adequate for 3 years only. Another site in the same area with a much larger capacity is being prepared with the aid of JICA and is expected to be adequate for the following seventeen years.

Future Management

The necessity of a sewerage treatment plant especially in the urban centres is periodically voiced. Not much action has resulted. Besides this, other factors such as the planning and control of urbanisation, attention to proper housing, the control of pollution, food hygiene come into it. The instituting of a multi-sectoral approach comes into it for proper functioning. Safe water supplies and sewage disposal will improve nutrition and decrease contamination of foods; thus bringing about remarkable improvements in health.

DISABILITY AND REHABILITATION

If one goes over the health papers one finds that as from 1971, the number of important studies on disability that have been carried out is as listed (61).

National Census 1971

- Sample survey of disabled persons in Nepal 1980
- National survey of blindness 1981
- National survey of mental retardation 1989
- National survey of the prevalence of deafness and ear disease in Nepal 1991
- A disability survey of Kanchanpur District, 1995
- Survey of persons with disability in Sindhuli District, 1998
- A situational analysis of disability by National Planning Commission, 2001

As per the Census of 2011, 2% of the population or 513,321 persons are disabled.

It was as late as 1981 that some awareness about disability was created in Nepal. The International Year of Disabled Persons (IYDP) prompted the Nepal Paediatric Society (NEPAS) to hold its first conference with this theme.

The IYDP ad hoc committee had in 1980 initiated the process for doing a survey regarding disability in Nepal. This pilot survey covered some 8001 families with a total of 45,358 persons in six districts of Nepal. The results and subsequent extrapolation suggested that the total number of disabled in the country could be estimated to be 376,479 or nearing 400,000. No exact figures for the major causes were searched for, but the disabilities were grouped into four categories:

a. Orthopaedic, (of limb, head, neck and spine)
b. Visual
c. Hearing (deaf & deaf/mute)
d. Mental.

Analysis then showed that hearing disability was the most common disability in the country and the main reason was the suppurative otitis media leading on to chronic otitis (62).

Introduction of a very comprehensive "Disabled Protection and Welfare Act, 1982" was a major attainment following the IYDP, 1981. This act defines the disabled person as one physically and mentally unable to lead a normal life.

Following the IYDP, GoN has become conscious of fulfilling its obligations towards the disabled. Subsequent Five Year Plans have included aspects of three programmes given below:

1. Prevention of Blindness Project.
2. Disabled Rehabilitation Programme.
3. Survey and Treatment of Deafness.

The educational requirements of the disabled children were initially looked after and catered for at the Laboratory School at Kirtipur. A blind school at Dharan, and two deaf schools of which one was at the Balmandir in Kathmandu and the other at Bhairahawa were the initial efforts. Presently the some of the blind and visually handicapped are integrated in the mainstream system. In conformity with the government policies of "Education for all & HFA 2000" the intention was to provide primary and basic education to all by then.

The IYDP was followed by the UN Decade (1982-93) for Disabled Persons. Some improvement has taken place can be claimed by stating that a number of integrated schools for the blind and visually handicapped have come up now. These are run by the Nepal Association for the Welfare of the Blind (NAWB) and are situated in different parts of Nepal.

Starting first at Bhaktapur a NGO had started a number of Community Based Rehabilitation (CBR) programmes at Lalitpur and also Palpa. These were later handed over to the Ministry of Women & Social Welfare and extended in a limited scale to all the 75 districts of Nepal.

Subsequent development was the conduction of 'A Situational Analysis of Disability' in Nepal by the National Planning Commission with the support of UNICEF and New ERA. It was completed in 1996 (63).

The research was based on the 4 broad categories of disabilities which has now world wide acceptance as a form of categorisation viz:

- communication
- locomotion
- mentally related
- multiple / complex disabilities

The communication category comprise of seeing, hearing and speaking disabilities. The locomotion one of mobility and manipulation. The mentally related consist of mental retardation, epilepsy and chronic mental illness. The fourth category comprises of various combination of these.

Following the first phase of the research, further work was done from Sept. 2000 onwards. The field workers covered 35 clusters spread in the Terai, hills and mountains over a period of 4 months and a total of 13,005 households were enumerated. It showed:

Table 2.4. Disabled Persons as Respondents by Type of Disability

Disabled as Respondents	12-19 yrs	20-59 yrs	60+yrs	Total Self Res.	%
Seeing	4	39	25	68	13.6
Hearing	1	7	1	9	1.8
Speaking	0	0	3	3	0.6
Mobility	29	116	14	159	31.9
Manipulation	17	65	17	99	19.8
Mental Retardation	0	0	0	0	0
Chronic Mental Illness	0	6	0	6	1.2
Epilepsy	23	65	7	95	19.0
Multiple Disability	12	39	9	60	12.0
TOTAL	86	337	76	499	100.0

Sample size is weighted to account for sample size.
Source: A Situation Analysis of Disability in Nepal.

Communication Disabilities

Visual Disabilities

It was the pioneering zeal of Dr. Ram Prasad Pokhrel and his supporters, which started the Nepal Eye Hospital on 13th April, 1974. Further work by other organisations and individuals in this field resulted in a good network of eye care services in the country.

As a feasibility study in 1979 indicated that 90% of blindness could be prevented or cured, the Nepalese government and WHO began the following year a major programme with a survey of the prevalence and causes of blindness (64).

Though cataract was the cause of 67% of the blindness, it was trachoma, which was the widespread potentially blinding condition. Active trachoma was seen in as much as 6.5% of the population (65).

A survey was carried out from Dec. 80 to Apr. 81 MOH/GoN & WHO to estimate the prevalence and causes of blindness. It became also necessary to categorise the state of blindness - those in whom both eyes were involved was estimated to be 0.84 per 100 population whilst those in whom only in one eye was involved was estimated to be 1.66/100 persons. The leading cause of unilateral blindness was cataract (40.7%) with trachoma as the second common cause at 13.6%. Of those blind in both eyes, cataract was responsible in 72%, retinal disease for 33% and glaucoma in 3.2%. Blindness was found to be much more prevalent in women than in men.

It has been reported by Brilliant et al that age and sex standardized cataract prevalence was 2.7 times higher in sites at an altitude of 185 metres or less than in sites over 1000 metres. Sites with an average of 12 hours of sunlight had 3.8 times as much cataract at sites with an average of only seven hours of exposure (66).

Of the several NGOs involved in the prevention and control of disability a large number are involved in eye camps organised in different parts of the country. Lions and Leo Clubs in various parts of the country are also doing extensive services for eye care. It is estimated that as many as 100 or so eye camps are organised every year and that about 1400 patients have operation for cataracts and restoration of vision.

During the course of these years GoN gave Nepal Netra Jyoti Sangh (NNJS), a local NGO, the authority to coordinate all eye care services in Nepal. During the course of the last three decades a large number of cataract surgery has been performed. A substantial number of the patients serviced have come from surrounding areas of India. The back log of cases awaiting operations has been considerably reduced.

Among the nations of S-E Asia, xerophthalmia had been shown to be a major problem in Nepal (67). It was shown to be of higher incidence in boys than girls of the pre-school age. The risk of xerophthalmia was shown to be inversely related to the elevation of the terrain, with it being maximal in children living in the Terai region.

There are in mid-2013, a total of 17 NGO's Eye Hospitals with a capacity of 1,415 beds. These are being utilised for the provision of eye care.

The National Assembly of the Nepal Blinds Association in 1995 estimated that there are 240,000 blind people in the country.

Hearing Disabilities

It has been estimated during the course of the International Year of Disabled Persons that hearing disabilities were the most common. A school for children with hearing difficulties was started at Naxal in the proximity of Bal Mandir. Such schools started on a regional basis are at Surkhet and Dharan. Another such facility, run with the support of Lion's Club, is the Aksheshwar Mahavihar Clinic at Lalitpur. The current practice is to integrate children with disabilities into normal schools.

The Tribhuvan University Teaching Hospital (TUTH) has been running a Speech and Hearing Clinic in the capital since 1994. Appliances for those with hearing defects are also been assembled there. Three children were the first to have cochlear implantations done at the TUTH in December 2004.

Locomotion Disabilities

Orthopaedic Disabilities

In 2011 almost 83% people lived in the rural areas and had a life style that required climbing trees for chopping wood for domestic fires or gathering leaves as cattle fodder it is not surprising that injuries as a result of falls were quite common. Walking along mountain trails in the dark can be the cause of falls leading to broken bones or even death. Even the manner of carrying goods by *doko* led to injuries as was observed and so reported by Taylor in 1951.

"At Lumpek, a village on a very steep ridge, there were several cases of traumatic arthritis of the knees which resembled Charcot's joints. They had none of the neurological stigmata of **tabes dorsalis**. The aetiology seemed to have been traumatic, the symptoms being associated with carrying heavy loads down the steep hills (68)."

Burn contracture brought about by picking up live coals from the open hearth fires or scalding by hot fluids in their homes is common. Study by Banskota et al reported in 1988 AD showed that extremity burns causing inability to use the hand or even walking were the most common disability encountered (69). Facial burns also seen, besides causing disfigurement often led to blindness following exposure keratitis. Rehabilitation is also being done for problems related to congenital disorders, burns contracture, tuberculosis, osteomyelitis and neglected trauma (70).

Mentally Related

Mental Disabilities

Sometime since September, 1978 a organisation in which some Maryknoll Fathers have been involved through day care centres for the mentally retarded. Subsequently, an organisation known as Human And National Development Services (HANDS) started working in Nepal with the same objective on a more permanent basis. Now however this organisation is no longer working in Nepal but other local NGOs have been started and the work continues on.

The Association for the Welfare of the Mentally Retarded (AWMR) came into being in 1981 and is now working in about 18 districts of the country.

The Disabled Protection and Welfare Act, 2039 BS was passed as long ago as 1982. It is surprising that though Nepal was one of the first countries in the SAARC countries to promulgate the law, the reality is that not much progress has been made in this regard.

Supply of Essential Drugs

Medical personnel prescribe drugs and people buy them. The tendency now is that because of the fairly large market, many drug companies vie for a share in this area. Whilst a major share of the market belongs to Indian companies, the local manufacturing concerns supply about 34% of the market. This has risen from the 28.5% that had been confirmed in 2000. Drug companies from Bangladesh and elsewhere are also seeking a foothold here.

The drug scenario has changed during course of the last twenty years. Stress has been laid by the Department of Drug Administration on single effective drugs with known beneficial effect. Marketing of brands with more than single drug is not generally allowed unless the effect of both drugs is enhanced and the effect is beneficial to the patient. The use of multiple drugs in combination to give what may be termed 'blunderbuss' treatment is being discouraged at all levels.

With Nepal's entry into the World Trade Organisation (WTO) in 2004, there was great activity in the pharmaceutical industry. More recently there has been a certain amount of 'one upmanship' by Nepali Drug

Companies stating that they have been approved under the WHO GMP (Good Manufacturing Practices) criteria. WHO at one time put in a notice in a local paper, stating that it was the local authorities who certified this and not WHO. What must be remembered is that the world market is now accessible to Nepalese pharmaceutical concerns in the same manner in which world industries can also enter the Nepalese markets.

What must be noted is that the average family spends quite a substantial sum on medication, be it by over the counter sales or by the prescribed format of the doctor. Ineffective drugs or medicines with doubtful beneficial effects e.g. Anti diarrhoeal, cough syrups, tonics etc should be discouraged. It is the large number of marketing personnel of the drug companies who decide which drugs rule the market. Because companies are generally divided into two or three units, representatives visit the doctor every fortnight or even weekly in lieu of the single person who came from India to visit the doctors once or twice a year. Over prescribing certainly occurs and it is in that context that the concept of 'Rational Prescribing' has come into vogue.

Enforcement of the Essential Drug List

The demand for drugs to cure disease continues to rise because of the increase in population and the health awareness of the people. The estimate in 1996 was that the value of this was about Rs. 2650 million, of which 80% was imported from India and about 18% was produced by local industries. By mid-2012 the figures were that 45% were locally produced by about 50 pharmaceutical companies of which 20 were WHO GMP certified. About whilst 55% are still being imported from India and elsewhere. (71) It is also estimated that the annual growth of sales of medicine is in the region of 18%. Bearing this ever-increasing use of drugs, it is fortunate that the government has been advocating the use of essential drugs.

The provision of the essential drugs has been put as one of the eight elements of primary health care. This is very important in the context of HFA 2000. The selection and the advantages of an essential drug list are as follows:

a. Reduction in the number of pharmaceutical products to be purchased, stored, analyzed and distributed;
b. Improvement in the quality of drug utilization, management, information and monitoring;

c. Stimulation of local pharmaceutical industries;
d. Assistance to the least developed countries in urgent need of high priority drug programme to solve their primary health care problems.

Though a master plan had been initially brought out in 1955 advocating the use of medicinal plants, it was only in 1961 that this was implemented. The Royal Drug Research Laboratory (RDRL) established in 1964 as per this plan started the manufacturing of modern drugs in 1968. Subsequently the manufacturing unit of RDRL was converted into Royal Drugs Limited (RDL) in 1972 for the production of modern drug formulations on a commercial basis (72).

It was at the initiative of the Royal Drugs Ltd. that a list of basic drugs had been initially made. The idea behind this was that the production policy of Royal Drugs Ltd. would be based on the drugs on that list. Subsequently the IoM revised that list and then a combined meeting of the NMA and the Nepal Pharmaceutical Association gave it its final shape, plus also categorised it into two groups. One group consisted of those drugs, which could only be used at the health posts. The second group contained these plus other preparations, which could be prescribed at the hospital level (73).

Later the Department of Drug Administration (DDA) was established in 1979 in accordance with the Drug Act, 1978. It had meetings with the Nepal Medical Council to have an approved schedule of drugs (74). In 1986, the following year, the DDA brought out the first Essential Drug List, 1986. Revised versions of this Essential Drug List were brought in 1992 and 1997. Further categorisation was done as:

a. Complementary List
b. District Hospital List
c. Health Post List
d. Sub Health Post List
e. Primary Care Treatment List

A third revision of the national essential drug list (EDL) was done in 2002. The EDL of Nepal now contains 310 drugs of various strengths and dosage forms. The DDA has been playing a major role in the maintenance of Good Manufacturing Practices (GMP) and discouraging the formulation of preparations with multiple compounds. A number of recommendations have been made following the workshop on GMP in December, 1995. The

DDA has also brought out a list of Life Saving Drugs. The DDA brought out Nepalese National Formulary in 1997. In 2000 a 'Standard for Pharmaceutical Regulation and Care' was brought out.

A National Drugs Policy - 2051 BS was announced in mid - March 1995. It specifies that the drug industry be considered a priority sector with a view to making the country self-reliant in the production of essential drugs. The objective was to make the country produce 80% of drug formulations by the year 2005 (72). A pharmaceutical unit is to be opened under the Ministry of Health so that all matters pertaining to medicine /drugs can be co-ordinated from there.

During the course of 12 years (2041-2053 BS) a total of 180 pharmaceutical concerns were registered with the DDA. Among the 180 companies 67.77% are allopathic, 17.22% ayurvedic, 5.56% consist of veterinary, 0.56% homeopathic, 8.33% consist of repacking and the remaining 0.56% consisted of Unani manufacturers. Of the 122 allopathic companies registered with the DDA, only 29 had taken production license till mid 1996. After this period there was a sudden upsurge in the number of domestic pharmaceutical companies. As of April 2004 there were 65 concerns of which 26 were producing traditional medication whilst the remaining 39 were producing allopathic medicines. These had produced a total of 6149 products of which 4930 were allopathic and 1219 were traditional. There were also a total of 83 importers of drugs who were bringing medication from various parts of the world to Nepal. There are also a total of 14,000 drug retailers in the country selling medicines to the public.

In Oct. 2008 about 35% of the annual drug requirements are estimated to be produced within the country. The total annual expenditure on drugs is estimated to be in the region of NRs. 12 Billions. Nepal Drugs Limited (formerly Royal Drugs Ltd.) used to have a major share of this but now this is not so now as it has stopped manufacturing for a number of years.

Present State

After dissolution of the Department of Health Services in mid 1986, the major reorganisation of the Ministry of Health led to the formation of five regional directorates and 75 District Public Health Offices. At the central level the MoH was composed of ten divisions and the two departments of ayurved and drug administration. Four years subsequently in July, 1990 the three projects viz. FP & MCH, EPI and the NMEO were also converted into divisions prior to being integrated.

The ultimate aim was that the preventive activities for health care would reach grassroots level in a well-organised manner.

Though the Decentralisation Act had been passed in 1982 it had not been effectively implemented. The intention during the Eighth Plan period was to make the District Development Committees effective to undertake the responsibility of planning, implementation and supervision of the District Health Services. It was for this purpose that three new Acts as given below were passed.

1. Village Development Committee Act, 1991
2. Municipality Act, 1991
3. District Development Committee Act, 1991
4. Local Self-Governance Act, 1999 (2055 BS)

In the "Common framework: second evaluation" document of 1990 the government's intention is expressed with the words:

"Full acceptance and understanding of primary health care has been achieved at all levels of the health system. It is in fact the approach to provide all the Nepalese people with the basic minimum health services in the form of preventive, promotive and curative services at *ilaka* and district levels. However it is felt that more orientation of the PHC concept should be provided to health workers associated with the referral system particularly at the hospital end." (75)

With the changes that took place after the *Jana Andolan I*, it is but natural that people's expectations increased. With the possibility of a more socially oriented society and with a more equitable distribution of resources, the expectation was but natural that budgetary provisions for the social sectors would increase markedly.

With the current state of affairs, it seems that neither the health workers nor the consuming public is satisfied with the health services that currently exist. The reason for this is that the money spent on health, usually 5% of the national budget, is negligible. Of this amount the major share is for the salaries of the health workers and so the actual amount spent for services and supplies is very little. Whilst the theory is that the health services are free, the reality is that it is just the doctors and other health workers services that the public does not have to pay for. More recently token payments for various services have been introduced by many of the hospital boards as a form of income generation for partial sustainability. The making of private wards, cabin service and shops for rental to pharmaceutical firms or even individuals seems to be the order of the day. Various medicines including tonics, other supplies such as dressings and even emergency drugs usually have to be bought. In the advantageous position that such medicine shops have, some even charge more than the marked price of the drugs! It is the public who ultimately pays for it.

Whilst the government of Nepal had always been committed to HFA 2000, it also claimed that the National Health Policy of 1991 was radically different from anything in the past in that it is a commitment to providing health care at grassroots level. The concept of reaching all the villages by way of the sub health post at the VDC level was then accepted and became official. The stress was on the district health services with the intention of upgrading the health status of the population, 93% of which is in the rural areas (76). With this reiteration to provide basic health services, a recent document stated that GoN tried to maintain a ratio of 40:60 in the allocation of resources.

Thus the Eighth Plan (1992-1997) laid stress on the provision of primary health care in an integrated fashion through the medium of different level health institutions such as primary health care centres, health posts and sub health posts. The focus of these was on family planning plus MCH services.

As regards the services in the rural areas, the point to note was that of the total number of 675 integrated and 141 static health posts, 198 in all were to be upgraded to Primary Health Care Centres over a 10-year period. With upgrading of various health posts to primary health care centres, the number of health posts was automatically reduced. But it was not just HPs only, for 3 sub health posts were also upgraded to PHC centres. Ultimately all the 205 electoral constituencies will have a PHC Centre with three beds, of which one will be for obstetrics. The new figure given for VDC is 4015 (77).

As has already been stated, one of the difficulties of providing Primary Health Care has been the scattered location of the population, especially in the rural areas. As health institutions are relatively few, the problem has been to provide the service to even a limited percentage of 10-15% of the population. An attempt to get around this problem was by way of mobile health camps and this had been put into to use on a limited scale since the mid-sixties. The health camps tended to be in the winter in the different parts of the country. Some of these camps were also conducted in the development regions of the country, which late King Birendra visited on a rotation basis. It was the practice to have a health camp every year. After the UML Government had been in power for about five months, the MoH decided to reintroduce the concept of mobile camps in different parts of the country. Such camps, which started from about April, 1995 had 20 to 30 doctors, lasted from 10-15 days and the number of patients seen at each camp was considerable. Such camps were held at Pyuthan, Myagdi and Taplejung and the patients seen during its duration was fifteen thousand, twelve thousand and nineteen thousand plus respectively. There has however been some questions raised as to whether these were populist measures which had been put into action and a lot of money spent.

However the effort to provide health services at the grassroots level goes on. With the involvement of the community it is envisaged that there will be 3199 sub-health posts with each providing services to about 4,000 of the population.

All said and done, PHC facilities for the urban dweller must also be thought about. The urban population is increasing in Nepal at a rate of 7.4% annually. The influx of people has led to inability of the system to cope with the huge demand for essential services such as housing, health facilities and sanitation. The new health policy makes a provision of having an Urban Clinic for every 50,000 population in a town, especially in areas of slums where the urban poor live. The concept of Urban Based Services (UBS) existed in 1994 in 15 municipalities of Nepal with coverage of about one million people. From the total number of 58 municipalities at the time of the 1991 census, the number has not officially increased as of October 1997.

The Urban Community Health Service Programme (UCHSP) of Kathmandu is a programme, which started in 1994 with the support of UNFPA & UNICEF. The Kathmandu Metropolitan City (KMC) authorities, with a view to develop the capital into a healthy city, established a public health department. This department has recently issued a strategy notice giving the three main components of an envisaged programme:

- Urban Health Care
- Environmental Health
- Health Research and Training

The action plan for 1997/98 too has been given:

- Preparation of Municipal Health Plan.
- Manage existing 15 Urban Health Centres and open new ones as per need.
- Initiate EPI to cover whole city.
- Initiate safe motherhood programme.
- Start health care programme for Kathmandu's sweepers who number over 1300.
- Initiate programme to tackle Vitamin A, iodine and iron deficiencies.
- Start school health programme to educate about hygiene, sanitation and public health.
- Assess conditions of eating places for drinking water, food preparation areas and toilets.
- Ensure that good quality food is sold.
- Launch programmes for control of seasonal epidemics.
- Co-ordinate with GOs, NGOs and other city authorities.

More recently there has been talk of liberalisation and privatisation. The talk is of public and private mix in the delivery of health care services. Though all details have not been divulged, the intention seems to be to hand over the curative services to the private sector and for the government to restrict itself to just promotive health care. Whilst this is an easier option this seems tantamount to washing ones hands from having to do the difficult task of providing reasonable health services to the people at large. It seems that some of the health indicators have shown some improvement. Many feel that whatever has occurred is due to the initiative taken by persons or institutions other than governmental that has resulted in this.

Table: 2.2 The basic indicators of Health: Past and Present Goals

Indicators	In 1997	As of 2011
IMR per 1,000 live births	82	39
MMR per 100,000 live births	515	170
U5 MR per 1,000 live births	116	48
Life expectancy at birth (Years)	56	69
TFR per woman	5.1	2.7

Source: UNICEF 2013 (59).

With the setting up of many VDCs and municipalities the stage was set, for some action regarding facilities such as water supply and sanitation not only in urban but also in the rural areas. The process of decentralisation, the giving of funds to areas other than the centre has started and hopefully will result in action at the grassroots level.

It is felt that though the Local Elections have not been held for last eleven years i.e. 2002, the Local Self Governance Act has been effective to a certain extent in certain parts of the country (78). The preamble of this act states:

- Institutionalize the process of development by enhancing the participation of all the people including the ethnic communities, indigenous people and down-trodden as well as socially and economically backward groups in bringing out social equality in mobilizing and allocating means for the development of their own region and in the balanced and equal distribution of the fruits of development.
- Constitute local bodies for the development of the local self – governance system in a manner that they are able to make decisions on the matters affecting the day-to-day needs and lives of the people, by developing local leadership.

POINTS TO PONDER

The climate of the Himalayas was said to be good and as a result many of the wise and learned men were said to come to the Himalayas to meditate. Because of the height and temperature, many of the diseases and the epidemics of the hot and torrid regions were not prevalent. Though infectious and vector borne diseases were present to a certain extent, the newly available drugs and vaccines have resulted in a marked decrease of these. The future will see a rise in the cancers and other non-communicable diseases plus also in road traffic accidents. As people live longer, as the environment changes, the diseases and their pattern within the country will change too.

References

1. Oldfield, H. A. Sketches in Nipal. 1880. W. H. Allen and Co., London.2 Vols
2. Selections from the Records of The Government of Bengal. No XXVII.

Papers Relative to the Colonization, Commerce, Physical Geography & etc of the Himalaya Mountain & Nepal. Brian H. Hodgson. 1857, John Gray, "Calcutta Gazette" Office.

3. Jordan, RR. From Missionaries to Mountaineers. Early Encounters with Nepal. 2010. Kathmandu.
4. Heydon, Susan. Modern Medicine and International Aid. 2009 Orient Black Swan.
5. Four Decades of Development. The History of US Assistance to Nepal 1951-1991. CA Skerry, K Moran, KM Calavan 1991.
6. West KP Jr et al, Efficacy of Vitamin A in reducing preschool child mortality in Nepal. Lancet, 1991; 338 (8759): 67-71.
7. Bista MB. A Review of Viral Hepatitis Infection in Nepal. J.Nep.Med. Assoc, 1994, 32 (112): 257-260.
8. Shrestha S, Non-A, non-B types of viral hepatitis. Nep Paed Soc J, 1985; 4 (2): 87-91.
9. Shrestha SM, Primary liver cancer in Nepal. J Inst Med 1988; 10(3): 177-189.
10. Shrestha IL. Hepatitis E virus, the commonest aetiological agent of acute viral hepatitis in Kathmandu Valley, 1998. Khoj-bin, J of NHRC, 23-28
11. Shrestha SM, Shrestha S, Tsuda F et al. Molecular investigations of hepatitis E virus infection in patients with acute hepatitis in Kathmandu Valley. J. Med. Virol, 2003; 69:207-214
12. Shrestha IL. Seroprevalence of antibodies to hepatitis C virus among IDU from Kathmandu. KUMJ. 2003, 1-1-103.
13. Joshi DD, Regmi DN, Relation of bite to bite, type of bite, type of animal bite and incubation period of hydrophobia cases. J Inst Med 1983; 5(2): 134-146.
14. Rabies Guide Book, 2012. Epidemiology and DIsease Control Section. DoHS.
15. Bahmanvar M, Present status of plague in Nepal. WHO Assignment reports, Nov. 1985.
16. Ogawa S et al. Serological & virological studies of Japanese Encephalitis in the Terai region of Nepal. 1992. Asian J Trop Med Pub Health; *23*(1) : 37-43.
17. Joshi AB, Banjara MR. Wierzba T. Should Vaccination be a priority for Japanese Encephalitis Prevention in Nepal ?, 2005, Issue 9, KUMJ, Vol. 3, No1, Pg 70 –
18. Annual Report of Department of Health Services 2011-12. Kathmandu.
19. National Dengue Guidelines for Clinical Management, Prevention & Control. Epidemiology & Disease Control Division. 2011.
20. Health Situation in South East Asia Region 2001-2007. WHO- SEARO 2008.
21. Annual Report of National Tuberculosis Centre 2011-12. Thimi

22. Joshi DD, Epidemiological situation of tuberculosis in Nepal. J Inst Med 1986, 8(2) : 115-128.
23. Country Health Profile Nepal. MoH, PPM&SD, June, 1988.
24. Nepal Health Survey, Shah NK & Worth RM, 1965. East West Center, Univ. of Hawaii.
25. Pedley JC, Transmission of leprosy - Recent concepts. J Nep Med Assoc (Souvenir), 1975, 13, 9-14.
26. Research in developing countries: will leprosy vaccine be produced in Nepal. Nord Med 1990; 105(12): 338-139
27. Brakel WV et al. Relapses after multi drug therapy for leprosy: a preliminary report of 22 cases in West Nepal. Lepr Rev 1989; 60: 45-50.
28. de Stiger DH et al. Leprosy: between acceptance and segregation. Community behaviour towards persons affected ..... Lepr. Rev. 2000. 71(4): 492-8
29. Annual Report of Leprosy Control Division 2068-69 BS, DoHS, Kathmandu
30. Pollitzer, R. Cholera. 1959, WHO.
31. Tuker, Francis. Gorkha, the Story of the Gurkhas of Nepal. 1957. Constable & Co., London.
32. Singh. HL. Nepal in Records. Educational Publishing House, Kathmandu. 2007.
33. Ise Tohru et al. Outbreaks of Cholera in the Kathmandu Valley, Nepal. J Inst Med, 1994, 16 196-204.
34. Bista MB, Shrestha K, Devkota UN, Meningitis in Nepal 1990-92, in Gastroenteritis, Encephalitis, Meningitis.
35. Dickenson JG, Thaller VT. Brucellosis in shepherds in Nepal. J Nep Med Assoc 1979, 17(1): 20-24.
36. Joshi DD, Epidemiological situation of human plague in Nepal. 1985, J Nep Med Assoc, 23(3) : 33-38.
37. Pandey MR, Ghimire G. Prevalence of various types of heart disease in Kathmandu: a 6-year survey of admitted cases. J Nep Med Assoc 1975; 13(3-4): 37-46.
38. Subedi BK. Sexually Transmitted Diseases in Nepal. J Nep Med Assoc, 1996; 34: 277-278.
39. Annual Report of Public Health Division 2047/48 BS. District Public Health Office, Surkhet.
40. Malaria Pre-elimination Programme Nepal. DoHS, Epidemiology & Disease Control Division. 2012.
41. National Malaria Treatment Protocol. DoHS, Epidemiology & Disease Control Division, 2009.
42. Joshi AB et al. Evaluation of Direct Agglutination Test (DAT) South Asian J Trop Med Public Health. 1999:30(3):583-5.

43. National Strategic Guideline on Kala-azar Elimination Program in Nepal 2009. Epidemiology & Disease Control Division, DoHS, Kathmandu.
44. Rai SK et al, J Inst Med, 1997, 19, 37-41.
45. Joshi DD, Epidemiological survey of human echinococcosis/ hydatidosis in Kathmandu. J Nep Med Assoc, 1985; 23(1): 1.27-1.35.
46. Cysticercosis in Nepal A histopathologic study of 62 cases. Am.J.Surg. Pathol. 1999.23(10), 1276-9.
47. Cardio-vascular diseases, Nepal. WHO Assignment report, 1979.
48. Pradhananga KK, Baral M, Shrestha BM, A Multi-institution hospital-based cancer incidence data for Nepal: an initial report. Asian Pac. J. Cancer Prev. 2009, 10(2), 259-62.
49. Basnyat B, Acute mountain sickness in local pilgrims to a high altitude lake (4154 m) in Nepal, J Wildernes Med 1993; 4, 286-292.
50. Current Paediatric Diagnosis & Treatment. Prentice Hall, 1997
51. Daulaire N et al. Childhood Mortality after a high dose of Vitamin A in a high risk population. BMJ 1992; 304(6821) 207-210.
52. Assessment of Technical Assistance in Health Sector. Vol. I Valley Research Group (VaRG), 1993.
53. Analysis of the content of the Eight Essential Elements of Primary Health Care. WHO, 1981.
54. Report of a study in the Primary Health Care Unit (District) of Tanahu, Shah M, Shrestha M, Parker RL 1977, IoM, Kathmandu.
55. Report of a study in the Primary Health Care Unit (District) of Nuwakot, Shrestha R, Shrestha M,1979. IoM, Kathmandu.
56. Oswald, IH. Are Traditional Healers the solution to the Failures of Primary Health Care in Nepal ? 1983. Soc Sci Med 17(5), 255-257.
57. Dhankuta District Community Health Survey, Shrestha M, Bhattacharya A, Phillips PA, 1985, IoM.
58. Dixit, Ajay. Putting Water in Taps. SPACES Magazine, July-Aug. 2008.
59. UNICEF. The State of the World's Children Report, 2005 & 2013.
60. Wright, D. History of Nipal.
61. Prasad, Lakshmi N. Status of People with Disability in Nepal. 2003
62. Common Framework - Third Monitoring of Progress, P&FAD, MOH, Feb. 1994.
63. A Situational Analysis of Disability in Nepal. National Planning Commission, UNICEF, Feb. 2001.
64. Madeley J, Programme with a vision, World Health, 1981 July, 24-27.
65. Pokhrel RP, Gilbert SS, Sustainable Programme Development for Blindness Prevention : Nepal. Seminars in Ophthalmology, 1993; 8(3) : 177-182.
66. Brilliant LB, Associations among cataract prevalence, sunlight hours and altitude in the Himalayas. Am J Epidemiol, 1983; 118(2) : 250-64.

67. Simmersbach F, Tilden R, Prevention and control of vitamin A deficiency, xerophthalmia and nutritional blindness in Nepal, 1986 WHO, SEARO, New Delhi.
68. Taylor CE, Medical Pioneering in Nepal. J Chris Med Assoc of India, Pakistan, Burma & Ceylon, 1951, 1-5.
69. Banskota A et al. Burn contracture and disability, J Inst Med 1988; 10(4): 247-254.
70. Banskota A et al. Paediatric orthopaedic rehabilitation in Nepal, J Inst Med 1988; 10(2): 93-126.
71. Brochure of Association of Pharmaceutical Producers of Nepal. 2012.
72. Thapa B, Development of Pharmaceutical Industries in Nepal. Souvenir - Royal Drugs Ltd. 1997, Pg. 13-16.
73. Dixit, H. Production of Modern Medicines, J Inst Med 1982; 4(2): 181-198.
74. Milestones of Nepal Medical Council in Medical Education in Nepal. Tuladhar TM. NMC, 1995
75. Evaluating the Strategies for HFA 2000. (Common Framework - 2nd Evaluation), PPM&SD, Dec. 1990.
76. Implementation of Strategies for Health For All by the Year 2000 - Third Monitoring of Progress. 1994. P&FAD, HMG/WHO.
77. Human Resources for Health Master Plan 2052 BS. HIMDD/ERPHC (ODA) 1995.
78. Local Self-Governance Act 2055 BS (1999).

3.

CHILD AND MATERNAL HEALTH POPULATION TRENDS

Jung Bahadur is said to have attempted to have a census taken during his tenure as prime minister. However it was only in 1911 when Chandra Shumsher was prime minister that the very first census was taken.

BASIC HEALTH STATISTICS

The Nepal related figures are taken from various sources. Other vital statistics taken from the UNICEF document State of the World's Children 2005 and also the State of Nepali Children 2012 (1).

Indicators	1990 UNICEF*	2003 UNICEF	2011 NPR+	2013 UNICEF# S.E.Asia
Total Population		25.16 m	26.49 m	30.48 m
Population under 18 yrs		11.7 m		12.88 m
Population under 5 yrs		3.7 m		3.45 m
Neonatal Mortality Rate			27/1,000	27/1,000 live birth
Infant Mortality Rate	94/1,000 live birth	61/1,000 live birth	39/1,000 live birth	39/1,000 live birth
Under 5 Mortality Rate	135/1,000 live birth	67/1,000 live birth	48/1,000 live birth	48/1,000 live birth

Maternal Mortality Ratio		540 in 1985-2002		170/100,000 live birth
Life Expectancy at Birth - Male	54 yrs	60 yrs	69 yrs	69 yrs in 2011
Life Expectancy at Birth - Female		59 yrs		69 yrs in 2011
Adult Literacy Rate M/F		59%/24%	60	60% in 2007-11
Total Fertility Rate		4.2 per woman	2.7 per woman	2.7 per woman in 2011
Crude Death Rate		10 / 1,000	6 / 1,000	
Crude Birth Rate		33 /1,000	24/1,000	
Annual Pop Growth Rate		2.3% yearly	2.2% yearly	2.2% in last two decades
Gross National Income		$ 2.40 per capita	$ 540	

*UNICEF –State of the World's Children – 2005
UNICEF SE Asia Data Pocket Book – 2013
+Nepal Population Report - 2011

NB. Total population of 2011 was – 26,494,505 as stated in the final report of the National Population and Housing Census 2011. Of this the Nepali Indigenous People were said to comprise 35.81% of the population.

The Neonatal Mortality Rate at 27/1,000 live births is still disheartening. However with increased literacy amongst girls, it is likely to go down. Furthermore increased community dynamics by women is also helping to bring down neonatal and maternal mortality. The life-span of the average Nepali has also commendably gone up in spite of the fact that the GDP of the country is low (2).

Family Planning Activities in Nepal

Family planning in Nepal started with the involvement of the Nepal Medical Association (NMA) in such activities as far back as 1959. The

Family Planning Association of Nepal was then formed with the active involvement of NMA and the support of the International Planned Parenthood Federation (IPPF). Technical assistance by the US was to get the government to have a Family Planning Policy by 1965 (3). Family planning was also integrated with maternal and child health (MCH) to form a FP/MCH Project, under the Department of Health.

Subsequent technical assistance for family planning activities started in 1966 with the support of the USAID to the MCH section of the Department of Health. This service was started in the three districts - Kathmandu, Lalitpur and Bhaktapur. In 1968, the Family Planning and Maternal Child Health Project with 4 regional offices was established for implementation of the plans.

The National Planning Commission (NPC) then constituted in 1974 a task force to develop a population policy for the Fifth Five Year Plan 1975-80. In 1975 a Population Policies Co-ordination Board was established for formulating and coordinating population policies and programmes. Three years later (1978), a National Commission on Population (NCP) was established under the Chairmanship of the Prime Minister to bring about better functioning. The secretariat of the National Commission on Population was made a division of the NPC. The desired results were not attained and so in March, 1982 the commission was reorganised and made independent of the NPC. The long term aim of the National Population Policy as stated then was to:

> *"attain the replacement level of fertility (Total Fertility level of 2.5 corresponding to annual population growth rate of 1.2%) by the year 2000 AD." (4)*

The National Commission on Population highlighted the acuteness and recommended that multiple factors such as political, social, economic, cultural be taken into account. It stressed the need to narrow down the gap between government's concern and the individual's perception regarding the population problem (5). In 1990, the FP/MCH project was converted into a Division under the Ministry of Health.

The population figures for 1991 and 2001 were 18,462,081 and 23,151,423 respectively. This meant a 2.3% increase per annum which, continuing at the same trend could lead to a doubling of the population in 33 years. The Population Reference Bureau of USA had estimated the mid

2010 population of Nepal to be 28 million.

Table 3.1 Census totals and implied population growth rates: Nepal, 1911-1976

Reference Date	Population	Implied annual growth rate(%)
1911	5,638,749	
1920	5,573,788	- 0.13
1930	5,532,574	- 0.07
1941	6,283,649	1.16
1952 / 54	8,256625	2.27
1961	9,412,996	1.64
1971	11,555,983	2.05
1981	15,022,839	2.62
1991	18,491,097	2.08
2001	23,151,423	2.25
2011	26,494,505	1.35

Source: Nepal Population Report – 2011 (6).

Initially a lot of importance was given to the permanent methods. The use of contraceptives was taken up as one of the strategies. Though improvements in availability and accessibility of contraceptives occurred between 1976 and 1986, its use did not increase markedly (7).

By 1988, sterilization was no longer emphasised. To prevent early pregnancies and better spacing, more stress was laid on the other temporary methods. The population growth rate stood at 2.7% with fertility rate at 5.66 and IMR at 112, denoting that family planning had not been very effective.

Further analysis showed that 42% of the population was under 14 years of age and that 21% were in the reproductive age group of 15-44 years. (8) The population growth of Nepal from the 11.6 millions in 1971 to 15.0 millions in 1981, to 18.5 millions in 1991 and to the mid 1990 figures meant an increase of 2.1%, 2.6%, 2.1% and 2.3% in the decades of the sixties, seventies, eighties and nineties respectively.

The 1991 census however showed that the population increase was not as had been projected. It was even suggested that the Total Fertility Rate (TFR) was also down. Without the current contraceptive usage rate of 20% increasing to 34% the TFR could not be brought down from the level of 5.8 to 4.0. In term of numbers it meant that the existing number of 68,000 users had to reach the figure of 1.4 million, an almost impossible undertaking.

In the past, a lot had been stressed on the permanent methods. Subsequently some attention was given to "birth spacing" with more stress on temporary methods together with the "cafeteria approach."

One conjecture is that the high rates of population growths in developing countries are due to falling death rates plus changing birth rates, which have not decreased but may even be rising.

In course of time the old Population Division was dissolved and the National Planning Commission had a Population and Health Division whose function was to monitor and guide the population activities. The new arrangement came into force from mid-July 1993 and its immediate task was to establish working relationship with the line ministries concerned.

The Nepal Fertility, Family Planning and Health Survey of 1991 came out in 1993. One positive development of all this was that the age at which women were getting married had gradually increased over the years.

Some changes occurred regarding fertility too in that there was some decline over the last decade. The TFR then was 5.1 meaning thereby that each woman tended to have 5.1 births during her entire reproductive period. Closer scrutiny showed that the legitimate TFR for women in urban areas was 5.3 births whilst it was 6.2 in the rural setting. Similarly whilst the uneducated woman had a TFR of 6.2 births, her compatriot with just secondary level education had a much lower level of 4.0 births during her reproductive span. However the ideal number of children desired was reported to be three. "Estimate indicates that between 1977 and 1995, the TFR declined from 5.80 to 4.95 in the country as a whole, from 5.82 to 5.17 in rural areas and from 4.98 to 3.22 in urban areas. By education, the TFR declined from 5.84 to 5.34 among women with no education, from 4.76 to 4.57 among women with at least some primary education, and from 3.63 to 2.67 among women with more than a primary education." (8) The target set was to reduce the TFR to 4.5 per woman in the Eighth Plan

Period (1992-97) and to 4 by the year 2000 AD. However in mid 2010 the TFR was down to 3.0.

In the effort to popularise family planning, the Nepal Contraceptive Retail Sales (CRS) company had been established in 1978. Though organised initially for the sale of pills, condoms on a subsidized basis through many outlets all over the country, it is now selling injectable contraceptives products plus rehydration salts. In May 2010, USAID awarded CRS the 'Happy Homes' project. This project is hoped to assist GoN in enlarging the depth reach and impact in social marketing; and providing low-cost maternal, child health, family planning and HIV prevention products and services. A recent presentation regarding Matri Suraksha Chakki (MSC) stated that post partum haemorrhage accounted for nearly half of all MMR. (*Source was* NDHS, 2006, based on Study of Maternal Disease and Death 1998.)

About this time some of the IEC work that had been done started showing results. A district health survey done in Surkhet in early nineties came up with figures of 32.7% literacy in a population of 5 years and above. There were also a very small number of females under 15 who were married (9). A study of the nutritional status of adolescent girls of three sites in two districts was reported. One site was Satbariya of Dang district. The other two sites in Rolpa district were at Jinabang and Thabang (10). The study confirmed that girls were attending schools less than boys and their literacy rate was much below that of boys. One positive finding was delayed marriage in the sample. Of 179 adolescents, only nine (5%) were found to be married. This differed markedly from the national average of 78% of girls getting married by the age of 18 years at that time.

At this time that the population of Nepal increased by 2.1% per annum during 1981-91 and would have doubled in 33 years if the existing trend continued. Perhaps because of this, the Nepali Congress government, elected in May 1991 came out with a new population and health policy. The major policy thrust of the Eighth Plan (1992-97) was "to create an environment, through socio-economic development, which fosters a demand for small family of two children." It envisaged integrating the poverty alleviation and population programmes so that the concept of a small family became the norm. In Dec. 1995, the new coalition government created a separate ministry for "Population and Environment".

In March 2002, Nepal's Parliament had approved legislation to permit abortion on request during the first 12 weeks of pregnancy for any reason, to 18 weeks of pregnancy for rape or incest and up to any gestation period in case of disability or risk to the woman's life or foetus deformity. The hope was that this access to legal abortion would in the long run reduce maternal mortality and morbidity by reducing unsafe abortion practices (11). In Sept 2002 this legalisation process was taken one step further by the 11th amendment to the Muluki Ain. The law stated that abortion was now legal under certain conditions, following the rules and regulations laid by the Procedural Order, which had been formalised in Dec. 2003. This Procedural Order demands that a trained and listed provider should provide the abortion services as per the limits set by the law (12).

Abortion is available on request during the first 12 weeks of pregnancy. The government started providing Comprehensive Abortion Care (CAC) from March 2002. As per IPAS data, there are now about 300 centres providing such service in the country. A recent survey shows that abortion services were utilised mostly by married women who already had the desired number of children. From mid June 2011 the MoHP provided skilled birth attendants (SBA) for abortion services in health post of 10 districts. However the reality is still that safe abortion is still beyond the reach of most villages.

In Feb. 2005 the Ministry of Population and Environment had been restructured and the papulation sector had been merged with the MoH and Environment sector to the Ministry of Forests. With the high population growth the current population of 25 million was expected to increase by about 60% as a result of which women of reproductive age was expected to increase by 71% (13).

A news item in mid-June 2010 reported that one-third of pregnant ladies in Chitwan get themselves aborted. However what now worries the authorities is the sex-selective abortion trend that is tending to occur.

In 2010/11 the Contraceptive Prevalence Rate (CPR) for modern family planning methods was 44%. There has been a decline in TFR from 3.1 in 2006 to 2.6 in 2011 (14). In June 2011 there were 487 places deemed as Safe Abortion Sites. It may be noted many are still advocating safe and affordable abortion as a right of women as unplanned and hazardous abortions can be devastating (15).

The 2011 Census

The final report of the National Population & Housing Census 2011 was officially released in Nov. 2012. The population stood at 26,494,505. Of this the Terai had 50.27%, hill 43.00% and mountain 6.73%. Kathmandu has a population of 1,744,240. There are a total of 125 castes and ethnic groups and the number of religions found in the country is 10. The urban population is 17.7%.

Immunisation

The MCH Under 5 clinic, started in Bir Hospital in 1965 was the first in the country to make some urban mothers aware of immunisation. Subsequently *Sajha Swasthya Seva* ordered the vaccines such as DPT and Polio (initially injections and later oral drops). The Central Chest Clinic was giving BCG. These facilities were therefore in fairly widespread use, before the government decided much later in 1977 to provide such services on a regular scale.

In Nepal EPI was introduced in 1977 with DPT & BCG in 3 Districts. By 1980 DPT & measles immunisation were introduced and by 1988, EPI was operating in all 75 districts. With the "token" coverage of the whole country it was stated that Universal Coverage of Immunisation (UCI), had been attained.

In the attempt to eradicate polio as per the Polio Pulse campaign supported by Rotary International, and National Immunisation Days (NID) have been held since 1997/98. Though stopped for a few years it has now been restarted. The objective was to give all children below the age of five years oral polio drops for a number of years and thereby eradicate poliomyelitis. The overall polio coverage is claimed to be over 90%.

It is heartening that the objective of the EPI Programme as stated yearly, has continued steadfastly in its objective. The National Immunisation Programme in 2013 provided immunisation for the under-mentioned vaccines throughout the country as given below:

- BCG
- Diphtheria – pertussis-tetanus- Hepatitis B & Haemophilus influenza
- Poliomyelitis (OPV)
- Measles with use of MMR
- TT vaccination is provided to all pregnant women
- Vaccination for Japanese Encephalitis is given where required

The stress is on safe injection practices in the immunisation programme. There are plans to continue adding new vaccines in the national immunisation programme in the future (14). The present coverage is as follows:

Table 3.2 Vaccine Coverage in 2013

Vaccine	Coverage (%)
BCG Vaccine	96.3
DPT Vaccines – Hep B –Hib3	90.3
Oral Polio Vaccine (x3)	90.2
Measles, Rubella Vaccine (MMR)	85.4

Source :

PHC FOR WOMEN AND CHILDREN

Many years ago, during the time of the Lichchhavi kings of Nepal, rules and directives were issued to be followed by the general population for safe motherhood. In the case of death of pregnant mother, she had to be separated from the baby in utero in the fashion of what was done in ancient Rome at the time of Julius Caesar.

During recent years, the stress has been on Safe Motherhood and on the health of women. What then are the Primary Health Care facilities that must be provided to the women and children of Nepal ? Everyone in the country is aware of the fact that though women contribute substantially in terms of domestic work and for livelihood, this reality is glossed over and generally overlooked. Now various womens' organisations are making people more aware of it.

Special Hospitals for Women and Children

Most women and children in the developing world are not getting basic health care. With the acceptance of the PHC concept by Nepal at Alma Ata (now Almaty) in 1978, and the ratification of the Convention on the Rights of the Child (CRC) at New York in 1990, it was hoped that the health status of women and children in Nepal would improve. The implementation of the Child Survival Strategies and focus on dissemination of health messages should have helped towards this. The start of 1995 was the provision of the Rules and Regulations for Child Welfare.

Various reports state that many parents in Nepal give much attention to the health of the male child rather than that of the female. This preference, in certain segments of our society, is true for education, legal rights and even material benefits. In certain areas of Nepal, notably in the Far Western Region, women do all the work. The ordinary woman of Nepal does not have a life of ease for even the housework is monumental.

Following the 1990 Summit on CRC there was hope that things would change. Nepal was the 23rd country in the world to confirm ratification of CRC. It is now obligatory for Nepal to report, every two years, and the compliance of the provisions to the UN Rights of the Child Committee. Since then another Convention has been held on the Rights of Persons with Disabilities (CRPD), and governments around the world have to take the responsibility of ensuring that all children, irrespective of ability or disability, enjoy these rights without any form of discrimination. As of Feb. 2013, 193 countries have ratified the CRC and 127 countries and the European Union have ratified the CRPD (1).

Later, 1990 was designated as the "SAARC Year of the Girl Child." During the course of that year there were a lot discussions, and recommendations that were duly propagated. The enthusiasm generated by the "SAARC Year of the Girl Child" led to the nineties being labelled as the "SAARC Decade of the Girl Child." The achievements of this decade of the nineties were not as per expectations.

It was in this context that following the *Jana Andolan I*[1] the Prime Minister of the Interim Government gave his assurance for the formation of a National Council / Commission for Children. Though initially there was a Council for Women & Children it was only in 1995 that such a council came into existence. These entities are not fully functional because of political considerations.

Recent figures however show remarkable improvements from conditions in the past. This may be due to a more liberal environment. It is mainly due to the markedly increased 'Private Sector' which has evolved over the last two decades. A special mention must be made of the medical colleges and other health related medical institutions that have come up in different parts of the country.

The Maternal Mortality Ratio in 2013 is still high and over 61% of the

1. People's Movement. *Jana Andolan I and II* took place in early 1990 and 2006.

maternal mortality is due to "obstetric causes": sepsis (28%), haemorrhage (22%) and toxaemia (11%) even in the mid nineties.

Curative Maternal Care Facilities

The starting of the Shree Panch Indra Rajya Laxmi Devi Prasuti Griha (Maternity Hospital) in 1959 played a major role in the development of services for women, the motivation for medical personnel to take up maternal care and a major role in the family planning and safe motherhood activities in this country. The hospital had started with just 40 beds for obstetric care. The name of the institution has now been changed to Paropakar Maternity & Women's Diseases Hospital. The breakdown of the beds is now a total of 415 of which 336 are for indoor admission and 79 service beds. The beds for indoor admissions comprise of obstetrics 241, gynaecology 61 and 24 for the special care unit for babies (16). The gynaecology beds comprise those for sterilisation programme, radium therapy and sub fertility clinic. A service for 'test-tube' babies has also been started.

In the assessment of services for maternal care, the Nepal Fertility, Family Planning and Health Survey of 1991 also showed that 82% of births over the course of the preceding five years had received no prenatal care, whilst 15% received some care from a trained medical or health personnel. Out of every 10 births, as much as nine were delivered at home. Only 7% of births were attended by doctors, nurses and ANMs, whilst 25% were attended by TBAs and as much as 48% by relatives.

The Annual Report of FPAN 2012 states that the percentage of deliveries attended by skilled birth attendants (SBA) and other health workers at the health facilities or at home in Nepal was 48% (17).

Safe Motherhood

In the effort to reduce the high Maternal Mortality Ratio (MMR) the stress now is on Safe Motherhood. The government in 1997 started this and now a 15-year plan (2002-17) is envisaged. The Family Health Division proposed the establishment of Basic Essential Obstetric Care (BEOC) in 50 hospitals by 2006. Extension of this service to PHC centres has taken place. Besides this, it is also proposed in the plan to propose the establishment of Comprehensive Essential Obstetric Care (CEOC) in another 10 hospitals by 2006 (12). The Aama Suraksha Programme had two components:

i. Safe Delivery Incentive Programme (SDIP), started in 2005 gave cash
ii. Free Institutional Delivery Care started in 2009.

DFID and UNICEF support the National Safe Motherhood Programme of GoN in 12 districts. This programme has been implemented in all government health facilities nationwide and some accredited non-state health facilities. The service component is the mechanism by which the objective to improve midwifery and essential obstetrics care in both hospitals and community are being met. Indicators for assessment have been laid down as also the minimum acceptable level of services. The reduction in the MMR will be reduced by the provision of skilled service at the time of birth either at home or at a health facility and also by timely access to emergency services when required. The inaccessibility to maternal services is still an important factor inspite of the many plans and programmes that have been made.

NB. Many women of developing countries such as Nepal die each year of complications connected with pregnancy. This is because they lack access to life saving care. For such woman, access to maternity care; to essential care for those at risk; to family planning; and - in the long run - social equity, including access to good nutrition, a basic education and economic opportunity would make the difference between life and death.

The Nepal Family Health Survey (NFHS) of 1996 provided information on maternal mortality for the period 0-6 years before the survey i.e. 1990-96. The figure was found to be 539 deaths for 100,000 live births. An estimate by an indirect method (with some adjustment) by MoH in 1993 showed this to be 515 deaths per 100,000 live births. The plan was to reduce MMR to 300/100,000 live births by the end of the Tenth Plan period. Health Sector Strategy (HSS) document of 2004 states the target to be 134 (13). In 2013 it is currently 170.

NGOs WORKING FOR WOMEN

With the stress on poverty alleviation in the MDGs, attention has been drawn on the exploitation of women and the abuse of children in various parts of Nepal. The Convention on the Rights of Children tackled this aspect. Voices have been raised regarding the Violence Against Women (VAW) or Gender Based Violence (GBV). Listed below and later in this chapter are the organisations working for the cause of women and children respectively.

Maiti Nepal

Maiti Nepal was founded in 1993 as a non profit, child rights and women rights social organisation to find sustainable solutions to issues related to trafficking. The organisation is engaged in the protection, rescue and rehabilitation of survivors of trafficking by promoting their human rights in diversified avenues. Maiti Nepal runs three Prevention Homes, eleven Transit Homes, two Rehabilitation Homes, two Hospices, and conducts Community Outreach and Awareness Programmes in different parts of the country.

Mothers' Club - Aamaa Milan Kendra

This is a national level NGO established in 1975 during the International Women's Year. It operates in 19 districts with 59 local branches. Its overall objective is to develop and promote women in general. It is involved in the social and economic upliftment of women from grass roots level. Its strong point is that it is volunteer based and works at the community level.

WOREC Nepal

Women's Rehabilitation Centre (WOREC) was founded in 1991 by women rights activists and works in partnership with grassroots people in order to resolve the major socio-economic, cultural and human rights and sustainable community development based on social justice. It is also addressing the issues of Violence Against Women (VAW).

Curative Child Care Services

The first hospital for children at Kathmandu was initially known as Kanti Hospital and started out as a unlt of the Bir Hospital where paying patients were kept. The hospital was converted into one solely for children in July, 1970 and soon after its name was changed to Kanti Children's Hospital (KCH). The hospital is utilised for the training of doctors, nurses and other categories of health personnel. In 2005, at completion of 42 years of existence, it was announced that it would be upgraded to Institute of Child Health (18). In mid 2008, the Institute of Medicine opened its own Paediatric Department at TUTH though it continued using the KCH for teaching/learning activities. The Nepal Paediatric Society initially based at Kanti Children's Hospital started its activities from there in June, 1981.

During the course of the Fifth Paediatric Congress in 1990, a commitment was given to the opening of a children' hospital in each of the five regions of the country. Subsequent thought was that some fifty beds would be added for children at the regional hospitals. This was very necessary, for whilst the Kanti Children Hospital had 150 beds at that time, the total number of hospital beds for children in the country amounted to no more than 400 at the very most.

The Japanese input into the KCH increased the number of beds for child care to 250. Subsequently another 50 additional beds were added by GoN. In 2013 the hospital has a total of 330 beds and the special services that it provides are NICU, Burns Unit and Cancer Treatment Centre for children. (18)

National Childrens' Eye & Ear Hospital & Rehabilitation Centre.

This hospital was started at Monohara in Thimi by B.P. Health Foundation.

Ishan Nursing Home

This is a private health care facility for children, which have been functioning for over a decade. It also provides facilities for delivery.

International Children's Hospital

This hospital is in Maharajganj, Kathmandu.

CHILD CARE FACILITIES OUTSIDE

Paediatric departmental beds have been increased at the BPKIHS in Dharan and the Regional Hospitals in the country. AMDA set up a hospital for Women and Children in Butwal. The total number of beds, specifically for children stood at 897 out of a total of 6,348 in the country in 2001.

Infant mortality rate has decreased from an estimated 233/1000 live births in 1960 and 150/1000 live births in 1970 to the current figures given at the start of this chapter.

The Health Sector Strategy document had stated the Child Mortality Rate or the Under 5 MR to be reduced from 162 in 1990 to 91/1000 in 2001 (13). It is now 39/1000. The target is to reduce present figures to 30 per thousand by the year 2015.

Hospital & Rehabilitational Centre for Disabled Children (HRDC)

This hospital started in 1985 with the help of Terres des homes of Switzerland was initially situated at Jorpati. In 1998 it was shifted to Banepa and has been functioning there. HRDC is fully committed to work with the community to help children with disabilities. It works now in 25 districts of Nepal. Its work was recognised in 2011 with the honouring of Dr. Ashok Banskota, its Chief with the World of Children Health Award.

Facilities for Children in the Offing

Neuro Hospital: The Children's Organisation of Nepal or the Bal Mandir, based at Naxal has for a number of years been advocating its interest in building a hospital for children. In early 2011 it came out with the announcement that it was going to build a 50 bedded Neuro Hospital for Children at Thecho in Lalitpur. The intention was to complete it in two years.

General Hospital: In September 2013 a National Daily reported that a building constructed with the aid of the Embassy of India at Dorahi in Dang to serve as a Children' Hospital was still non functional. It was built in 2064 BS at a cost of about Rupees 95 lakhs but is still vacant with just one room being utilised by the police for their 'Police Beat'.

NB. Incidents such as this illustrate the lack of co-ordination prevalent in Nepal. Past instances were the Bir Hospital OPD building and also the Trauma Centre at the same site.

Children's Diseases

With the signing of the Rights of the Child by GoN in 1990, a commitment was made to cater to the welfare of children. The current figures which were attained by 2011, are as below:

IMR To 39 per 1,000 live births

U5MR To 48 per 1,000 live births

In 1998, a pilot project on "Integrated Management for Childhood Illnesses" (IMCI) was started in two countries of Asia - the Philippines and Nepal. The strategies of IMCI were:

i. Improving case management skills of health workers
ii. Improving the health system to deliver IMCI
iii. Improving family and community practices

Initially IMCI was implemented mainly in Mahottari and in parts of the district of Gorkha. It is felt that IMCI belongs to the group of cost effective interventions with potential to make the greatest impact on the global burden of childhood diseases.

It had been estimated by WHO in 2004 that more than 7 out of every 10 deaths in the world's children was in Africa and South East Asia. (19)

In 2004/05 the major killers of children were diarrhoeal diseases and pneumonia. As an estimated 30-40 thousand children died each year from each of these major causes the stress has been on specific policies for both diarrhoeal diseases and acute respiratory infection (ARI). The practice is to refer to ARI cases as severe pneumonia. The government has been conducting programmes for the control of both diarrhoea and ARI. PHC health workers and even mothers were being taught signs of impending severity in both conditions. The Community Based-IMCI components are: i. ARI ii. Diarrhoea iii. Measles iv. Malaria and v. Malnutrition and the plan was to incorporate new items so as to revise IMCI from time to time. Accordingly, Low Osmolar ORS and Zinc treatment in diarrhoea was incorporated in IMCI in 2005/06. The expansion of CB-IMCI was completed in 2009/10. Now the CB-Newborn Care Package (NCP) is scaled up in 39 districts and is due to be implemented in all 75 districts by 2015. Beyond 2015 it is hoped to include this in the Safe Motherhood programme.

The conventional health care system does not tackle the multiple causes of ill-health, which is the synergistic outcome of factors like malnutrition, infection, unsafe water, poor sanitation, little education, depressed status of women, early marriage, frequent child births and lack of health-related education.

In the context of Nepalese children, health and sanitation are inseparable. Water-borne diseases are the most common of all childhood diseases, and are a major killer of children. Respiratory infections, which have not been much researched are only slightly less fatal to the young. Though attempts at eradication are being done the vaccine-preventable childhood diseases - diphtheria, pertussis, tetanus, poliomyelitis, tuberculosis and measles are sometimes seen in the country. There is great stress now on immunization for the prevention of measles in children. The concept of "Prevention is better than cure" is being followed.

The children of Nepal come face to face with a number of hurdles or obstructions as they grow up. A large number fall by the wayside and those fortunate enough to survive may be disabled or not in the best of health. They do not attain their full potential.

We have since the last five decades been thinking of Family Planning as being the panacea of all our problems. Some success has been obtained because of the development of new vaccines, child survival and smaller families as a result. Furthermore, as the literacy rate, especially that of women rises and as economic conditions improve, both the birth rate and population growth will decrease.

Following the Convention on the Rights of the Child and the signing of the document it is obligatory for Nepal to submit periodic reports. Nepal has made two 10-years National Programme for Action (NPA) i.e.(i) 1992-2002 and (ii) 2004-2014. It is acknowledged that some progress has been made. More is expected to take place on completion of the State's 10-year National Plan of Action for Children (2005-2015).

The only way to make the public conscious about measures for child survival, without gender bias is by massive media campaign, which must be sustained. The whole nation must be aware of the fact that child survival is a fundamental right to which everyone is entitled We must remember that Lord Buddha has said, *"Children are the greatest asset of mankind."*

Millennium Development Goals for Health

As has been described in other chapters too, these goals are a blueprint agreed by 149 countries to be reached by 2015. These goals though meant for everybody dealt primarily for children. In fact six of the eight goals relate directly to children. Some vital statistics in comparison with the present goals are as given in Table 3.4.

Table 3.4 Millennium Development Goals (MDG) for Health*

Indicators	1990	2001	2006	MDG for 2015*
MMR	539	415	281	134
Child MR	161.6	91	61	54
Malaria PR /100,000 persons	196	52	25	Halve or Reduce
TB PR /100,000 persons	460	310	280	Halve or Reduce
HIV in 15-49/ 100,000 persons	NA	290	500	Halve or Reduce

* Round table on "MDG and Children". Ministry of Women, Children

and Social Welfare and Central Child Welfare Board, SOS Children's Village Nepal and Action Aid Nepal.

The importance of the MDGs and its implementation has become very important in the care of both women and children of Nepal. It is felt that Nepal has made good progress despite a decade long (1996-2006) armed conflict taking place in the country. The period after this has been one of uncertainties. This is partly due to the fact that MDGs are well integrated in the country's plans. Dr. Bal Gopal Vaidya of New Era, in a recent presentation on the subject (20) in 2013 summarised the situation as follows: "He felt that the 8th Goal concerning global partnerships was something which Nepal was not in a position to control. Of the 24 indicators concerning the first seven MDGs he felt that nine (37%) had already been achieved by 2011 and of the remaining, he felt that achievement by 2015 would be:

Likely	6 (25%)
Possible	4 (17%)
Unlikely	5 (21%)"

INGOs & NGOs WORKING FOR CHILDREN

Save The Children Fund (UK)

SCF (UK) started work in Nepal in 1975 after having signed an agreement with the Nepal Children's Organisation (NCO) and the Social Services National Coordination Council (SSNCC). The first Mother and Child Health project were set up at Surkhet (1976), Dhankuta (1977) and Baglung in 1977. The Nutrition Unit attached to the Clinic at Dhankuta did remarkable work. A fourth project on MCH, with special boarding facilities for students was started at Chautara, Sindupalchowk in 1982. All projects of SCF were run in collaboration with MoH and the Institute of Medicine. An agreement regarding all four projects was signed with the MoH in 1983 and subsequently renewed for five year periods in 1986 and also in 1991.

Over the course of the years that the projects had been functioning a certain set pattern had emerged. There were in fact three interlinked components to each project:

i. A MCH Clinic, which included a Nutrition Unit
ii. A Health Post Support Programme
iii. A Child Health Support Programme

Following the Bhutanese refugee influx into Nepal, SCF (UK) worked in collaboration with the United Nations High Commissioner for Refugees (UNHCR) since mid-1992. After 1995 SCF handed over the projects and that was completed in mid-1996.

Redd Barna

This is the Norwegian name of the SCF based in Norway and started to work in Nepal from late 1983 after an agreement with the SSNCC in July, 1984. Redd Barna has been working in Nepal with a long term aim of community development. Its main objectives are:

- improving the quality of life of the children and the disadvantaged in the areas where it is working
- increasing awareness of child issues on a national perspective and doing some activities on a national scale.

SCF (Japan)

This member of the SCF has only been working in community development in the Dhanusha area of Nepal for about two years.

SCF (USA)

Following an initial agreement with the SSNCC in November, 1980, SCF (USA) started work in the Gorkha district and gradually increased its area of activity. It had also been involved in AIDS awareness programme in Nuwakot district. During 1993-95 it was coordinator of 17 NGOs involved in AIDS related work as a result of American Foundation for AIDS Research (AmFAR) grants in Nepal.

SC Alliance

Initially SC (UK) and Redd Barna co-ordinated their work. After !st April 2009 the four SC organisations which had been working in Nepal decided to work with a common objective. It is now Save the Children International with its headquarters in London (21).

The Saving Newborn Lives (SNL) initiative in Nepal, implemented by Save the Children (SC) with support of the Gates Foundation was launched in Nov. 2000 with the objective of improving the health and survival of the newborns in Nepal. One phase has been compeleted and the current second phase started in October 2005.

Bal Mandir - Nepal Children's Organisation

This organisation, known as Balmandir is one of the oldest organisations set up for child welfare as long ago as 1964. Its objective is to provide food, shelter and education to the disadvantaged children in the country. It is looking after the conflict affected and orphan children in various parts of the country. It is currently running 11 Children Homes and has district committees in each of the 75 districts of the country. Nepal Children's Organisation also has sponsorship and adoption programmes.

Child Workers in Nepal (CWIN)

The International Year of the Child (IYC) had been celebrated in 1979. Some student leaders in the country wanted to celebrate the decade from 1980 for furthering the cause of child rights. CWIN was established as a NGO in 1987 and initially it was working for the children on the streets. It had a number of centres where children have access to come and stay occasionally. Over the course of the last twenty-five years CWIN has been fighting for the cause of child workers – their rights, their neglect and for stopping their exploitation. It has highlighted the child abuse that has been taking place.

Child Development Society (CDS)

This NGO formed in 1991, has been working in the area of Child Rights and also against child labour. It has been helping in child education by starting and helping in schools. It has brought out various publications in this regard.

SOS Children's Villages

This is an international organisation that has its Central Office at Imst in Austria. The first SOS village in Nepal was at Sanu Thimi, Bhaktapur and opened in 1973 by Queen Aishwarya. Since then nine other villages have been opened in different parts of Nepal. A tenth one SOS is being built at Dhangadi. The main focus of SOS Children Villages of Nepal is to provide long term family based care to orphaned, abandoned and destitute children. It runs 10+2 schools within or in the proximity of villages. Thus it gives education, training, health care and has other outreach programmes to help needy children and mothers from neighbouring communities by way of schools, youth facilities, vocational training and community centres. In recent years the focus has been shifted to Family Strenthening Programmes. There is also a sponsorship programme.

Child NGO Federation

This federation has at the end of September 2013 a total of 118 members and is pursuing its perspective to bring about co-ordination amongst all NGOs and INGOs working in the field of child health.

CORE

Some of the External Development Partners (EDP) have formed what has come to be known as the CORE group. This is a consortium of 5 different organisations involved in what is called Child Survival Collaboration and Resources Group. It comprises of the SCF(USA), CARE, PLAN, World Vision and ADRA. Besides childcare activities the group is also concerned with strengthening PHC services delivery system at the community level.

Adolescent health

After the International Conference on Population and Development (ICPD) in 1994 some thought started being given to Adolescent Reproductive Health, mainly because adolescents were very vulnerable to reproductive health problems. To address this GoN formulated the Adolescent Health and Development Strategy 2000 with the object of improving the health and socio-economic status of adolescents. Teenage behavioural, sexual, drug abuse are some of the problems at this age. A large number of children of both sexes may be on the streets and as a result get into trouble of various sorts. Because of the poor socio-economic status, broken homes and loneliness in a strange environment they are prone to many hazards. As adolescents are neither children nor adults as such, it has been realised that special facilities must be started for them. This awareness, having now been created, has led to the setting up of adolescent friendly facilities in some health institutions of the country.

Family Planning Association of Nepal (FPAN) with the support of UNICEF & DANIDA etc has a Six-Year Strategic Plan (2010-2015). FPAN programmes focussed on five thematic areas including Adolescents, HIV/AIDS, Abortion, Access and Advocacy. Adolescent and youth focussed Sexual & Reproductive Health (SRH) programmes have been implemented to empower them on informed choice and decision making regarding their sexual and reproductive health (17).

VAW & GBV

An important development is the Violence Against Women and Gender Based Violence. The MoHP has so far designated 15 hospitals in different parts of the country where women subject to VAW assaults can be taken for medical examination and admission for a few days. Hospitals where such cases can be managed have a 'One-step Crisis Management Centre' (OCMC) protocol and are dealt in this fashion. A number of police stations can also keep such cases for a day or two. In fourteen districts of the country there are also 'Safe Homes' where such females care allowed to stay for a day or two at the time of crisis. More details on VAW are in the article by Joshi S (22).

Future Directions

As from International Women's Day (March 8th, 1995) when the formation of a Women and Child Committee was announced, it was expected that some concrete steps would be taken in this area. Thus besides the Safe Motherhood initiative, the Ministry of Health decided in June 1995, to accept in principle the WHO offer of implementing the Integrated Management of the Sick Child.

An event of importance was the Supreme Court of Nepal's directive of 5th August, 1995 (18th Shrawan, 2052 BS) on the two-year-old petition of Ms Mira Dhungana and Ms Mira Khanal, both advocates, pleading for non discrimination against women as this was against the Nepalese constitution of 2047 BS. The Supreme Court had issued a directive to the Government (then UML) to bring forth and enact legislation protecting the rights of women, especially property rights. Subsequent Coalition Governments had not, till mid 1998 been able to achieve much. Such legislation, if implemented, can go a long way towards improving the lot of women. However the UML government of 1995 created a task force for the setting up of institutions like:

a. Institute of Obstetrics & Gynaecology
b.Institute of Child Health

Later a three party coalition government, installed on 22nd September 1995 showed its commitment to women, and presumably to their health also, by having a separate ministry for Women and Social Services. As stated already it was only in March 2002 that legislation was approved legalising abortion. It was implemented only in 2004. The proposals for the new institutes mentioned above have still not materialised.

Nepal has signed and ratified international human rights treaties, including the Covenanant on Economic, Social and Cultural Rights and the Convention on the Elimination of All Forms of Discrimination against Women (23).

Nutrition & Health Education

The first health survey of Nepal, done in 1965/66, tried to get information on the diet and nutritional status of the Nepalese people (24). A total of 6,321 people from 957 households from nineteen different sites within the country were covered. It was found that the diet as a whole is lacking in protein, calcium, Vit. A, riboflavin and ascorbic acid. In view of the high under five-mortality rate (U5MR), its conclusion was that marginal malnutrition was prevalent. On the whole however; the clinical nutritional status of the population was pronounced as satisfactory by the investigation team from the University of Hawaii.

In 1974 Pourbaix conducted a survey to assess the nutritional status of Nepalese children. The survey was limited to 1042 children between 6 to 72 months from 17 areas of the country. Clinical criteria including weight for age and weight for height were used to grade the status.

Nepal National Nutrition Status Surveys

Subsequent to this a Nepal National Nutrition Status Survey was done in 1975 by GoN with the aid of the Centre for Disease Control, Atlanta with the financial support of USAID. In this survey some 6,578 children under 6 years of age were surveyed in 221 sites. Of the total child population there were 52.5% boys and 47.5% girls. The feeling is that the boys were over represented in this study as this is not the usual male to female child ratio in the population.

In 1975 with the aid of WHO and UNICEF, recommendations for malnutrition and goitre control were made part and parcel of Country Health Programme exercise.

In 1976 GoN established a National Nutrition Policy Co-ordination Committee (NNPCC) with a member of the National Planning Commission (NPC) in charge of health and social welfare as the Chairman.

In 1978/77 a survey of 749 children, between one to five years of age, was done using UNICEF provided Sakir tapes. The findings of this survey in Bara and Parsa districts divided into three grades in the percentages as given below (25):

Table 3.5 Status of Nutrition

Degree of Malnutrition	%
Severe malnutrition	11.8
Mild malnutrition	36.4
Good nutrition	51.6

In 1978 the NNPCC in collaboration with WHO and UNICEF organised a workshop on food and nutrition planning. The prevailing state of malnutrition was identified, strategies decided and measures which could be undertaken to combat malnutrition stated at the National Nutrition Strategy Workshop at Pokhara (26). As a prime example of good intentions, it drew up a multisectoral strategy for improving nutrition. This culminated in the so-called Pokhara Declaration and resulted in the formation of nutrition focal points in 4 ministries viz. Health, Agriculture, Education and Panchayat. It led to the establishment of Nutrition Section under Department of Health Services in the MoH. The Joint Nutrition Support Programme (JNSP) was then put into action to implement the major activities of the four ministries but as not much was achieved the JNSP was finally dismantled as a result of donor dissatisfaction.

There was the awareness that malnutrition per se was not primarily a clinical disease but a social one with multiple causes. The health sector realised that for interventions for the eradication of malnutrition to be successful it was essential to have the necessary political commitment.

Work by personnel of the United Mission to Nepal with a community-oriented approach has been reported in 1980 in local journals. Such workers believed that whilst nutrition education is an essential component, others factors such as anthropological, psychological and social have to be taken into consideration for any change to occur.

The Nepal Demographic and Health Survey of 2011 (NDHS-2011) showed that 41% of children are underweight and 11% of children below 5 years are wasted. Most common form is PEM. Malnutrition is not evenly distributed. Hopefully with the increasing road network there will be a decrease as food will be transmitted much quicker to areas of deficiency.

Report shows that stunting, underweight and wasting are more common in mid and far west hills and mountainous regions of the country.

SCF (UK) Work in the Rural Areas

SCF (UK) started working in Nepal with an agreement with the Bal Sangathan. The initial work was done at Dhankuta where it was noted that most of the cases seen in children between 12 and 23 months presented during the monsoon season when stocks of food was low. Most suffered from infectious diseases such as diarrhoea and respiratory infection (27). Valuable work on malnutrition in children of Nepal has been reported from time to time as a result of this group's study in this and three other rural districts of Nepal, viz. Surkhet, Baglung and Sindhupalchowk. Work in Chuliban village in east Nepal showed that growth faltering started at 3 months of age, and that prevalence of wasting and stunting also varied with ethnic group. This work also suggested that the combination of influences associated with seasonal reduction in children's growth rates is not the same as the combination, which precipitates wasting malnutrition (28).

In 1987 an unpublished study by Sullivan at the SCF clinic in Surkhet compared the nutritional status findings with those found ten years earlier at the time of the initial survey. There was an overall improvement with marked reduction in levels of acute and chronic malnutrition.

Investigations and Research

As much as 54% of the crude birth rate of the country was due to the U5MR, the major cause of which is malnutrition. Work in the community showed that mortality and morbidity rates could be reduced by educating mothers in the proper use of locally available foods, breast milk included (29). Action on these lines will reduce the chronic protein-calorie malnutrition prevalent in Nepalese children.

A study of 4,600 singleton babies at Patan Hospital in mid eighties showed that the birth weight in Nepal in this series was 3010 grams for males and 2900 for females in a relatively well off population. This study also showed a lack of haemoconcentration during the last eight weeks of pregnancy, indicating that the iron stores in the mother had been depleted (30).

A study regarding Vitamin A was one done by West and his co-workers (31). This randomised, double blind trial showed that overall children taking Vitamin A supplements had lower mortality rates in age specific groups in both most malnourished and well-nourished children.

Other Activities on Nutrition

It is noteworthy that the first nutritional assessment of the population was only done in 1975. Not much followed and even in 1990 the figures of 1975 were being quoted as "the latest ones". Finally a review of a total of 111 materials which had been generated as a result of various investigations done in the nutrition field during the course of the period 1975-90 was done. The various fields are shown in the Table 3.6.

Table. 3.6 Some Investigations in the Nutrition Field over various years

Field of Investigation	No. of Studies done in period			
	1975-79	1980-84	1985-90	Total
PEM	9	26	22	57
Vitamin A	0	5	12	17
Iodine	2	3	6	11
Iron	3	1	3	7
Health	2	7	10	19

Some time later a review of the various smaller studies was done and a working document was complied to give a composite picture of the state of nutrition in Nepal (32).

On the basis of these reports the general impression was:

1. The nutritional status of children in Nepal was showing a worsening trend. Suggestion was made to assess the nutritional status regularly with the objective of seeing the impact of child health and nutritional programmes.
2. Vitamin A deficiency is a public health problem in Nepal and needs to be addressed.
3. Iodine deficiency disorders (IDD) have also public health importance. There is now a declining trend of these, because of salt iodations and iodised oil injections.
4. Not much work has been done in Nepal regarding micronutrient deficiencies. Anaemia is very common in women of reproductive age and is a major public health problem that needs to be tackled.

National Seminar on Nutrition, Kathmandu, 1991

It has been stated that the state of malnutrition in a country is reflected in the state of nutrition of the children. In 1991, 44% of the population was under the age of 14 years. Proper treatment of childhood diseases, overall child care and child feeding practices were expected to bring about major reduction of malnutrition in our part of the world. The 1991 National Health Policy drew attention to breast-feeding, weight measurement of children, control of Vitamin A deficiency and nutritional education being important (33). This same document stated that the four forms of malnutrition existing in the country were:

- Protein Energy Malnutrition
- Xerophthalmia due to Vit. A deficiency
- Iron deficiency anaemia
- Iodine deficiency disorders

The Family Health Survey of 1996 (34) showed that on the basis of height-for-age there was considerable chronic malnutrition among Nepali children - overall 48% of children under 3 years were stunted and 20% severely stunted. Female children were prone to be stunted (50%) or severely stunted (22%) than male children (47% and 19% respectively). Stunting was seen more often among children of higher birth order or with a short birth interval.

Much stress was laid in the 1990s to the important role of Vitamin A in the development of children as well as on the preventive role in bringing down the high mortality and morbidity rates. Vitamin A, besides preventing night blindness is now credited with bringing down the morbidity of communicable diseases plus also diarrhoea. A survey, combined with the distribution of Vitamin A capsules twice a year to children between 6 months and five years has been done in 27 districts of the Terai and Far Western region of Nepal.

Nutrition Assessment and Gap Analysis

In 1998 a task force was created by the National Planning Commission with the help of UNICEF to develop a new National Plan of Action in Nutrition (NPAN) taking into account child care practices, women empowerment, food security and responsive health actions. Though a draft NPAN had been prepared in 2007 the imperceptible decrease in the prevalence of under weight, stunted and wasted children in the country was very worrying. A Nutrition Assessment and Gap Analysis report was submitted in Nov. 2009 and endorsed by MoHP. Recommendations have been sent to NPC.

An estimated 50% of Nepali children under 5 are stunted – too short for their size as per the report 'Tracking Progress on Child & Maternal Nutrition in Nepal – 2010' launched by the DoHS. Far flung areas such as Rukum are in this category.

Research is currently underway in a nutrition and agriculture multi-sectoral programme to assess pathways linking agriculture to nutrition, food production, access and security and diet with nutritional status in Nepal. The investigators from both Nepal and USA are doing a panel survey of 5,000 pre-school children from 2013-15.

Suaahara[2] is an integarted nutrition programme which is supported by USAID and covers a 5 year period from Aug. 2011 to Aug. 2016. The purpose is to improve the nutritional status of women and of children under two years of age in 20-25 target districts The Suaahara group includes three national NGOs and will also co-ordinate with INGOs covering all the 25 districts in the 5-year period.

Iodine Deficiency Disorders - Iodation

Dr. V. Ramalingaswami had carried out a countrywide goitre prevalence survey in 1965-66. The survey in the three geographical regions showed that 55% of the population had goitre (35). Another survey in 1969 found rates of goitre prevalence to be between 74 and 100% in Jumla and Trishuli.

The Goitre Control Project set up in 1973 became subsequently the Goitre and Cretinism Eradication Project. Mass iodised oil injections were given in the remote mountainous and hilly areas where cretinism was widespread. During the programme a substantial number of females in the child bearing age, in 40 such districts had been given injections some twice or even three times. GoN also launched a salt iodation programme as early as 1972 as a result of which the number of cretins born has decreased. Contrary to this a report in 1985 stated that two surveys done in mountainous areas of Northern Nepal showed cretinism to have disappeared before the start of the Goitre Control Project of GoN (35). The reason suggested for this is that the population increase caused a food deficit in the area and that to deal with the problem, food with higher iodine content was transported from the lowland areas. The author however stressed the necessity of continuing the Goitre Control Project

2. The acronym stands for *Suddha Santulit Aahar, Hamro Jeevan Rakchhya ko Baliyo Aadhaar* meaning good nutrition.

and the iodation programme. The MoH was then giving iodine capsules in only eight districts of the country and laying stress on the provision of iodised salt (34).

An overall study supported by UNICEF (36) in 1984 had made the following suggestions regarding salt iodation in Nepal:

- The level of iodation should be 30 ppm of potassium iodate
- Iodation plants should be established in Nepal
- Salt should be packed in wire woven bags to minimise wastage
- There should be quality control
- The prevalence of goitre and cretinism should be monitored
- The iodine oil injection programme should be repeated
- Financial support should be extended
- Salt Trading Corporation should continue to be responsible for the salt iodation programme.

Regarding the problem of the Iodine Deficiency Disorder (IDD) the MoHP's plan of action has five components:

- policy formulation
- universal salt iodisation
- targeted iodine supplementation
- monitoring and evaluation, and the
- IEC component.

The situation as regards iodation is that there are currently three such plants established at Birgunj, Biratnagar and Bhairahawa. There is a mobile unit at Nepalgunj. Thus whilst we talk of tertiary care and high technology, the fact remains that for whatever may be the reason, we have not been able to provide iodised salt to all the Nepalese. Besides the Salt Trading Ltd. private parties are also being allowed to import iodised salt. Currently, iodised salt in manageable 1 kilo packing is now being sold. Presently there is one urinary iodine monitoring laboratory and four salt iodine-monitoring laboratories in Nepal.

Legislation has been enacted making it mandatory to have only iodised salt made available for sale. Though there is a virtual absence of disease of visible goitre among the population, there is still a high rate for palpable goitre. It has been recommended that sustained IDD control activities continue as a high priority.

Nepal Micronutrient Status Survey, 1998

That people in parts of Nepal were aware of the necessity of micronutrients is shown by the fact that even now it is customary in many districts of the Northern belt of Nepal for people to drink fresh yak blood about twice a year. The yak herders bring the animals to the grazing grounds where the interested individuals are waiting. The vein of the animal is lanced and people collect the fresh blood in their mugs and drink the fluid immediately. The belief is that as the yak grazes on Himalayan herbs, it has a lot of essential nutrients, which are beneficial also to humans. The effect is said to be increased by drinking *rakshi* or alcohol immediately after this.

This micronutrient survey had been undertaken after a gap of twenty-four years. The overall objective was to assess the distribution and severity of micronutrient malnutrition and to measure the progress so far of the various interventions done. Data collected were to determine the prevalence of:

- Iodine deficiency disorders (IDD),
- Iron deficiency anaemia (IDA) and
- Vitamin A deficiency (VAD).

A number of factors have been identified and future course of action was based on these findings (37).

Iron Deficiency Anaemia

Nutritional anaemia is very prevalent and a public health problem in Nepal. A large percentage of preschool children, pregnant and non-pregnant women were found to be anaemic. It had been discovered in 1997 by the Nepal Multiple Indicator Surveillance (NMIS) that only 10% of women had received iron and folic acid during their previous pregnancy. The recommendation of this NMIS survey is to give iron supplementation to adolescent girls, pregnant and non-pregnant women. It was suggested that special efforts be made and alternative strategies taken to bring this about.

Iron deficiency anaemia is the most common nutritional problem in Nepal and as per the Nepal Micronutrient Status Survey (NMSS) report 75% of pregnant and 67% of non-pregnant women suffer from anaemia. A survey was done in the 3 districts of Kathmandu, Bhaktapur and Lalitpur in the Central Development Region to elicit the level of anaemia in adolescent girl. The prevalence of anaemia among the community adolescents was

46%: the prevalence of mild anaemia was 38%, moderate 8% and severe 0.4% (38).

Vitamin A Deficiency

There was improvement in the Vitamin A status in that the prevalence of Bitot spots and night blindness has decreased appreciably from what it was 25 years ago. It is now only sometimes seen in women and pre school children. The National Vitamin A Programme (NVAP) covers currently 42 districts. The recommendation is that the bi-annual Vit. A capsule supplementation should be continued and expanded to cover all the 75 districts of the country.

As a large propoltion of Nepalis work in the agricultural sector, mostly on subsistence farming, investigations are under way to measure, classify and understand pathways by which agriculture with input of health and nutrition involvement can be effective to improve nutritional status of women and children.

POPULATION TRENDS

The average Total Fertility Rate (TFR) of Nepal 3.0 in 2010 was a great improvement though the rural Nepal is still high (6). The annual increase rate in 2011 was found to be 1.35%.

As 48.9% of the population in 2011 was between 15 and 19 years old, it means that one can, as a general rule, expect high fertility and declining mortality. Because of early marriage and short birth spacing in younger women it means that the MMR and IMR may not decline quickly to desired levels. The percentage of elderly persons i.e. those who are 60 or above, in the population has been gradually increasing over the years e.g.

1952-54	5.0 %
1991	5.8 %
2001	6.5 %
2011	8.13 %

In 2012 those over 65 years of age constituted 6.1 % of the population. Elderly persons in Nepal, because of the joint family system are generally found to be quite active in their advancing years. They may be involved in fairly unstrenuous tasks such as childcare, cattle herding, handicrafts and light farming activities. It may be also noted that the census of June 2011 also marked 100 years of population recording in Nepal.

Transmission of Health Messages

In the effort to tackle the problem of malnutrition a preventive and curative approach to the health of a child is necessary. In this context, a study at Santang near Dhankuta showed that the causes of malnutrition and ill health, which could be tackled, were lack of knowledge related to health and nutrition and economic constraints (40).

Some improvement has occurred since 2000 as the government has encouraged the airing of health messages in the electronic media. The banning of tobacco advertisements and that of alcohol during prime time has helped considerably.

It is a known fact that social-cultural factors influence many nutrition programmes in the rural areas. Many of the feeding practices may be of negative nature. To counter these, as well as to give nutrition education, much work needs to be done. A study of this in the PHC setting (39) showed that the low impact was due to:

a. Too many unrealistic messages.
b. Messages conflicting with cultural and traditional practices.
c. Western oriented content of message.

POINTS TO PONDER

The IMR, U5MR and MMR figures were very high at one time in Nepal. Over the course of the last two decades all these have come down and people are now living much longer. The increased Literacy Rate and the prolonged life span, especially amongst women is having a marked effect. This improvement in the health status can only increase and get better.

References

1. State of the World's Children, 2005 & 2012. UNICEF / State of the Nepali Children
2. World Health Report 2008. PHC Now More Than Ever.
3. Assessment of Technical Assistance in Health Sector, 1993, Valley Research Group (VaRG), Kathmandu.
4. National Commission on Population. GoN. A Profile. (undated)
5. David AB, Zivetz L, The Population problem of Nepal: causes and treatment. 1983. National Commission on Population, Kathmandu.
6. Nepal Population Report. 2011.

7. Thapa S, A decade of Nepal's family planning programme: achievements and prospects. In Studies in Family Planning 1989, 20(1): 38-52.
8. Fertility Trends in Nepal 1977-1995. Rutherford ED, Thapa S in Fertility Transition in Nepal. July, 1998, CNAS, Kathmandu.
9. Surkhet District Health Profile, 1991. Health Development Project, Kathmandu.
10. A Study on the Factors influencing Nutritional Status of Adolescent Girls. Regmi SC, Adhikari R. 1994. New ERA, Kathmandu.
11. Protecting Women from Unsafe Abortion. 2004. Souvenir 8th Nat. Conf. of NESOG.
12. Women's Right to Life & Health. Sharma S, Chaudhary P, Sharma SK. 2002. UNICEF, Kathmandu.
13. Health Sector Strategy – An Agenda for Reform. MoH, GoN, 2004
14. Annual Report of Department of Health Services, 2011/12 (2068/69 BS)
15. Upreti, Mellisa. Safe & Affordable Abortion. The Himalayan Times. 24 May 2012.
16. Souvenir of 54th Anniversary of Paropakar Obstetric & Women's Diseases Hospital, 2013.
17. Annual Report of Family Planning Association of Nepal, 2012.
18. Kanti Children's Hospital Souvenir, 2012.
19. The Global Burden of Disease. 2004 Update WHO.
20. Vaidya, Bal Gopal. MDG Roundtable in 2013 at SoS.
21. Save the Children . Bhutan & Nepal. Annual Report 2012.
22. Violence against women in Nepal: Role of health care workers. KUMJ 2009. 7, (2), 89-90.
23. Pradhan, Sapna M. The Urgent Need for Comprehensive Law. The Himalayan Times. 19 Oct. 2012.
24. Brown ML, Worth RM & Shah NK. Health Survey of Nepal. 1968; Am. Jou. Clin. Nut. 21, (8), 875-881.
25. Sharma PR, Child nutrition yesterday, today and tomorrow. 1979; Narayani Health J, 2(1) : 5-8.
26. Report of the National Nutrition Strategy Workshop. 1978 Pokhara.
27. Padfield N, Nabarro D. The Management of Children with PEM in Nepal: Results of Dhankuta Nutrition Unit. J Inst Med 1984; 6(1): 1-14.
28. Nabarro D. Influences on the growth of children. Nep Paed Soc J 1983; 2: 167-205.
29. Krantz ME, Nutrition problems and programmes in Nepal. J Nep Med Assoc 1979; 17(1) : 45-53.
30. Ulstein M et al. Some fetal and pregnancy parameters in Nepal. Acta Obstetrica et Gynecologica Scandanavia, 1988; 67(1): 47-52.
31. West KP Jr et al, Efficacy of Vit A in reducing preschool child mortality in

Nepal. Lancet 1991; 338(8759): 67-71.

32. Adhikari, Ramesh. Trends in Nutritional Status in Nepal since 1975. 1991, UNICEF, Kathmandu.
33. Third Monitoring of Progress - Common Framework. P&FAD, MOH, Feb. 1994.
34. Family Health Survey 1996. Family Health Division, MoH, Kathmandu, 1997.
35. Achard T, Some aspects of iodine deficiency in Nepal. 1985 J Inst Med 7(1) : 43-6.
36. Subramanian P, Control of iodine deficiency disorders by salt iodation in Nepal. 1984, UNICEF, New Delhi.
37. Nepal Micronutrient Status Survey. 1998. HMGN, UNICEF, WHO.
38. Rikimaru, Toru, Nira Joshi, Sharada Pandey, Anaemia in Adolescent Girls. 2004. Nutrition Section, Child Health Division.

4.

HRH, ACADEMICS AND RESEARCH

Historical research has shown that King Pratap Malla and Malla kings of Bhaktapur and Patan encouraged Ayurvedic system of medicine by asking to prepare books in Ayurved and creating opportunities for professional training (1).

The Early Years of HRH Training

It has been stated that Dr. Ratna Das Baidya was the first Nepali to have become a doctor as per the news cutting in the local Gorkhapatra newspaper of 20th Shrawan, 1959 BS (1902 AD). He is credited to have done the equivalent of the LMP course in Bengali language at Calcutta and come back to work at Singha Durbar at Kathmandu.

During the time of World War I, to cope with the increasing number of wounded army personnel, the British authorities in India started the category of health workers known as Licentiate Medical Practitioners (LMP). This four-year course with a pre-requisite of Matriculation was conducted at the Campbell Medical School (now National Medical School), at Calcutta and two Nepali students were enrolled into this. These two who came back after qualification in 1918 were Dr. Devi Prasad Upadhaya and Dr. Ganesh Lal Maskey and whilst the former opted for general practice, the latter did pathology.

Later Dr. Siddhi Mani A Dixit did the matriculation examination in 1914 and passed the MB in 1921 from Medical College, Calcutta. Dr. Yagya Man Baidya also qualified soon after.

In the meantime the LMP course, which became the Licentiate of the Medical Faculty (LMF), was done by most of the Nepali students who went to study medicine in India. Following independence in 1947, all the LMF doctors had to do a condensed medical course to be upgraded as MBBS doctors. Nepali doctors so qualified went too, for upgrading courses to India. By this time the entry requirement for MBBS became Intermediate in Science (I.Sc.).

As far as ladies are concerned Ms. Rajabhai S. K. Chauhan qualified from the Lady Hardinge Medical College at Delhi in 1935 and after marriage to a Nepali came to work in Nepal. Dr. Mrs. Rajabhai Rana may therefore be taken as the first Nepali lady doctor.

In the first half of the twentieth century, almost all of the Nepali health personnel were trained in India. The first four Nepali girls to be trained in midwifery were sent to Allahabad in 1928 for the eighteen months training then considered necessary. On their return, they were employed in Bir Hospital.

Health personnel education started in Nepal with the formation of the Nepal Rajakiya Ayurved Vidyalaya in 1933/34 (1990 BS) for the training of baidyas and other categories of ayurvedic personnel (2). The ayurvedic personnel trained there, from the time of its establishment and its much later incorporation into the Institute of Medicine (IoM) in 1972 can be categorised into three grades viz:

- Baidya Vinod / Madhyama
- Baidya Bhusan / Shastri
- Baidya Ratna / Acharya

Training for compounders and dressers also started in 1934 in the newly opened Civil Medical School. This institution was probably so named as there was a trend in India to train the local people over a period of three to four years, often at the state level in the local language in so called "medical schools". Such health personnel in India were known as Licentiate Medical Practitioners (LMP). In distinction to this, the students trained in the Western type of degree course (MBBS) were produced by the "Medical Colleges" (3).

Health services in the pre-World War II Nepal were minimal and confined to some of the bigger towns. Expatriate doctors, mostly Bengalis, staffed almost all the posts. The 238 compounders and 213 dressers, trained within the country by the Civil Medical School over the course of the first thirty years effectively ran the hospitals and smaller units under the supervision of the doctors (4).

Students continued to be sent to India for training. An innovative step was when two Nepali girls were sent to India in 1952 with the idea that they would be utilised as teachers in schools contemplated for middle level health workers (5). Thus a programme for the middle level-nursing workers began with the formation of a nursing school in 1956 under the Directorate of Health Services, Ministry of Health (MoH). The course was of three and half year's duration and the first intake was of fifteen girls (6). However, because of the existing shortage of nurses, the Development Board of the Bir Hospital in the early sixties recruited as many as twenty-two Indian nurses (7). Separate school for training another category viz. Health Assistants started in the same year with a two year course. Entry to it was after ten years of basic schooling. This training was started with the objective of having a category of health personnel similar to the Licentiate Medical Practitioner (LMP) of the British ruled colonial India. Such personnel, after having worked for a few years as health assistants, would be entitled to compete for a place and undergo further training to become doctors. A total of 65 personnel were trained under this scheme.

Soon after this, an AHW School was started under the aegis of the Ministry of Health in 1962 and trained 43 health assistants. Later it was felt that a single training school, producing a category between the health assistant and the compounders and dressers would be more economical. This school went on to train 341 AHWs over the course of the next eight years.

Other institutions for the production of these and other categories came to bc established during the course of subsequent years. The training of a cadre to provide midwifery care was started in 1958. Later, a woman's Auxiliary Health Workers Training Programme was started under the Directorate of Health Services, with the support of USAID (1). This training of three batches produced a total of 43 female health workers. Subsequently, with a view to give it a community focus, this programme was shifted from Hetauda to the hospital compound at Bharatpur. Later it was converted to cater for the training of ANMs in 1963. Thus the AHW and the ANM came into being in the health care setting of Nepal (8). ANM schools were started subsequently at Biratnagar in 1965 and at Nepalgunj in 1967.

The idea of starting a medical school in Nepal had first been suggested in 1963 by a WHO Assignment Team led by Prof. W. M. Arnott. Later in

October 1965, another team from India, led by Dr. P. M. Bhandarkar, then Surgeon General of Maharashtra State, gave a similar suggestion. A medical school was planned to be constructed during the course of the then current Five Year Plan.

Some months later, in June 1968, a committee headed by Dr. D. N. Baidya was constituted with the objective of starting a medical college that same year with an annual intake of 25 to 30 students. A 5-member team travelled to various medical colleges at Berampur, Ranchi, Lucknow and Benaras in India for purposes of planning. Two Nepali doctors too were sent for training in the pre-clinical sciences.

Subsequent rethought brought about a new concept of providing rural health services through middle and basic level workers, with the idea that such health personnel would be more effective (9). The medical school project was thus temporarily shelved.

Institute of Medicine (IoM)

Up to this period the basic health pereonnel training institutions within the country were under the Ministry of Health. In mid-July 1972 (1st Shrawan, 2028), Tribhuvan University was reconstituted with a total of ten institutes, four research centres and a Central Office. It was under the New Education Systems Plan (NESP), that the Institute of Medicine was established. A new educational policy envisaged the concept of vocational training and its implementation. Thus, the IoM, which had its origins in, the Civil Medical School of 1934 by way of the Health Assistants School of 1956 and the AHW School of 1962, finally reached the existing set up in July 1972 AD (10).

Soon after the establishment of IoM to make health personnel education more widespread, it started campuses for different grades of health workers, in each of the then existing four development regions i.e. Eastern, Central, Western and Far Western. These campuses were as follows:

1. ANM extension campuses at Tansen, Palpa (1973) and at Chhetrapati, Kathmandu from 1973-1979.
2. AHW campuses at Birgunj (1975), at Surkhet (1978), at Tansen (1978) and at Inarwa from (1978-1979). The Inarwa campus was relocated to Dhankuta in 1984.

3. A Certificate level Campus started in 1978 at Dharan was relocated within a year at Maharajgunj and the batch of students amalgamated with the HA batch there.

Besides the training programmes for AHW & ANM health workers, IoM had six certificate level programmes, in general medicine, nursing, pharmacy, radiography, health laboratory and traditional / general medicine. Four of these certificate level programmes were of two and half years duration, while nursing and the ayurvedic programmes were both of 3 years after the ten years of basic schooling. In terms of career development, there was to be provision, for a four year "Diploma Level" course in medical sciences at a later date.

These middle levels of medical personnel who worked in the field for specified periods of time, would then be given opportunities to go on to become community oriented physicians at the end of four years of study and one year of internship.

The auxiliary and certificates level programmes at the IoM have changed from time to time. New programmes in physiotherapy and health education and sanitation were started and later stopped. The entry level for auxiliary programmes has varied from an "eight class pass" to a "class ten pass". Some upgrading courses of three months duration were done for the old AHW. Later, post SLC auxiliary course of one year was started for Community Medical Auxiliary (CMA). Students who completed this course and then worked in the health field for a specified time were allowed to take upgrading courses to become Health Assistants at a later stage.

Ayurved Personnel Training

With the implementation of the NESP the training of the *baidyas* was taken over by the Ayurved Campus of Tribhuvan University (TU) with the programme based at the Ayurved Hospital at Naradevi. IoM at that time was training also the Ayurved Assistants and later the Bachelor grades of Ayurved known as Bachelor of Ayurved Medicine and Surgery (BAMS). Later the Sanskrit University started the training of baidyas and BAMS at Dang also. IoM discontinued the lower level training and the Council of Technical Education and Vocational Training (CTEVT) took over the training of these levels of HRH. The Sanskrit University is now only doing the Bachelor programme.

In 2006 the Ayurved Campus of TU shifted to its own building at Kirtipur and conducted the BAMS course. It was reported as having 75 beds. The BAMS course has been recognised by the Council of Indigenous Medicine in India and so our graduates in this field can do further studies in India too. As from 2011 Ayurved Campus has started the MD (Ayurved) also.

Nursing Programmes

With the establishment of the IoM in 1972, the certificate level courses in nursing were only conducted at the Mahaboudha Nursing Campus and at the Shanta Bhawan Nurse Training Programme. Subsequent years saw the conversion of the CMA campuses or upgrading of the ANM Campuses so that the net result was the establishment between 1981 and 1987 of four additional nursing campuses in the order given. These were at Biratnagar 1981, Pokhara 1984, Birgunj 1986 and Nepalgunj 1987 (10).

The Mahabouddha Nursing Campus was shifted in 1986 to the Tribhuvan University Teaching Hospital site as the Maharajgunj Nursing Campus. The Shanta Bhawan Nursing Programme became the Lalitpur Nursing Campus in 1990. A new Nursing Campus was started at Bir Hospital in 1988.

The certificate level nursing curriculum was revised in 1987, with stress in community orientation, to enable nurses to work not only as staff nurses of the urban hospitals but also in the rural settings.

In 1978, the IoM started higher grades of study in nursing and medicine on keeping with Tribhuvan University (TU) policies then, the BN was initially referred to as a 'Diploma' level program. Later with change of university policy and increased duration of course these programmes became known as bachelor degree programs in nursing, medicine and ayurved respectively.

In 1992, following a change in policy the auxiliary courses conducted by IoM were discontinued. It should be noted too that from 1993 the entry to certificate level courses had been made to be intermediate science or 10 + 2 or equivalent. In 2013 entry is almost totally by 10+2 with science subjects.

The nineties also saw the starting of the BN course at the Lalitpur Nursing Campus. The B. P. Koirala Institute of Health Sciences (BPKIHS) at Dharan started a BSc in nursing with both male and female students. The Pubanchal University (PU) has also started a Bachelor grade course in nursing. Later in the 2nd millennium BSc Nursing courses of study were started under TU, Kathmandu University (KU) and PU. The KU started in 2010 a Post Basic course for those who wanted to do a degree, but with a science background. This Bachelor in Nursing Science (BNS) programme is comparable to the BN.

NB. Entry to Technician Certificate in nursing continues to be still SLC pass.

Human Resources for Nursing

Nepal Government had, during the time of the agreements for setting up medical colleges, stipulated that all such institutions must have a nursing programme of their own. The colleges in their turn have started a number of programmes of both Certificate and Bachelor level. A major producer of PCL nurses is however the CTEVT which has two colleges of its own and hundred and four others affiliated to it. Recently the Nepal Nursing Council is trying to enforce a rule making it obligatory for nursing colleges to have their own hospital beds or access to such. The various nursing programmes and where they are conducted are as shown below:

Table 4.1 Nursing Programmes by Institutions

Institution	ANM	PCL	Post Basic BN	Post Basic BNS	BSc Nursing	MN-Master Nursing	MSc Nursing
CTEVT	41	102					
BPKIHS		1	1		1	1	1
TU – IoM		5	8		6	3	
Kathmandu Univ.		(DMI)*		3	9		
Purbanchal Univ.			21		19		
Pokhara Univ					2		
NAMS (Bir Hosp)		1	1				
TOTAL	41	110	31	3	37	4	1

* Dhulikhel Medical Institute

Nursing can be taken as an empowerment of women and is important in the context of Nepal. Furthermore one has only to think of Kerala state in India, which improved its health status as a result of the mass interest of girls to take up nursing as a profession. This interest is almost worldwide now. Many have done so in Nepal and are going abroad either as nurses or as care givers in Old People's home in North America, Europe or even Australia to provide nursing care to the elderly. This enthusiasm has also furthered the aims of female education in Nepal.

Table 4.2 Production of Nurses and ANMs

Category	End of 2004	Up to mid-May 2013
Nurses	5,664	22,038
ANMs	6,161	20,056
Total	11,825	42,944

This includes 750 foreign nurses, registered and working in Nepal. Currently there is an average of 3,560 studying to be ANMs or nurses in Nepal.

Of this total number of 42, 944, it must be noted that the current renewed status up to 15th May 2013 is:

Nurses: 6,050
ANMs: 2,599
Total: 8,649

The number of nurses working within the country has to be periodically checked and verified by the Nepal Nursing Council (NNC). A number of those trained may leave the profession once they get married and have children. The tendency now-a-days, as stated already, is for a number to go abroad to UK, USA, Australia or Canada to work as 'care givers' at old people's homes. It cannot be denied that the private sector has made considerable effort in this. However some questions have been raised as to the quality of training that the girls have received and whether they have done adequate and appropriate on job training. A recent survey by a health magazine stated that out of 88 nursing colleges in the country only 37 had their own hospital. In term of teaching beds for nurses, India requires five beds per student, China seven and Thailand eight beds per student. (11) There has recently been a trend of going out of the country, mainly India for nursing training. Whilst there are many good institutions, there are others where clinical skills training, so important in this field are nonexistent (11).

National Health Training Centre (NHTC)

National Health Training Centre (NHTC) is the apex body of MoHP for human reasource develeopment to cater to the training need for various centres and divisions of DoHS, Department of Drugs Administration (DDA) and Department of Ayurved (DoA).

With the concept of providing an integrated community oriented health services, a number of Regional Training Centres had been started in the five different regions of the country at varying periods of time under the aegis of MoH. Four of these at Dhankuta, Pathliaiya, Pokhara and Surkhet were started in 1982 whilst the one at Dhankuta was only established in 1990. The NHTC now has one sub-regional training centre at Sapahi, in Dhanusha district, 30 districts level training facilities and 14 training health posts in 13 districts.

Following the introduction of the National Health Policy of 1991, a National Training Co-ordination Unit was established in the MoH. The initial training of VHWs /MCHWs has been phased out. The NHTC is doing upgrading courses for MCHWs, ANMs and AHWs. Its focus now is on the training of skilled birth attendants (SBA) (12).

Council for Technical Education and Vocational Training (CTEVT)

A Council for Higher Secondary Education plus another Council for Technical Education and Vocational Training (CTEVT) had been established in 1989. Then, following the change in policy the auxiliary courses conducted by IoM were discontinued in 1992. The CTEVT has now taken over the responsibility of running the auxiliary and Proficiency Certificate Level (PCL) courses. It is responsible for policy formulation and is the co-ordinating body for technical education and vocational training in Nepal.

During the course of the last twenty years various private institutions of differing capabilities suddenly mushroomed all over the country. Their objective was to fulfil the expected shortfall in the lower levels of health personnel.

In November 2008, besides the Engineering and Agricultural fields, a number of students in the health field of Nursing, General Medicine, Dental, Pharmacy and Ophthalmology had been in the CTEVT affiliated institutions for the training of the basic levels of health personnel such as CMA, ANM etc. Of this number five were the Regional Training Centres of Nepal Government for CMA training and the others are all private institutions. There are currently in 2011, according to the CTEVT Website the under mentioned number of institutions conducting various courses.

Table 4.3 Schools conducting PCL & Auxiliary Courses by Types as of 2011

Level	Types of Courses	No of Schools	
		Constituent	Affiliated
Basic	Community Medicine Auxiliary (CMA)	2	72
	Auxiliary Nurse Midwife (ANM)	4	40
	Laboratory Assistant	-	30
	Ayurved Auxiliary Health Worker (AAHW)	-	5
	Amchi (Tibetan Medicine)		1
Middle	PCL Nursing	2	77
	PCL General Medicine (HA)	1	46
	PCL Medical Laboratory Assistant	1	20
	Diploma Pharmacy	1	43
	Diploma Radiography	-	15
	Diploma Dental Science	-	5
	Homeopathy	-	1
	Ayurved	-	2

Health Assistant courses are also being conducted at Bharatpur, Nepalgunj and Dhulikhel. The Sanskrit University is planning to produce different grades of ayurvedic personnel.

Whilst intake requirements vary from a SLC to SLC test passed, the numbers enrolled vary between 20 and 120 per intake at each institution. The course duration varies too, from one year to two years and five months with the certificate issued at the end being labelled as that of a Technical SLC to denote a CMA, ANM or an AHW. Grave concern is being expressed regarding the quality of the products as much deficiency exists in the equipment, training facilities and teachers of these teaching institutions. The inadequacies for practical training, the large numbers of intake in each batch are just two of the causes for further worry. At a lower level a six months PHC course is also in existence.

Institute of Medicine's MBBS course & its Influence

The concept of the basic community oriented doctor was the philosophy of the course of study that the IoM started with in 1978. Its first batch came out in 1984 (13). Initial opposition to the programme was that this being "WHO inspired and community oriented" would lead to the production of sub-standard medical personnel. The opening of the Japanese aided Tribhuvan University Teaching Hospital helped tremendously to dispel the doubts regarding the training of the MBBS programme. The initial five batches into the MBBS course were candidates who were middle level health workers but subsequently entrants were of two groups viz. those with an I.Sc or those who had been middle level health workers. From 1999 candidates who after twelve years of schooling had passed I.Sc. or 10+2 with Physics, Chemistry and Biology or its equivalent were admitted into the programme.

The general hope was that doctors produced by IoM would be more ready to go out to work at rural postings e.g. the district hospitals than doctors who had been produced outside of Nepal. The standards and capability of the IoM produced medical graduates is no longer in doubt as many have been going out to different countries of the world for further training and study. Even a number of the graduates of the new medical schools are going out of the country.

Community Oriented MBBS Course

When the MBBS course at the Institute of Medicine was started in 1978, there was a great deal of opposition in the sense that what was being envisaged for Nepal was something new, not traditional and something which was not accepted in the world in general. What has happened is that the concepts then advocated e.g. community medicine, problem solving, system wise instruction and integrated teaching have now been accepted in many countries. A recent paper on Community Oriented Medical Education (COME) stated that IoM had, to a certain extent incorporated these concepts in its teaching learning activities. COME has had a positive impact on the education of physicians in Nepal in that later programmes of MBBS at BPKIHS and KU have taken it up. KU has introduced what has been termed the SPICES model type of curriculum, which is based on the principles of:

S – student centred/teacher centred approach
P – problem based/information gathering approach
I – integrated discipline based
C – community oriented/hospital based
E – elective included

S – systematic approach to curriculum planning/apprenticeship based

Now the Patan Academy of Health Sciences (PAHS), as from 2010 has been conducting this same type of medical education. As from 2011, KU has incorporated Problem Based Learning (PBL) from the start of the course and this is being implemented in all its affiliated colleges.

Present and Future Problems

Though successful efforts were made for the recognition of MBBS of IoM by the countries of the SAARC region and further afield the work has not been completed yet. The situation however has changed now. Nepali medical graduates have to sit for a licensing examination during the course of their internship year. The products of the medical colleges of Nepal are allowed to sit for the USMLE, PLAB and other licensing examinations of foreign lands. Many are leaving soon after, thus constituting a 'Brain Drain'. The Nepal Medical Association (NMA) has drawn the attention of the authorities to this.

The Medical Colleges Situation

The medical course at the IoM was started in 1978. The first batch of IoM's basic community oriented doctor came out in 1984. Even in those early years (1980), there was interest by various groups from outside of Nepal to set up medical colleges. Bearing in mind the fact that as the MBBS course of the IoM had just started, the Nepalese authorities were not keen to allow such efforts. Thus it was only in the nineties that it was decided to set up the B. P. Koirala Institute of Health Sciences (BPKIHS) at Dharan with the help of the Government of India. At about this time the idea was mooted that having private medical colleges will not only bring about a boost in the economy but that a good service sector could be created in the health field. Besides decreasing the amount of money being spent outside of the country for the health care of the Nepalese, the government would be providing health services to a substantial portion of the population, at no cost to itself. The opening of private medical colleges became a reality in Dec. 1994 when the Manipal College of Medical Sciences was started at Pokhara. The total number of medical colleges in October 2013 is nineteen. Thus different medical colleges came into being in the order given in different parts of the country. The fear now is that there might be too many to be sustainable.

Table 4.4 Medical colleges in the country.

Name of Medical College	University	Year Estd	MBBS Class Started	Annual Intake in 2013	Masters PG started
Institute of Medicine, Kathmandu	Tribhuvan	1972	1978	75	1982
BP Koirala Inst. Health Sciences, Dharan	Deemed	1993	1994	100	1999
Manipal College of Med. Sciences, Pokhara	Kathmandu	1994	1994	150	2007
College of Medical Sciences- Nepal, Bharatpur	Kathmandu	1996	1997	150	2007
Nepalgunj Medical College, Nepalgunj	Kathmandu	1996	1997	150	2007
Kathmandu Medical College, Kathmandu.	Kathmandu	1997	1997	100	2009
Nepal Medical College, Kathmandu.	Kathmandu	1997	1997	100	2009
Universal College of Medical Sciences, Bhairahawa	Tribhuvan	1997	1998	125	
National Medical College, Birgunj	Tribhuvan	2000	2000	150	
KU School of Medical Sciences, Dhulikhel.	Kathmandu	2001	2001	60	1999
Janaki Medical College, Janakpur.	Tribhuvan	2003	2003	100	
Nobel Medical College, Biratnagar.	Kathmandu	2005	2007	150	

Lumbini Medical College, Tansen.	Kathmandu	2010	2010	75	
Patan Academy Health Sciences, Lalitpur	Deemed	2008	2010	60	
KIST Medical College, Lalitpur.	Tribhuvan	2008	2009	80	
Chitwan College of Medical Sciences Bharatpur	Tribhuvan	2008	2009	75	
Gandaki Medical College, Pokhara.	Tribhuvan	2009	2010	75	
Nepali Army Institute of Medical Sciences, Kathmandu	Tribhuvan	2011	2011	100	

Deemed University -2 TU + Affiliates – 1+7 KU + Affiliates – 1+7

NB. NAMS is an autonomous institute for post graduate studies

The Institute of Medicine was the first medical college to be set up in the country. As of now there are four and fourteen medical institutions for MBBS course in the Public and Private sector respectively. It is noteworthy that seven of the private medical colleges are affiliated to Kathmandu University which also has its own medical school KUMS. There are now four dental colleges affiliated with it. Tribhuvan University besides its own Institute of Medicine has also seven other medical colleges and four dental colleges affiliated to it. BPKIHS has its own medical and dental college.

1. Institute of Medicine, Maharajgunj (IoM).

Some information about the IoM has already been given. Besides the main teaching hospital with its free beds and cabins it has now proliferated into different sections and specialities. The total number of functional beds in 2013 is now 627 plus 70 in the compound at Maharajgunj, and the occupancy is 86%. Thus TUTH includes the following:

i. B. P. Koirala Lions Centre for Ophthalmic Studies (BPKLCOS), which recently celebrated its 17th anniversary, has so far produced 100 ophthalmologists and 62 optometrists. Most of the work is on OPD basis but it is now in the process of building a new indoor too.

ii. Man Mohan Cardio-Thoracic Vascular and Transplant Centre (MCTVTC)

iii. Ganesh Man ENT Centre.

The total number of beds will reach 802, thus making it the largest hospital in the country. A new emergency block has also been opened. (14).

2. B. P. Koirala Institute of Health Sciences (BPKIHS), Dharan

An Act of Parliament on 18th Jan, 1993 started the process for the setting of this autonomous institute, not under any University. It was subsequently established on 16th July, 1993. Its first intake in 1994 was of 30 students but this has gradually increased to 75 over the first decade and from 2005 it is now 100 students annually. There are special provisions for local candidates and also for those from foreign lands paying regular fees. After the first phase of the project was completed, the official opening of the hospital was done on 9th September 1999. Following additions done periodically to the original 150 beds it has now been turned into a 700-bedded complex. Post graduate courses such as MD/MS are also conducted.

BPKIHS is a Centre for Infectious and Tropical Diseases. It School of Dentistry started the BDS programme in 1998 and now also conducts the MDS in various specialities. The School of Nursing conducts the Certificate, BSc and MSc programmes. Another School for Allied Health Personnel does the laboratory technician course. An amendment to the original act gave it the status of a deemed university in Oct. 1998. A School of Public Health started from the academic year 2005 and runs a two year MPH programme.

3. Manipal College of Medical Sciences (MCOMS), Pokhara (KU)

This college started with its first intake of students in Dec. 1994 with the Western Regional Hospital being utilised for clinical training. Buildings of the new hospital are complete and functioning. With the increased facilities and using the facilities of the Regional Hospital at Pokhara the student intake has been increased to 150 with intakes in August and February in an academic year. There are, besides the Nepali students, others from SAARC countries and abroad.

MCOMS is also running courses in Masters grade for the Basic Sciences for both medical and non-medical personnel. MD/MS courses in clinical subjects started in Feb. 2007. There is also a nursing Certificate program school as per the CTEVT curriculum and a BSc Nursing program affiliated to KU.

Post Graduate Medical and Dental programs of KU were started at Bangalore, Mangalore and Manipal, India in collaboration with Manipal Academy of Health Education (MAHE) - later Manipal University in 2003 The Master's Dental programs were however conducted only for 4 years (16).

4. College of Medical Sciences - Nepal, Bharatpur (KU)

The medical college was allowed to start functioning as from August of 1996 and its first institution day was celebrated on 14th December, 1996. Its ninth intake was in August as with the other medical colleges under Kathmandu University. There is a clause in the agreement of this college by which the Nepalese students account for about 25% of the annual intake. There are also special provisions for local candidates. Currently there are about 25 Nepalese students in each year. Others are mainly from India. MD /MS in various clinical subjects from Feb. 2007. Its first super specialists passed out in 2013.

5. Nepalgunj Medical College, Nepalgunj (KU)

This, GoN approved medical college has been set up by a group of Nepali entrepreneurs grouped together in a body known as Lord Buddha Educational Academy. Established in 1996 this medical college started functioning from December, 1997 with the first intake of 75 students, with an increase to 100 from the following year. As from 2005 it admits 150 students per year. Masters PG studies in clinical areas started from Feb. 2007. It has recently produced some super-specialists. A nursing school as per the curriculum of CTEVT is being run.

6. Kathmandu Medical College, Kathmandu (KU)

This medical college too started functioning from Dec. 1997 with a first intake of 75 of which around 33% were Nepalese. The college now has its Basic Sciences set up at Duwakot, Bhaktapur and its clinical set up at Sinamangal. It is currently taking 100 students per year. MD in pathology is running as from 2003 and postgraduate studies in other clinical areas started from Feb. 2007. A Bachelor course in nursing started in 2006 and its first batch graduated in Feb. 2010. It started the Bachelor programme in Dental Surgery in 2012.

7. Nepal Medical College, Kathmandu (KU)

This private medical college too started functioning from the 1997/98 session with an annual intake of 75 of which most were Nepalese. The formal opening was on 28th Dec, 1997 on the occasion of late King Birendra's birthday. Whilst the initial plans are to use some of the hospitals of Kathmandu valley, the future hospital of this medical college has been constructed at Attarkhel, Jorpati. Its annual intake of students is now 150. It started the Bachelor programme in Dental Surgery in 2011.

8. Universal College of Medical Sciences, Bhairahawa (TU)

The Universal Institute of Advanced Studies & Research Inc. established a medical college and hospital at Bhairahawa, near the birthplace of Lord Buddha and was granted affiliation by Tribhuvan University. It is officially known as Universal Institute of Medical Sciences, Nepal. Its initial intake was 60 but now has an annual intake of 150. A dental college also functions in the same premises.

9. National Medical College, Birgunj (TU)

This college, affiliated with TU started classes in 2000 with an initial intake of 60 students and has currently four batches of MBBS students. Its intake is now 150. It conducts MD/MS PG programmes in clinical areas.

10. Kathmandu University School of Medical Sciences (KUSMS), Dhulikhel

Kathmandu University School of Medical Sciences (KUSMS) was established in 2001 with joint effort of Kathmandu University and Dhulikhel Hospital. The hospital had in fact been opened in 1996 by late King Birendra as a community based institution. It is a not for profit and autonomous programme, established to produce technically competent and socially responsible medical graduates by way of Problem Based Learning (PBL). In 2013 it now has a total of 375 beds and trains doctors, nurses, laboratory technicians and physiotherapists (16,17). As from 2011 KU decided to implement PBL in all its affiliated colleges too. KUSMS runs the BDS dental programme, the nursing programmes BSc Nursing (2005), BNS and BPT, a bachelor programme in physiotherapy, both in 2010.

The Dhulikhel Medical Institute trains middle level personnel such as nurses and laboratory technicians.

11. Janaki Medical College, Janakpur (TU)

This college, which is run by the Ram Janaki Health Foundation, is a private sector undertaking and is based at Ramdaiya Bhawadi, Dhanusha. Its first batch of sixty MBBS students qualified in 2007. It currently has an intake of 100.

12. Nobel Medical College, Biratnagar (KU)

The Nobel Medical College was started at Biratnagar in 2005 for the training of medical doctors. Affiliation by KU was given in 2007. In the early years there were some teething problems and the management changed hands periodically. It now has an intake of 100.

13. Lumbini Medical College, Palpa (KU)

This college was given affiliation by KU in 2010 and its first two intakes were 60 per year. It also runs a nursing programme under CTEVT guidelines.

14. Patan Academy of Health Science, Lalitpur (Deemed Univ.)

Patan Academy of Health Sciences, though started in 2008 with its own Vice Chancellor was able to start MBBS classes from June 2010 only with an initial intake of 60. Though preference was to be given to personnel who had been health workers, there were very few in the first two intakes.

15. KIST Medical College, Imadol, Patan (TU)

Based at Lalitpur and started from the 2010 session with an initial intake of sixty. Currently it has a 300 bedded hospital. It has also started its own dental college as from 2011.

16. Chitwan College of Medical Sciences, Bharatpur (TU)

The hospital of this teaching institution started in 2008. It was however only in Nov. 2009 that the medical college started functioning with an initial batch of 60. Now it has the BDS, BSc Nursing, BMLT and B.Pharm too.

17. Gandaki Medical College Teaching Hospital & Research Centre, Pokhara (TU)

The Charak Hospital at Pokhara was started in 2009. The medical college, affiliated to Tribhuvan University was allowed to function with an initial intake of 75 as from December 2010.

18. Nepalese Army Institute of Medical Sciences, Kathmandu (TU)

One major development is that the Nepal Army started its own Health Sciences Academy as from 2011. Presently this comprises of Medical and, Nursing components and intends to have a Medical Polytechnic and Dental College soon. The medical college is affiliated to TU and the nursing school to CTEVT. This Institute and the Medical College was officially opened by President Dr. Ram Baran Yadav on 23rd May 2012 (10th Jestha 2069).

Other ventures

Because of the large number of aspirants for medical studies within and from regions around Nepal it is likely that other colleges will come up in the future.

The Nepal Government has because of its remoteness and lack of health facilities decided to set up the Karnali Academy of Health Sciences (KAHS) and has even appointed a Vice Chancellor. What programmes the Academy will conduct still remains to be announced. GoN is also in the process of starting a Medical College in the Far Western Region. It is expected to be at Geta VDC in Dhangadi near to the Eye Hospital which has been running for a number of years. It is along the Dhangadi – Attaria highway. Furthermore the MoE and TU have informed the applicants for starting medical colleges that preference will be given to the one ready to set up a college in the Far Western Region. Nepal Police Hospital is also in the process of starting its own medical college.

The Purabanchal University has been planning for a number of years to start a medical college at Mrigauliya, Morang district.

Though a special expert committee formed by the MoHP under the Chairmanship of Prof. Bimal Sinha had recommended that there should be a distance of 50 kilometres between two medical colleges in the hills and 100 kilometres in the Terai area, this has not been adhered too. The committee also recommended that there should be no more medical colleges in the capital.

The Man Mohan Memorial Co-operative University which includes the Man Mohan Memorial Hospital and medical college are raising funds for the same as from Oct 2009 when Mr Madhav Kumar Nepal, then PM inaugurated a '*Hom*' organised in support of it. This and the Pushpa Lal Medical College are awaiting approval. The Janamaitri Health Foundation at Balaju, Kathmandu has also applied for permission (18). The Norvic International Hospital based at Thapathali in Kathmandu had a letter of intent issued previously and has now announced its tie up with Medanta Medicity in New Delhi and that it will start its own medical college by 2015. The Khetan group of industries has announced that it will open a medical college at Tripureshwar area, Kathmandu .

Two pending applications on the verge for starting medical college are those of Birat at Biratnagar, and Devdaha in Rupandehi. Other pending are at Ilam, Rajbiraj, Hetauda and Birgunj where the projected Aswini Medical Colleges is sited.

National Academy of Medical Sciences (NAMS)

The National Academy of Sciences was started in 2002 by the government of Nepal and started its own PG Programme soon after. It was announced as a deemed university with the aims of quality service and production of specialists and super-specialists. Priority of admission was given to those doctors in government service who have served in remote areas. It was however only in July 2004 the Ministry of Health's (MoH) announced the setting up of an autonomous post-graduate National Academy of Medical Sciences (NAMS) based at Bir Hospital. The body responsible for this will be the Valley Group of Hospitals and its programmes are being currently run in a number of hospitals in the Valley. It is thus the Post Graduate Medical Institute of the Government. It also awards Fellowships following experience and academic training.

The nursing courses that it runs are of Certificate (CTEVT) and Bachelor of Nursing (TU).

Tilganga Institute of Ophthalmology

The hospital which is doing remarkable eye care and producing lens on a large scale was converted into an institute. It is running the MD in Ophthalmology course in affiliation with NAMS.

Nick Simons Institute

This is an Institute funded by charitable organization in New York in memory of Nick Simons who had come to Nepal in 2002 and worked with a NGO involved in water resources. Following his experience in Nepal he intended studying medicine and work for sometime in Nepal. However it so turned out that he was drowned in 2003 whilst swimming in Bali. The Nick Simons Institute was established in 2006 with a view to help in medical education, not only in Kathmandu but all over Nepal. The concept is a Medical Training Network with a view to furthering continuing medical education amongst all levels of health workers in Nepal.

DENTAL COLLEGES

At one time there was a great shortage of dental surgeons in the country. Over the course of the last decade a number of students have taken up study in this area. The number of dental colleges in the country has reached eleven.

Table 4.5 Number of Dental Colleges in the country

Name of College	University	Year Estd.	BDS Annual Intake 2013	Masters PG started
Peoples Dental College, Kathmandu.	Tribhuvan	1997	60	Yes; 2010
BPKIHS- College of Dental Surgery, Dharan	Deemed	1999	40	Yes
Universal College of Dental Sciences, Bhairahawa.	Tribhuvan	2001	75	Yes
MB Kedia Dental College, Birgunj	Tribhuvan	2005	60	
Kantipur Dental College, Kathmandu.	Kathmandu	2007	60	
KIST MC - College DS	Tribhuvan	2011	40	
KU - School of Dental Surgery	Kathmandu	2011	30	
Nepal MC - College DS	Kathmandu	2011	50	
Nobel MC - College DS	Kathmandu	2011	60	
Chitwan MC - DS	Tribhuvan	2011		
Kathmandu MC – Dental College	Kathmandu	2012	50	

Deemed University -1 TU Affiliated – 5 KU + Affiliated – 1+4.

NB. Though NAMS and IoM do not have BDS programmes both are conducting MDS in certain areas.

a. College of Dental Surgery, BPKIHS, Dharan

Though BPKIHS started its MBBS course in October 1994, the first batch of dental students was only taken in August 1999. Initially the dental college was functioning from the medical complex, but later the College of Dental Surgery had its own buildings and the first batch of students completed the BDS course in 2004.

b. People's Dental College, Kathmandu (TU)

A project, which was started with the intention of starting another, medical college at Kathmandu was later established in 1997 as the People's Dental College, affiliated to Tribhuvan University. The first batch of this institution qualified in 2004. The management of this college is in the process of starting a medical programme soon.

c. College of Dental Surgery, Bhairahawa (TU)

The Universal College of Medical Sciences at Bhairahawa started classes of its first batch of BDS students in what was initially the Dental Wing of the Medical College in November 2001. Subsequently it was changed into the College of Dental Surgery in 2003.

d. MB Kedia Dental College, Birgunj (TU)

This affiliated dental college was started in Birgunj in 2006 with an initial intake of 30 students. Its first two batches have graduated.

e. Kantipur Dental College, Kathmandu (KU)

This is the first dental college affiliated to Kathmandu University and was started in 2007.

f. KIST Dental College, Imadol, Lalitpur

This is affiliated to TU and the BDS course was started in 2011.

g. KU – School of Dental Surgery, Dhulikhel

This is the college of Kathmandu University and is based at Dhulikhel.

h. Dental College of Nepal Medical College

This is affiliated to KU and was started in 2011 with an initial intake of 50.

i. Dental College of Nobel Medical College of Medical Sciences – Nepal, Biratnagar.

This is affiliated to KU and the BDS course was started in 2011 with an initial intake of 50.

j. Chitwan Dental College, Chitwan, Bharatpur.

This is affiliated to TU and was started in 2011 with an initial intake of 50.

k. Dental College of Kathmandu Medical College

This is affiliated to KU and was started in 2012 with an initial intake of 50.

National Requirements for Doctors

Till Nov. 1996, Nepal had just two institutions producing doctors. The sudden spurt of activity to open private medical colleges spurred the Nepal Medical Council to express concern about the quality of graduates to be produced by health / academic institutions which did not have proper facilities neither for service nor for training. This led to widespread concern about standards. Another worry was whether there would be enough work for graduates produced as this would lead to under utilisation of doctors. The desire of many young students to study in the medical or engineering fields within the country has attracted many entrepreneurs to meet this demand.

Because of the excessive amount of capitation or medical "fees" in India, the trend had been for students to go to Bangladesh, Philippines and more recently China where the costs were said to be less. The large number of Nepalese going to the former USSR or to the Commonwealth of Independent States (CIS) and some of the newly founded Republics to study medicine decreased markedly as a result. As standards of medical education vary in different countries and between the public and private institutions in the same country, there was a lot of sorting out to be done. This led to the NMC to propose to the Government to have licensing examinations, which was started in 2002. Since 2008/9 these examinations are held twice a year and the newly qualified doctors, who have completed six months of internship are allowed to sit for the examination. The certificate of passing is given on completion of the internship.

In view of the fact that numbers of students wanting to study medicine was still large and to discourage students who may not yet be ready to take up this study, the Nepal Medical Council got the GoN to agree in 2011 that only students who had appeared and passed the entrance test conducted by any of the universities of Nepal or the Ministry of Education for medical studies would be assisted to go abroad for study. Such a step should help in ensuring that standards are maintained.

A study of the NMC records till end of December 2012 suggests that out of the 11,359 currently registered Nepalese doctors, 7615 are male and 3544 female. Of this perhaps about 500 or so are out of the country studying or working elsewhere. This figure also includes those in Nepal who are retired and not doing any professional work. The number of dental surgeons in the country at the end of 2012 was 507 males and 715 females making a total of 1,222. These are the medical and dental personnel who are catering to the health needs of the current population of 2.5 million as per the Population Census of 2011 (18). Of this 12.9 million and 13.7 million are male and female respectively. The breakdown of the population in terms of residence is Terai (50.2%), Hill about 43% and Mountain (7%). There is however no reliable statistics to calculate the doctor : patient ratio of the population. Of these numbers about 20% or 2617 are currently registered as specialists of whom 1938 are male and 679 female. There are also about 300 expatriate doctors and dental surgeons, who have been given temporary registration and are working within the country. Of this 200 are working in the Basic Sciences Section of different medical colleges and the remainder in clinical subjects in different parts of the country. (19, 20)

The scenario for the production of doctors is changing and currently about 1800 Nepalese students are being trained annually in medicine in Nepal. Another 500 or so are being educated in China, Bangladesh or Philippines. Is it because the doctor's life is seen to be financially attractive and the profession lucrative?

The current enthusiasm for starting new HRH producing institutions shows that uncertainties regarding viability of medical colleges are not a deterrent to prospective entrepreneurs. Are institutions of capable and reputable standards being set up? Will there be adequate number of teachers? Queries of this sort are coming to the NMC and the Universities of Nepal. Some of these pertinent issues have been addressed by the new guidelines of NMC (21).

Presently the intake of about 220 students by the three government institutions (IoM, BPKIHS & PAHS) will produce this number annually. The 14 private medical colleges currently functioning, have an intake of about 2400 students of which approximately one fifth are students from outside the country. If one includes doctors trained outside of Nepal, there will be a minimal addition of about 1000 doctors a year. Of this number the government gets about 200 trained doctors as a result of scholarships of which as much as 150 will be from the scholarships within country at the private medical colleges. If the government makes it mandatory for every one who has had a scholarship in medicine to work for a maximum of one year at a government institution, then the problem of non-availability of doctors at government health institutions will no longer exist. Whilst this is being done to a certain extent, the practice is to post these doctors at the urban centres. The result of all this is that the rural or backward areas are still without doctors. Talking to some of the government scholarship holders, one hears also that the institutions where they are posted lack supporting staff or other logistics. It is the same old story being repeated again and again.

The main concern of the NMC and the Nepal Medical Association (NMA) is with regards to the quality of the doctors produced by the private medical colleges. This applies also to some institutions outside of Nepal, where the facilities for training are said to be grossly inadequate. NMC guidelines lays down that there should be a minimum of 300 beds at the time of starting the institution in Nepal. The departments necessary, tbe number and quality of faculty and the breakdown of beds required for the particular number of students being admitted as shown in the table below (20):

Table 4.6 Revised NMC guidelines on beds requirements by speciality as of 2013

SN	Speciality	For 50 students	For 100 students	For 150 students
1	Internal Medicine	60	90	130
2	General Surgery	60	90	135
3	Obstetrics & Gynaecology	60	90	120
4	Paediatrics	60	60	95
5	Orthopaedics	30	60	90
6	Ophthalmology	30	30	30
7	Otorhinolaryngology	30	30	30
8	Psychiatry	30	30	30
9	Skin & STD	10	15	15
10	Emergency & Observation	30	30	60
11	Dental Surgery	5	10	15
	Total	**405**	**535**	**750**

These new guidelines replace those of 2010. There has been revision too in the numbers of faculty required for the different departments. Visiting faculties are also being allowed.

What are Rational Requirements?

The doctor population ratio as prevalent a decade ago has changed completely now. The establishment of the medical colleges and the nursing homes has led to a greater Public / Private mix in the urban centres of the country. On top of this the central region of the country had 445 of the 874 government posts for doctors. A very rough estimate of hospital beds in Kathmandu valley then (1992) was put at about 2000 out of the total number of about 5000 beds in the whole country at that time. The number of hospital beds in 2002 was stated to be 4458. Now the doctor per population is 1 for every 1,000 persons and the number of beds in the country is about 26,000. (See details in Chapter 6).

The general refrain about government services is the overcrowding, long wait and poor services that seem to be the standard. A question that immediately arises is whether the Government supported hospitals and teaching institutions are so overstaffed, that under utilisation of the technical personnel occurs? Considering the relatively smaller numbers of personnel that they employ, are the private and semi-private institutions providing substandard services? Or is it better? Have the nursing and paramedical staffs at such institutions been adequately trained in recognised institutions and are they registered in their respective Councils?

Table. 4.6 Health Workers Population Ratio (per 10,000 populations) in some SEA Countries (22)

Country	Doctors	Dental Surgeons	Nurses	Pharmacists
Bangladesh	3.0	0.2	1.4	0.6
Bhutan	2.0	0.2	8.0	0.3
India	7.0	0.6	8.0	5.6
Indonesia	2.0	0.6	13.0	0.3
Myanmar	3.0	0.3	4.0	N A
Nepal	2.0	0.1	2.0	0.1
Sri Lanka	6.0	0.6	14.0	0.6
Thailand	3.0	1.7	14.0	2.5

Source: Health Situation in South East Asia Region 2001-2007.
Data of about 2005 generally. NA. - Not available.

In the above Table, the number of doctors and other HRH working in Nepal per every 10,000 of the population has been compared with some of the countries of South-East Asia round about the year 2005. For Nepal it means that there are about 20 doctors for 100,000 population or one doctor for every 5000 people. In rural areas the ratio is probably 1 per one hundred thousand populations! This ratio has probably changed now considering the large number of institutions producing various grades of HRH. It will improve further only when pay and facilities for living, lodging, and career development for those serving in rural areas are better than for those in the cities. As concession on these matters is seen as "being soft" by the government authorities, it is likely that the staffing of governmental posts will never be satisfactory. Proof of all this is evident in the fact that many of those selected for posting in government health institutions out of the capital have not taken up the posting. Even the passage of the Health Act is not helping much as there is no real enthusiasm to join government services. The Health Act was revised by the New Constituent Assembly. To try to provide services in the rural areas, Nepal Government has come with a proposal to send doctors there on contract basis, giving special facilities.

Though there has been a marked increase of doctors produced in the country every year, a substantial number of new graduates are sitting for USMLE and PLAB tests with the hope of going out of the country. To counter this, Nepal Government has specifically stated that, " A special programme will be brought forward by the government to prevent the brain drain of the scientific and technical personnel from the country".

Future Projections of Physicians

Future projections for Nepalese doctors registering with the NMC can be estimated. It is difficult at any time to project accurate figures for the requirements of not just physicians but also other categories of health personnel. This is because there are no certain plans for the future though attempts have been made from time to time. The updated Human Resources Master Plan draft document of June 1995 had made a detailed estimation of doctors and specialists requirements for the government sector, and projections for the future (23). The figures may be out of date or even incorrect for serious consideration had not been made of the requirements of the private sector such as nursing homes, private hospitals etc. The strategic plan for HRH of 2003 is more specific (24).

With the new medical schools and the new specialised Institutes plus the nursing homes of the urban centres vying for the services of the doctors, there are not going to be very many left for service in the districts as per the intention of the government. The numbers of middle level workers such as nurses, laboratory technicians etc required is not going to be easily available as there are not enough for the present existing services. The private sector is more attractive than the government one and so there may be a gross shortage of middle level workers. In such a situation, the planned new institutions will not be able to function and the standards in existing ones may drop because of inadequate numbers of staff. This is being temporarily, partially solved by HRH students in training who do 'on job training' or OJT and contribute to keep the services just functioning. To continue functioning, certain compromises will have to be made, leading thereby to undesirable functioning. Staffing of the hospitals in the districts is still more difficult. The district health system and the health services at the grassroots level are generally functioning with lack of appropriate staff, absence of monitoring and total lack of effective and supportive supervision. The non holding of local elections for years has partly contributed to this. Alternative arrangements or options will have to be taken up.

When Nepal signed the Declaration of Alma Ata in 1978, our commitment was to HFA 2000 with the determination to provide Primary Health Care. The National Health Policy was laid down in 1991 with stress on the rural areas. When the IoM was established and the community-oriented course was started, the stress too was on the concept of "health teams" providing care to the people. As developments in Nepal unfolded, the stress was laid more on the training of physicians with more emphasis on tertiary care. The concept of a health care team seems to have fallen by the wayside. The new catchwords introduced were the "public / private mix in the delivery of health care". The identification of the district as the unit of health care is the requirement of the day as health is now a birthright. The presence of a single doctor at the PHC Centre in an electoral constituency does not spell the delivery of primary health care. The health sector reform which has been put into action has to be expedited.

One way is to be philosophical and say that the process of decentralisation of the health services is on the move. Instead of coming to the capital there are going to be better tertiary care facilities places where there are medical colleges. With facilities a little bit nearer to where people live, incidental costs such as travel, temporary accommodation for attendants have decreased. Hopefully with better facilities within the country, the numbers of the ill that go to India and abroad will also decrease. Commitment to this concept must come from the top. As far as eye care is concerned patients are coming from India to Nepal and this is a healthy trend.

Coupled with the existing reality of personnel shortages in the health field, there is a desire of many students to take up medicine as a career. This has led to an increase in the number of institutions for imparting medical education. Worries about the direction medical education may take exist as many medical colleges are being opened without really knowing what the country's actual requirements are.

With such a background, many new Nepalese medical graduates produced here are now going out to other countries for further study and training. Should this be a cause for worry? Is this a drain of scarce resources that the country cannot afford or a blessing in disguise in that the personnel which the government cannot employ nor the country sustain is going elsewhere? The hope is that they may send remittances back or at least come back to the home country once they retire, where ever they may be. The introduction of 'dual citizenship' may perhaps be an incentive to them.

In 2012 we heard about a possible new health policy to replace that which had been enunciated twenty years ago in 1991. The new political developments, together with reports of various aspects / activities e.g. MDG in the past and the political acceptance of Health Rights as a Basic Right in the constitution have necessitated this. The basic components are: promotive, preventive, curative and rehabilitative services. This envisages a healthy Nepali community. As far as curative services are concerned, primary health care will be free to every citizen.

Post Graduate Studies in Medicine

Postgraduate study programmes run on traditional lines and imported from out of country institutions are mainly adapted towards international recognition, rather than meeting the community needs and local realities. It is also more costly. It was these thoughts, which prompted steps to try to ensure that most of the Nepali doctors do their postgraduate studies in Nepal.

Postgraduate studies started in the country as early as 1982 with the MD in general practice for those referred to as 'generalists'. The MD(GP) programme of IoM, had the support of the University of Calgary till March, 1995. The course of action followed in subsequent years by the IoM was that the different degree/diploma courses started were as per the requirements of the country and according to priority basis. This general practice programme is being conducted at BPKIHS and also by NAMS as family practice.

The two years M.Sc. (PH) was started at IoM in 1991 and continued till 1998 when it was converted into a one year MPH.

In the post *Jana Andolan I* period a number of meetings were held with the object of starting post-graduate studies in a number of specialities. Dr. S. K. Kakkar, then Director of the All India Institute of Medical Sciences, came in Dec. 1992 as a WHO consultant to help guide the process. Three programmes, on a much lesser scale than then envisaged, started in 1994. The course of studies was to be done at the valley group of hospitals and the degree awarded would be that of Tribhuvan University.

In the initial days of post graduate instruction there were also one year Diplomas and three years Degree courses. The new policy regarding degrees and diplomas by the MoH is that only doctors with postgraduate degrees will be posted in hospitals, which are centres for postgraduate training. This decision and the establishment of other medical colleges also meant that there is a large requirement of doctors with postgraduate degrees in different specialities.

Considering the fact that there are about 1,500 new medical graduates entering the service sector in Nepal, extensive thought should be given to their utilization in the country. As there are now a total of eighteen medical colleges in different parts of the country, all must be encouraged to develop post graduation and also sub speciality facilities and training in Nepal. To encourage PG studies within the country, Nepal Government could make national postgraduate degree a minimum criterion for getting government specialist and academic positions. There should be a National PG Board for regulating and conducting the final evaluation for PG and super speciality candidates.

The institutions conducting post graduate medical courses within the country are:

Table 4.9 Post Graduation Courses conducted by different institutions

INSTITUTION	MD/MS	MSc	MPH	M.Phil	PhD	DM/MCH	MDS
TU - IoM	Yes	Yes	Yes	Yes	x	Yes; 2010	Yes
TU - Affiliated	Yes	x	x	x	x	x	Yes
BPKIHS	Yes	MSc	Yes	x	x	x	Yes
NAMS	Yes	x	x	x	x	Yes	Yes
KU - SMS	Yes	Yes	x	x	x	x	x
KU - Affiliated	Yes	Yes	x	x	x	Yes	x
PAHS	x	x	x	x	x	x	x

x - Not being currently conducted

Status of PG & Specialist Requirements

A paper by a WHO consultant had documented in 2003 that the distribution of specialists in government and private sector was as given below:

Number of different specialities: 30

Number of specialists: 1544

Public Sector: 363 (23.5%)

Private Sector: 1181 (76.5%)

There are no specialists in the district hospitals except for the MDGP who too must be accepted as a specialist in his field. Some district hospitals have the MDGP. Because of the lack of specialists in the country the GoN is considering the proposal for setting up a Board for PG studies. There is also a plan to provide specialist services at the district level by using the specialist of the various medical colleges periodically. The GoN is also thinking of restarting Diploma level courses in some areas as obstetrics and anaesthesia.

Registration of specialists by Nepal Medical Council till end of 2012 shows a total of 2617 specialists of which 1938 are males and 679 females. A paper by a WHO consultant had documented the distribution of forty-one types of specialists in Nepal in 2003 and forecasted requirements for 2017. The current figures of registered specialists are shown in column six.

Table 4.10 Nepali Specialists registered with NMC

S No	Speciality	GoN estimate 2003*	NMC Registered			Projection for 2017	
			mid-2006	2007 end	2012 end	Govt.	Private
1	Anaesthesia	37	43	59	153	62	90
2	Anatomy	-	-	-	2	-	-
3	Biochemistry	-	-	-	1	-	-
4	Cardiology	16	50	53	77	16	49
5	Clinical Path.	44	18	36	101	69	6
6	Com.Med/PubHealth	98	11	21	59	106	24
7	Dental - Masters	-	23	43	148	-	50#
8	Dermatology + Ven.	17	18	32	81	17	53
9	Endocrinology	2				2	1
10	ENT & HN Surgery	53	26	39	87	39	60#
11	Epidemiology	-	-	-	-	3	12
12	Forensic Medicine	-	3	3	8	-	30#
13	Gastroenterology	14	11	12	19	6	16
13A	General Practice	30	39	64	144	43	34
13B	Family Medicine	-	-		4		
15	General Surgery	129	86	144	275	93	145
16	Geriatrics	1	-	-	-	1	0
17	Hepatology	-	-	-	1		
18	Cardio Tho. Surgery	11	-	-	-	4	12
19	Neuro Surgery	11				4	12
20	Internal Medicine	118	50	88	277	87	134
21	Tropical Medicine	11	-	-	-	3	12
22	Microbiology	-	1	2	16	-	30#
23	Nephrology	8	4	4	10	3	9
24	Neurology	7	7	8	21	3	8
25	Nuclear Medicine	5	2	3	5	6	0
26	Obs & Gynae	205	115	156	287	140	181
27	Oncology	-	3	3	-	-	-
28	Oncology Surgery	-	-	-	15	-	-
29	Ophthalmology	106	43	60	145	44	121
30	Orthopaedics	60	47	95	207	32	68
31	Paediatrics	177	84	121	235	129	201

32	Paediatric Surgery	8	-	-	-	3	9
33	Pharmacology	-	5	7	19	15#	15#
34	Pulmonology	-	-	-	1	-	-
35	Psychiatry	32	16	25	53	13#	36#
36	Physiology	-	-	-	4	-	-
37	Plastic Surgery	7	-	-	-	3	8
38	Radio / Imaging	59	37	58	135	52	38
39	Radiotherapy	-	-	-	2	-	-
40	TB, Resp. Disease Pulmonology	30	4	5	8	11	34
41	Urology/Uro. Surgery	16	8	9	17	6	18

*- Estimates are only of active and retired personnel as per government records.

- Estimates required for Medical / Dental Colleges within the country.

Adapted from various sources: Health Sector Support Programme - GTZ/ Nepal (25) and NMC Register.

This specialists number as of end December 2012 and provided by NMC is a total of 2,617. In terms of gender breakdown it is 1,938 males and 679 females. Whilst at present the current popular speciality choices are Cardiology and Radiology/Radiotherapy, the top seven specialities in which doctors registered with the Nepal Medical Council as specialists till the end of December 2012 were:

Table 4.11 Number of some specialists registered with NMC, 2012

S.N.	Specialities	Number
1	Obstetrics & Gynaecology	287
2	Internal Medicine	277
3	General Surgery	275
4	Paediatrics	235
5	Anaesthesia	153
6	MDGP	148
7	Clinical Pathology	101
	Total	**1,476**

It may be noted that the number of doctors taking up the Basic Sciences as specialisation is still limited as most have still to qualify.

HRH in Pharmaceutical Sciences

Though the Institute of Medicine had started the Proficiency Certificate Level (PCL) training in pharmacy in the seventies, the Bachelor grade personnel had to be trained outside the country. It was the Kathmandu University, which started the Bachelor, and subsequently Masters in this area. Some years later IoM also started training in the Bachelor level. The Nepal Pharmacy Council Act requires that all the personnel in these areas have to be registered.

There are 25 colleges under CTEVT with an average of 40 per year that conduct the three year Diploma course in pharmacy with the idea that these personnel would go into the market and be employed in the retail pharmacy sector. This means an annual intake of about 1,000 students.

Break down of the twenty colleges under four universities running the Bachelor in Pharmacy programme is as given. KU has its own college only, TU has its own and 7 affiliates, Pokhara University has its own and 3 affiliates, Purbanchal University has seven affiliates only. A total of 560 students are produced per annum.

There are some problems with the Bachelor level of Pharmacy products. Most are employed in the 45 + 8 pharmaceutical industries producing drugs for both human and veterinary consumption. In 2010 there were 44 members of the Association of Pharmaceutical Producers of Nepal of which 16 have been certified with WHO-GMP. These companies produce about 35% of the national pharmaceutical requirements (26).

Thus there has been remarkable development in this field because a large number of institutions have started the production of the 'Bachelor' and Masters level graduates. The numbers registered till end of Sept. 2013 are:

1. Pharmacy Assistants 3,214 of which 2,005 are males and 1209 are females.
2. Pharmacists 1,273 of which 840 are males and 433 females.

Their area of work is as given in table 4.12:

Table 4.12 Number of Pharmacy Personnel by their Place of Work

Place of Work	Number of Pharmacists	Number of Pharmacy Assistants
Industry / Laboratory	102	1
Education	15	3
Govt. Service	23	14
Pharmacy	22	19
NGOs	9	1
Others	36	11
TOTAL	207	49

Many of the products of the colleges are probably self employed too. The Department of Drug Administration (DDA) and its branches at Biratnagar, Birgunj and Nepalgunj, in their efforts to implement the Drug Act of 1978 have up to June of 2012 registered the under mentioned outlets for the supply of medicines to the public:

Table 4. 13 Number of outlets for the supply of therapeutic drugs

Types of outlets	Wholesaler	Retailer
Modern Medicines	1,688	8,800
Veterinary	265	1,767
Ayurved	116	1,821
Homeopathic	19	422
Unani	0	21
Total	2,068	12,831

Source: Drug Bulletin of Nepal 2012 Vol 24. No1 Pg. 7-12

Other Categories of Human Resources for Health and their deployment in Nepal

There are many and comprehensive lists with specific job description and terms of employment which have to be compiled and put into effective use if proper health services are to be provided to the people.

As per the MoHP website (www.mohp.gov.np) the number and breakdown of persons employed by Nepal Government or working as volunteers in the health sector at the end of 2009/10 was as follows:

Table 4.14 No of health workers in the public sector by types, 2009/10

S.N.	Types of Health Workers	Number
1	Doctor	1,627
2	Nurse / ANM	11,637
3	Paramedic / Health Assistant	7,491
4	Village Health Worker	3,985
5	Maternal & Child Health Worker	3,190
6	Pharmacist	21
7	Pharmacy Assistant	15
8	Ayurvedic Physician	394
9	Ayurvedic Baidya	360
10	Female Community Health Volunteer	53,999
11	Trained Traditional Birth Attendant	14,951

The MoHP is the largest ministry employing the largest number of Human resources. There are now 31,628 personnel, but of this there exists about 4,000 vacancies. Somehow or the other, there always seems to be a shortage in the government health institutions. One reads in the papers of shortage of ANMs, AHWs, HAs and doctors periodically. This is very ironic considering that Health Rights of every Nepali as a birth right is going to be incorporated in our constitution.

Many categories of HRH are produced by the Private Sector under the supervision of CTEVT which itself is under the MoE. They are in the fields of Nursing, General Medicine, Dentistry, Pharmacy and Ophthalmology workers in many CTEVT affiliated institutions. Except for two, all the others are private ones, conducting various types of programmes to produce Basic and Middle level health workers is as follows:

Table 4.15 Number of institutions producing different types of HRH by levels

Level	Type	No of institutions
Basic	CMA	74
	ANM	44
Middle (PCL)	Nursing	104
	Health Assistant	47
	Laboratory Technician	21
	Pharmacy Assistant	44
	Radiography Assistant	15

Health Professional Council

Other categories of health professional registered by the Nepal Health Professional Council are laboratory technicians, physiotherapists, radiographers plus some other categories. A combined figure of those registered by the Nepal Health Professional Council until the end of May 2013 is as follows:

Nepali Health Professional	=	52,404
Foreign Health Professionals	=	16
Total	=	**52,420**

Nepal Ayurved Council

The Nepal Ayurved Council Act took many years to be implemented and the two major grades of workers produced are both by the public sector institutions run by the government. There are also institutions in the private sector for the training of Homeopathic doctors.

Nepal Pharmacy Council

The Nepal Pharmacy Council as per the provisions of the Act of 2057 BS monitors the quality of educational institutions and registers pharmacy personnel. At present Diploma in Pharmacy, Bachelor of Pharmacy, Master of Pharmacy, Doctor of Pharmacy and PhD courses are conducted within the country.

4.16 HRH Producing Institutes and their Programmes

Institution	MBBS	MD/ MS	DM	BPH/ MPH	MSc	MPhil	Cert N	BN	BSc	MN
TU- IoM	Yes	Yes	Yes	Yes	Yes	Yes	Yes	Yes	Yes	Yes
BPKIHS	Yes	Yes	?	Yes	Yes	x	Yes		Yes	x
MCOMS	Yes	Yes	?	x	Yes		Yes	x	Yes	x
CMS-S	Yes	Yes		x	Yes		Yes			x
NepalG MC	Yes	Yes		x		x	Yes			x
KMC	Yes	Yes	x	x	x	x	x	x	Yes	x
NMC	Yes	Yes	x	x		x				
UCMS	Yes									
Nat MC	Yes									
KU-SMS	Yes	Yes	x	x	Yes	x	Yes	x	Yes	x
Janaki MC	Yes									
Nobel MC	Yes									

Lumbini MC	Yes									
Patan AHS	Yes	x	x	x	x	x	Yes	?	x	x
KIST MC	Yes									
Chitwan MC	Yes									
NAMS	x	Yes	Yes	x	x	Fellow	Yes	Yes	x	x

See also Table 4.9

Future Projections and HRH Issues. Private and Public Mix

What must be realized is that the Ministry of Health and Population (MoHP) has the largest number of government employees. Roughly about one fifth of all those employed by the government are under the MoHP.

Considering these facts it is realistic for health personnel planning exercises to have been done in the past. A master plan for Human Resources for Health (HRH) was prepared in 1996 and 2002. Ultimately a more comprehensive document on HRH was published in 2003 (27).

The requirement for various grades of personnel is going to increase markedly due to demands of the private nursing homes, the medical colleges and the specialist hospitals/ institutes. The area of the most acute need is possibly going to be in nursing as the major requirement of nurses will be great as more health care institutions are opened. Though no figures are quoted as optimal ratios, the World Development Report 1993 recommends as a rule of thumb that nurses should exceed physicians by at least two to one. Another figure mentioned is that of the State of California in the USA which is trying to have a nurse to patient ratio of 1:5 in its hospitals. The reality in Nepal is far removed from this and the most recent factor for the shortage is the increased demand for nurses in developed countries such as UK, USA, Canada and Australia where most of our nurses are going as caregivers in old age homes.

There is desire by many students in Nepal to take up a career in the health field. This is welcome in the context of personnel shortages in this area but a fear exists that excessive production of different grades of HRH may be at the cost of skill and capability. With the policy of liberalisation there has been the granting of permission to open a variety of schools for different grades of workers. This existing demand has led to an increase in the number of institutions imparting education for service in the health sector. Many feel that clinical exposure is lacking. There are also doubts about cost, quality and over production that have been raised because of the increased privatization in health professional education.

Some of these new institutions, which have been sanctioned by the CTEVT, are very substandard and should not be functioning. But they exist, and are going to produce workers who will be practising at grass root levels with drugs about which their knowledge is not adequate. What will be the standard of the doctors, nurses and other categories of health workers produced does not seem to be the worry of the authorities.

Table 4.16 Private and Public Institutions Producing HRH in Nepal (28)

S No	Universities & Institutions	Programme		Level
		No	%	
1	CTEVT and its Affiliates	224	76.2%	T-SLC, PCL & Diploma
2	Purbanchal University (PU)	32	10.9%	Bachelor Level
3	Tribhuvan University (TU)	18	6.1%	PCL to PhD
4.	Kathmandu University (KU)	10	3.4%	PCL to PhD
5	Pokhara University (Pok. U)	6	2.0%	Bachelor Level
6	Patan Academy of Health Sciences –(PAHS)	1	0.3%	Bachelor Level
7	Nepal Sanskrit University (NSU)	1	0.3%	Bachelor Level
8	BP Koirala Inst of Health Sciences –(BPKIHS)	1	0.3%	PCL to Master Level
9	National Academy of Health Sciences (NAMS)	1	0.3%	Bachelor to Master Level
	Total	**294**	**100%**	

RESEARCH

Health Statistics

Nepal, being one of the least developed countries in the world, has many health problems. Statistics about Nepal, vital or otherwise, are hard to come by. The quoted infant mortality rate or maternal mortality ratio varies from source to source and from publication to publication. Is it the incorrectness of the methodology or approach or are the figures just "cooked up"? Many researchers, irrespective of the credibility of the principal investigator have to depend on figures supplied by basic level workers or research teams who have not been adequately trained. Instead of striving to obtain correct figures their whole attitude to the result may be lackadaisical or "this will do". Nepal aside, such practices are known to be prevalent in institutions of greater credibility and learning found in other developing countries too. The variation of figures makes one doubt the correctness of all the statistics.

Few medical doctors seem to be interested to be involved in research. Is it because it is less lucrative? Hopefully with the increased number of medical colleges there will be in the future a corresponding increase in research.

Health Research

Research in Nepal has been done under various institutions. Before 1950 not much research was done and in the sixties it may have been regarded as a form of luxury. Accounts of diseases seen by the various Resident - Surgeons at the British Residency do exist.

A survey of sorts regarding malaria in Kathmandu valley was done with the support of USOM in 1950. A more detailed health survey of Nepal was done in 1965-66 with the support of the University of Hawaii and the Dooley Foundation. It is a milestone of research activity in Nepal. Subsequent to this, some medical research work was done by some teams, which usually got permission from the Nepalese government as a result of some tie up with the infrastructure existing, to enter Nepal. Such tie-ups were either with the TU's Research Centre for Applied Science and Technology (RECAST), TU's Centre for Nepal and Asian Studies (CNAS) or the National Council of Science and Technology. Universities or other institutions in their home countries in turn usually supported the expatriate researchers. They did their research and went back. The results were published in the West.

With the formation of the various institutions and research centres of Tribhuvan University, a new method of research operation came into being. Any expatriate wanting to do research had to get the concurrence of the concerned institute e.g. medicine and the research section of Tribhuvan University. It was at this time suggested to the researchers that they should publish their findings in Nepal, besides in their own countries.

At that point in time if any local Nepali was motivated enough to do research, he could get some support in one of the under mentioned ways:

a. Through university funds, allocated to the institute. Though relatively limited, one had to have proper proposals and so there were not many who applied.
b. From National Council of Science and Technology
c. From WHO
    i. SEARO. Said to be relatively easy to obtain but in reality not so.
    ii. Geneva originating Tropical Diseases Research. In special areas like malaria, leprosy, kala-azar and schistosomiasis. Institutional support provided, but not many applications.
d. From USAID funds. Know of cases that applied, were short-listed but later did not succeed.

Again, operational research was encouraged during this period of the early seventies. It usually centred around the benefits of integrated health service delivery vs. uni-purpose vertical health services delivery concept. A national effort in the form of the Nepal Fertility Survey (NFS) with the support of the University of California at Berkeley took place in 1976. During all these years and subsequently, USAID has been involved in various types of research in conjunction with the FP/MCH Project of Nepal Government.

In late seventies workshops were held at Kirtipur under the aegis of TU to try to kindle interest in research. It might have generated some interest but not enough. This led to the IoM conducting a workshop with WHO support on Research Methodology in Sept. 1982.

The Royal Nepal Academy of Science and Technology (RONAST), was established in 1982 and was then the responsible body for scientific and technological research, policy and planning (28). With this setting up of RONAST a new chapter was started. The giving of certain awards by RONAST to young scientists in the medical field generated some interest to think in terms of research and of its subsequent publication. National conferences on research are being held in the country. When Nepal became a republic in 2006 the name was shortened to Nepal Academy of Science & Technology or NAST.

Research Activities

One thought about research in this part of the world is that it is a luxury and should not be undertaken until health service problems have been solved. The contrary view says that research is necessary to enable those trying to solve the problems to accomplish more with fewer resources. This should be the line of thought if we are to make any headway in the future.

Nepal is a virgin territory as far as research is concerned. We do not, for example have standard figures regarding the health status of the Nepalese. Answers are lacking for many of the biomedical and public health problems in the country. It is for this that both the IoM and the Ministry of Health have at various times, in unison or separately brought out lists for suggested areas of research. The most recent one put out by the NHRC is given later in this chapter.

Research conducted so far may be said to have been influenced by the Nepal Medical Research Committee. This seven-member body formed on 15th April, 1982, was to be the National Focal Point on Health Services Research. The fact that the Health Secretary was the Chairman meant that it was directly under the Health Ministry. Later in September 1982, this committee was expanded to 10 by including members from other areas related to health, e.g. Ayurved, Pharmaceutical etc. After this an Ethical Review Body (ERB) was formed whose function was to review the project proposals submitted to NMRC.

The function of NMRC was to encourage research, help in making proposals and elicit funding, help in publishing and disseminating results. It held workshops directed towards solving these problems. Some increase of research activity took place but was not adequate. The undertaking of research and publishing of findings needs to be encouraged to a much greater extent, especially in areas outside the capital.

Whilst research conducted locally had been helped in the past by the National Council of Science and Technology (NCST) and RONAST, a number of research projects underway have been supported by various overseas organization or institutions, e.g. WHO, IDRC, JICA and so on.

As mentioned earlier, most of the research done in Nepal, especially those with external support are not published within the country. Even local researchers would give preference to this, for this is the only way that the work conducted is noticed. The usual excuse that access to recent research reports is not available is no longer valid with the Internet, Medline and other options that are now available. More recently some of the Nepali medical journals are being excerpted outside and have been given ISSN numbers. Since 2004 the Journal of Nepal Medical College, Kathmandu University Medical Journal and the Journal of the Nepal Medical Association were listed in Index Medicus and PubMed.

Priorities and Plans in the Past

A new chapter was started with the establishment of the Nepal Health Research Council as an autonomous body on 29th April 1991, as per the Nepal Health Research Council Act of the same year. It was given the responsibility to promote and co-ordinate health research for improvement of the health of the people of Nepal as detailed:

- Promote a health research culture within health and related sectors with special emphasis on the young scientists
- Maintain ethical, scientific and technical standards in health research
- Update the research priorities and establish national health research agenda
- Coordinate research within health and related sectors and avoid duplication
- Evaluate and promote the utilisation of research findings in policy development and service delivery
- Fund and facilitate researchers to enhance their research skills

In the November of its first year of functioning, the Nepal Health Research Council did a review, long overdue of research done between 1986 to 1991 (29).

Due to various reasons the Nepal Health Research Council found itself in the doldrums and very little occurred in the way of activity over the course of the next two to three years. Subsequently, the NHRC, being a focal point for Essential National Health Research (ENHR), held a national conference in June 1997 to endorse ENHR as an integral part of national policy development and proposed action plan. It was felt that the process could be strengthened by way of the six under mentioned themes:

- linking of health with equity and social justice
- "People First" concept - making health a public agent: empowering

process for the people with special focus on women

- health rights, health service user's rights / patients rights
- regulatory process development - transparency and accountability in health care
- health sector reform
- envisioning health research for the 21st Century / future.

Making a compilation of its activities during 1991-97 the Nepal Health Research Council (NHRC) reported that a total of 202 research proposals were accepted during this time and that 85 of these had been completed. The results of these have not been published nor the findings disseminated. Why one does not know.

Whilst the NHRC has been supported with ad hoc grants by GoN, it has been supported over the years by WHO in Health System Research. There is also an Environmental Health Centre which has been established. Maryknoll Fathers & Brothers (MFB) has personnel working with NHRC since 1977.

In 1998 a conference was held at Kathmandu for prioritising essential national health research agendas. These were categorised in four broad areas: Clinical Research, Health Policy and System Research, Behavioural and Social Research and Technology & Product Research. The following year 1999 saw the identification of research priorities under 14 headings (30).

In 2000 the NHR received the Rockefeller Foundation Award for the 'Capacity Strengthening of the Health Research Network in Nepal'. A number of activities were held over the next two years in the form of workshops and seminars with the involvement of academicians, medical colleges, Govt / Private hospitals, NGOs / INGOs with the objective of increasing the research capacity.

A "National Ethical Guidelines for Health Research in Nepal" was brought out in 2001 in the hope that such a document will help to promote medicine and science, whilst at the same time protecting the dignity, rights, safety and well being of research participants (31).

The new set of office bearers brought out a document "National Health Research Policy for Nepal" to cover the period 2003-2008 (32). The policy aims stated therein were as follows:

1. To emphasize ethical practice in all health research to achieve equity and social justice.
2. To augment health researches in the priority areas set by the National Health Policy and to provide advice based on evidence to HMG/N for formulating appropriate health policies.
3. To promote health research in all aspects.
4. To facilitate collaboration and networking with all major stakeholders involved in health research at the national level.
5. To enable, support and sustain human, financial, technical and other resources required for health research.
6. To promote inter / intra-sectoral participation in health research.
7. To secure international linkages and collaboration for health research.
8. To establish a National Health Research System.

The current activities of the NHRC are:

a. Support researchers with grants
b. Conduct workshops - training and programme
c. Disseminate health research findings
d. Provide capacity strengthening trainings
e. Bring out publications.

The National Health Research Policy institutes the National Health Research System (NHRS) and the objectives of NHRS are to:

a. Develop a broad strategic vision for health research including short-term and long-term health research strategies.
b. Develop a National Health Research Policy, Health Research Agenda and Health Research Priorities.
c. Link health research to national and local health priorities.
d. Develop standard procedures and a mechanism to ensure ethics, equity, accountability and transparency in the health research system.
e. Promote co-ordination, collaboration and partnership in health research (31).

The NHRC has also been involved since 2003 in trying to bring about active participation of health research councils of South Asian countries. A South Asian Forum for Health Research (SAFHeR) was established in econd meeting of SAFHeR was organised by NHRC in 2008 at K... u. This meeting concluded with preparation of the "Kathmandu Declara..on" the objective of which was to get the participating countries to evolve and pursue some common strategies. A later meeting was in June 2009 to try to strengthen this further. (33). A third meeting was held in August 2010 prior to Nepal handing over the Chairmanship to India.

Since its establishment, NHRC has focussed its activities in the following areas:

- Capacity building and strengthening for research
- Ensuring conduct of ethical health research
- Networking and collaboration
- Resource mobilization
- Knowledge management.

The most recent activity in June 2012 as referred to already was to evolve national consensus to "Define Health System Research priorities (PHASE –I)

Current Research Opportunities for Health Research in Nepal

1. Communicable /Infectious Diseases
2. Non communicable Diseases
3. Neonatal & Child Health
4. Reproductive Health
5. Geriatric Health
6. Nutritional Diseases
7. Health Care Delivery System
8. Environment & Occupational Health
9. Injuries & Accidents
10. Substance Abuse
11. Mental Health
12. Traditional Medicine & Herbs
13. High Altitude Sickness / Illness
14. Ethics
15. Urban Health
16. Epidemic Outbreak
17. Hospital Management (effective, efficient & quality service delivery)

POINTS TO PONDER

The policy for the production of Human Resources for Health (HRH) changed drastically from the last decade of the 20th Century. The mushrooming of nursing, medical and other health professional training within the country has brought out a situation in which Nepal has trained HRH not only for its own needs but to work in other countries also – both developed and developing. The hope is that with the increased number of personnel to work in the health sector, the health status of the people would improve. This seems to be already happening if the statistics that have presented by the concerned authorities are correct. Research should be done regarding all levels and types of HRH, their training, capabilities and effectiveness.

References

1. Marasini BR. Health and Hospital Development in Nepal: Past and Present. JNMA 2003, 42, 306-311.
2. Shrestha, IB. Health Personnel Training in Nepal. J Inst Med 1979; 1(2):155-172.
3. Medical Education Re-examined. Medico Friend Circle, 1991, Bombay.
4. Dixit H. Training to meet health needs in Nepal. Indian J Pediat 1986, 49: 481-486.
5. Das, Uma D. (Personal communication).
6. Factors Affecting the Roles and Functions of Staff Nurses in Nepal. Thakur, Laxmi. 1993. Nursing Education Dept. IOM.
7. Prasad, Mahendra. Bir Hospital reminiscences of a challenge. Bir Hospital Centenary Souvenir, 1990, 86-90.
8. Four Decades of Development. The History of US Assistance to Nepal 1951-1991. CA Skerry, K Moran, KM Calavan, 1991.
9. Dixit H. Role of the Institute of Medicine: A Review of Perspectives. Tribhuvan University Journal, 1980, Vol. 11, 1, 5-13.
10. Annual Report of the Institute of Medicine, 2009 / 2066
11. Nursing Education without Skills (Nepali) Swasthya Khabar Patrika, Kartik 2067 BS.
12. Annual Report of DoHS 2011-2012.
13. Innovative Programmes of Medical Education in South-East Asia, 1993, WHO, SEARO Publication No. 21.
14. TU Teaching Hospital. 31st Anniversary Annual Report 2013.
15. KU Diary – Pocket Pal 2009
16. Dixit H. Development of Medical Education in Nepal. KUMJ 2009, Vol 7 No 1, 8-10.
17. Adhikari Sitaram. Chitsa Sikshama Fadko, 2013
18. Basnet MB. The Business of Affiliation. Nepal Weekly, Bhadra 2070 BS.
19. National Analysis on Human Resources for Health, 2012, MoHP.

20. Dixit H. Role of Private Sector for HRH Production in Nepal. JKMC, 2013 Vol 2. No2 97-103
21. Nepal Medical Council Guidelines, 2013. NMC, Kathmandu.
22. Health Situation in South-East Asia Region 2001-2007. WHO-SEAR, 2008, New Delhi.
23. Human Resources for Health Master Plan. June, 1995. HIMDD/ERPHC (ODA)
24. Adhikari R. Privatisation of Technical Education: The case of Education of Health Professionals in Nepal. Regional Health Forum. 2006. Vol. 10 (1), 59-64.
25. Policies for the Development & Deployment of Medical Specialities in Nepal. 2003 Health Sector Support Programme - GTZ Nepal.
26. Pharma Nepal – Special Issue 2010.
27. Strategic plan for Human Resources for health 2003-2017 MoH.
28. Gupta R.P. Investing in Human Resources for Quality Health Services in Nepal. HRH Conference, 2013, Kathmandu
29. Health Research Review. 1991. NHRC/WHO.
30. National Consensus Workshop to Define Health System Research Priorities (PHASE – I) 2012
31. National Health Research Policy, 2010. NHRC.
32. National Ethical Guidelines for Health Research in Nepal. 2001. NHRC.
33. Regional meeting of South Asian Forum for Health Research (SAFHeR), June 2009 NHRC.

5.

DEVELOPMENT OF HEALTH SERVICES

The present health status of the people is the result of efforts, which followed the ushering in of a democratic government after 104 years of Rana feudal rule in February of 1951. The pre-plan period was followed by the first elections and the installation of the government. Stability was not attained and the removal of the duly elected government in mid-December, 1960 was the start of 30 years of Panchayat rule. This indigenous system of government, said to be in tune with the conditions existing in the country saw a total of six plans over the course of three decades. The *Jana Andolan 1* or "peoples' movement" in April of 1990 was expected to bring about major changes in the matter of governance and benefits to the people. The new health policy, with stress on rural health care, put forward by the Nepali Congress government, led to great expectations. Later the official documents of the Ninth and Tenth Plans and the Second Long Term Health Plan were introduced. The plans, though high sounding, lacked proper implementation. The political changes that followed and the installation of various coalition governments resulted in some modifications of the original plans for health, prior to attempts at implementation. The last decade of the 20th Century also saw the setting up of many medical colleges across the length and breadth of the country. This is the start of the Public and Private Mix, which had been discussed for some years.

Jana Andolan II[1] of 2006 led to further changes of governments. UML-Maoist led government announced the introduction of free health services at the District and VDC levels. The intention was good but the services could not be provided fully during the tenure of the government. It was disappointing, considering that Health has been termed a basic right of the people. Furthermore what had been regular plans were even

1. People's Movement

curtailed. One hopes, for the sake of the Nepali people, that whichever party forms the next government, will advocate for Nepal being turned into a country with strong education and health sectors.

As of 2013 there are three departments in the MoPH and these are:

(i) Department of Health Services (DoHS),
(ii) Department of Ayurved (DoA) and,
(iii) Department of Drug Administration (DDA).

The DoHS is responsible for providing preventive, promotive and curative services throughout Nepal. This is a tremendous task as health has been listed as a 'Basic Right of the People' in the interim constitution and will surely be included in the new constitution that is due to be promulgated. The DoHS has been re-organised now into six divisions:

1. Management
2. Family Health
3. Child Health
4. Epidemiology and Disease Control
5. Logistic Management
6. Primary Health Care Revitalisation.

Although this is the new setup, the problem is in trying to visualise what will happen in the next five years. How many regions, provinces or districts will there be? How will the health services be provided to the people? By the Central government or by the local authorities as health is now a Basic Right of the people? What will be the role of the Public / Private mix that the parties and others are talking about? Is this all talk only until the next government is formed and the constitution written? As for real effective change one cannot be confident as the local elections was last held in 2002 and no new effective leaders have emerged.

There are five centres with some degree of autonomy. These are:

1. National Health Training Centre (NHTC)
2. National Health Education, Information & Communication Centre (NHEICC)
3. National Tuberculosis Centre (NTC)
4. National Centre for AIDS & STD Control (NCASC)
5. National Public Health Laboratory (NPHL)

Currently at the National level there are Regional Health Directorates which in turn are supervising the districts. As far as the existing 75 districts are concerned, sixty-one are managed by the District Health Office (DHO) together with the support of the District Public Health Office (DPHO). The remaining fourteen districts are managed by the DPHO only.

The country wide health service delivery outlets as per Annual Report of DoHs 2011/12 are:

Central Level Hospitals	8
Regional Hospitals	3
Sub-regional Hospitals	2
Zonal Hospitals	8
District Hospitals	70
Public Health Care Centres	205
Health Posts	822
Sub-health Posts	2,987

It will be rational to consider the development of the health services in the context of the various Plans, which have been made and implemented since 1951 (1, 2). Two institutions BPKIHS & PAHS are both deemed universities under the government.

Breakdown of the 47 years

The Pre-plan Period, 1951-1956

During those years stress was laid on training of doctors under the Colombo Plan in India. A nursing school, based at the Bir Hospital was established with the aid of WHO. The first NGO hospital to be started was one by the United Mission to Nepal, in a part of the government Cholera Hospital.

In 1951 a plan was made for establishing a number of well-staffed health institutions in different parts of the country. The categories included health posts, health centres, district, and zonal, central and national hospitals. Whilst the health posts would be manned and run by a health assistant there was a provision for a physician at the health centres.

The number of hospitals providing curative health care in 1952 was just 33 with some basic level workers called compounders distributing medicines and giving injections. The dressers applied dressings to wounds. The doctors, just about 50 in the whole country, supervised both these groups.

Because of such limited facilities, the number of individuals availing of the health facilities provided by the government was a small percentage of the estimated 8.47 million populations. The life expectancy at that time was just 28 years and the IMR was 255/1,000 live births (3).

There were few urban centres, as there were just 18 municipalities in 1954. The capital had limited piped drinking water facilities by way of the reservoirs at Sundarijal, Panipokhari and Pharping. Ordinary folk used water from the various *dhunge dharas* or the stone waterspouts in their vicinity. Some of the other urban centres had minimal water supply facilities.

Decision was taken to clear some of the Terai areas of the dreaded malaria and make the land agriculturally productive. The expected growth in population and possible migration from the other hilly areas gave further impetus to this task. A project for Malaria Eradication in Chitwan valley was started in 1953. The Rapti Valley Multi Sector Development Project started the following year in 1954.

The health statistics in the country prior to the starting of the First Five Year Plan in 1956 were as follows (4):

Hospitals 34 with a total of 625 beds.
Dispensaries were 24 in number.
Ayurved *aushadhalayas* were 63.

The First Five Year Plan, 1956-61

During this first plan period emphasis was laid on the curative aspect of health. The Nepal Malaria Eradication Organisation (NMEO) programme in the Chitwan valley went into full swing and geared towards the eradication of malaria and resettlement of the hill people in the Terai region.

Keeping in mind the expansion of the health services, re-organisation of the Ministry of Health was done in 1956.

Though the decision to start a training school for nurses at the Bir Hospital had been taken in 1954, the first intake of girls took place only in 1956 and the first batch of thirteen nurses was produced in 1960 (5).

To provide basic health care in the rural areas it was decided to start the training of middle level health workers. Thus a Health Assistant Training School (HATS) was started in 1955.

A Nurses' Training Centre, established in Hetauda in 1958 was later moved to Bharatpur in the Rapti Valley for the training of Assistant Nurse Midwives for service in the rural areas (3).

With the focus on curative aspects some upgrading and even modernisation of the existing hospitals was done. At the same period there was also further re-organisation of the NMEO in 1958.

Additional curative facilities included the building of the first Maternity Hospital (Prasuti Griha) in 1959. Though there were 34 hospitals with 160 doctors, the number of health posts in 1961 was 24 and the estimation was that only 7% of the 9.4 million people in the country were being served by a health facility (3).

Second Plan Period, 1962-65

At the start of this plan period in 1962, the population was 9.8 million with a life expectancy of 33 years. During the course of this three-year plan period the emphasis on the curative aspect was continued but more stress was laid on the preventive aspects of health.

The preventive or the public health aspects were stressed by a smallpox survey being started in 1962 with the objective of eradication of the dreaded disease. Subsequently pilot projects for control of two other major diseases were started:

Leprosy control in 1963.
Tuberculosis control in 1965.
Royal Drug Research Laboratory was established in 1964.

The Assistant Nursing Midwife Programme began in 1962 with the establishment of a training school at Bharatpur. Manpower records of health personnel showed that there were a total of 450 auxiliaries trained since 1934. The different schools, which imparted this training, were - Nepal Rajakiya Ayurved Vidyalaya, Civil Medical School, Health Assistant Training School (HATS) and Auxiliary Health Worker (AHW) School.

The number of health posts opened in 1964 was 9. By 1965 the National Health Survey, which had been done recently by Shah and Worth, was made public. Government records showed that, there were by this time a total of 102 health posts in existence. The number of hospitals providing very minimal health services was 36. Some vertical projects such as malaria eradication, smallpox eradication, TB and leprosy control projects and FP/MCH services were in place.

Third Plan Period, 1965-70

Stress was however still on the curative aspects of health care but it was accepted that more focus on prevention was necessary and provision was made for this in the planning and the budgeting process. The concept in 1966 was to have as many as 32 - district health centres categorised into two groups A and B. The sixteen of Type A were to have a posting of two medical officers, of which one would be female. There would only be one male doctor in the remaining 16 health centres of Type B.

The concept of provision of rural health service led to more health posts. The building of additional new health posts in 1970 resulted in a total of 113 at end of this period.

The stress on prevention led to the establishment of vertical projects such as:

Leprosy Eradication Project launched in 1965.
Smallpox Eradication Project in 1967.
Family Planning & Maternal Child Health Project in 1968.

Though investigative pathological support for the patients at the Bir Hospital was available, the starting of the Central Health Laboratory in 1967, initially within the precincts of the hospital compound heralded the establishment of laboratory facilities on a countrywide basis.

Fourth Plan Period, 1970-75

The life expectancy had gone up to 42.3 years and the IMR had come down to 157/1,000 live births. The population which stood at 11.4 million in 1971 had gone up to 12.9 million in 1975. Planners were sensitised that population control should be taken seriously.

More emphasis was laid on preventive aspects of health care with the provision of some curative services. The HRH training institutions for various grades of middle and basic level health workers was shifted in 1972, from being under the Nepal government to the Institute of Medicine under the Tribhuvan University. Training of various new categories plus upgrading courses for existing health workers were started not only in the capital but also in other parts of the country.

In 1971 a pilot project was started in Bara district under the name of Integrated Basic Health Services. Objective was to provide the basic minimum health services to the maximum number of people. A similar project was started in Kaski in 1972. Finally, an evaluation of both the projects was done in 1975. It was as a result of this that the old health post gradually became converted to integrated types. These and the new integrated health posts became the peripheral unit of the health services, providing not just simple curative services but also stressing on preventive and promotive aspects of health care. This was the start of the provision of an integrated health service to the people (6).

Previously it had been customary for the different vertical projects to send in separately their health statistics. These statistics now came in an integrated fashion and for the overall impact to be assessed. Thus whilst a total of 2,500 cases of malaria had been seen in 1972, what was disheartening was the recurrence of malaria in 1974. The notification and the recording of the last case of smallpox seen in Nepal was in 1974. Karki in a review of global smallpox eradication stated that Nepal had been classified as non-endemic since 1973 (7). This particular case was thought to have been due to importation from adjoining areas of India.

During this period the Community Health and Integration Division (CHID) was set up to reduce duplication and to make health programmes cost effective. This division also tried to integrate vertical projects under the administrative body.

Health personnel in 1971 consisted of 311 physician, 900 nurses and some auxiliaries. A subsequent count by a separate source put the number of doctors at 288 in 1974. A year later in 1975, there were said to be a total of 348 physicians.

A total of over 1,000 health workers of the basic level (paramedics such as AHW, ANM) and middle level such as health assistants had been trained by IoM. During this time the DoHS trained the village health workers (VHW), the FP/MCH section of the DoHS trained panchayat based health workers (PBHWs).

Towards the end of this period a Long Term Health Plan of 25 years was contemplated. An initial effort was later modified to make this into a 15-year plan for the years 1975-90. This particular document stated that at the end of the Fourth Plan Period the existing health institutions numbered:

Hospitals:	62 with a total of 2,174 beds.
Health centres:	33, where services of a doctor, was available in the out patients.
Health posts:	351, all over the country had health assistants as the personnel in charge.
Ayurved *aushadhalayas*:	82 in total.

Country Health Planning (CHP)

As from 1974 the WHO introduced the CHP concept in Nepal. The first exercise for this had nine Nepali and six foreigners as participants. The exercise was used to prepare the First Long Term Health Plan (FLTHP) for the period 1975 to 1990.

Fifth Plan Period, 1975-80

Population increased from 12.9 million in 1975 to 13.9 million in 1978 and to an estimated 14.0 millions in 1979.

Estimates in 1977/78 showed that the life expectancy had gone up to 46 years and the IMR had been reduced to 145/1,000 live births.

Further steps were also taken to integrate vertical programmes into a health infrastructure capable of providing effective services to the people.

The IoM increased its efforts on health personnel production to meet the expected increased requirements of the expanding health services.

The manpower for the health services showed in 1978 a relatively larger increase in the lower basic and middle levels. The official figures were about 1,000 VHW, 450 FP/PBWs, 2,000 middle level workers at the health posts and hospitals, over 3,000 malaria workers. Physicians numbered 375.

Nepal signed the HFA 2000 document at Alma Ata in 1978 and accepted primary health care as being an effective method by which essential health services were to be provided to the community in an acceptable and affordable way, and with the full participation of the people.

By 1979, the number of physicians in the country had risen to 457. The number of hospitals at this time was 69 whilst the number of health posts was 483, of which 233 had been integrated.

Estimated IMR in 1976 was 134/1000 live births.

First Long Term Health Plan (FLTHP), 1975-1990

The Long Term Health Plan (LTHP) for the period 1975-90 was developed and officially adopted as continuation of the previous policy of gradual expansion of basic health care of the population living in the rural areas. Popularising family planning, plus stress on maternal and child health was stressed.

A midterm evaluation of this FLTHP was nevertheless so critical that the actual document regarding this was not made public.

Sixth Plan Period, 1980-85

Life expectancy at birth estimated to be 53 years for men and 50 years for women.

Among the stated objectives were increasing food supply plus the provision of clean drinking water. With this objective Nepal started observing the International Drinking Water Supply and Sanitation Decade (1981-90) at the call of the United Nations. The idea was that with the improvement in water supply and sanitation, a major part of the causes of ill health would be done away with. Major steps were to be taken for the checking of population growth as this would lead to improvement in the health status of the people.

The number of urban centres e.g. municipalities had reached 29 by the year 1983 and some form of health facilities were provided at these urban settings. Up to this time there were still eighteen districts without a hospital. There were a total of 745 health posts in the country. Of the health posts 450 were integrated and provided a full range of health services including field visiting by VHW. By the end of this period a total of 26 health centres were to be upgraded to hospitals or downgraded to health posts or even phased out as per the Long Term Health Plan. The concept of Basic Minimum Needs (BMN) was to be followed.

Health care at the grassroots level was to be provided by way of VHWs at the health posts, be they integrated or static. After extensive debate the concept of VHWs was accepted and effort were to be made for inclusion in future.

The Basic Minimum Needs goal was officially enunciated in 1985 and the Nepalese were promised that they would reach the vague Asian Standard. The National Planning Commission later produced a "Basic

Needs" list. It was on the basis of this that the caloric value of the average Nepali diet was made the yardstick to segregate people into those above or below the poverty line.

Even at this early stage discussions were underway for "attracting private investors in the development of rural and urban health services."

Seventh Plan Period, 1985-90

Organisational integration had been completed more or less by 1987 at the peripheral level and by 1990 at the central level. Because of this, data reporting had been integrated in 27 out of the 75 districts of the kingdom by this time.

A national Health Information System, developed by GoN with WHO collaboration, had been functioning since 1988. It was tested out at Dhading and Sarlahi. The number of Health Institutions by types that existed in September of 1985 was:

Table 5.1. Number of health institutions by types

Health Posts	744 plus 1 (IoM)
Health Centres	26
District Hospitals	44
Zonal Hospitals	9
Central Hospitals	5
Other Hospitals	23
Total Hospitals in the country	**81***

* Corrected figure in later documents was just 79.

Emphasis was on basic minimum health needs (BMHN) of the people of which primary health care and sanitation were but two of them. The objectives of the plan included reducing IMR to 98/1000 live births, Total Fertility Rate (TFR) to 4.00 and increasing life expectancy to 55.4 years by the year 1990. Estimated IMR then was 111/1000 live births.

Bed: Population Ratios of Nepal

At the end of the Seventh Five Year Plan period there were 12 districts without any hospitals and thus no facilities for patient admission. The old health centres, though having a post for a doctor, had no facilities for admission like that of the PHC Centres of the post *andolan* period. The total number of hospitals, governmental and non-governmental, including private ones, at the end of 1990 was 123 with a total bed capacity of 4,717 beds (7). This in terms of a population of 19 million worked out to just 2.4 beds for every 10,000 population.

In 1986, during the period of the Seventh Five Year Plan, the Department of Health Services was dissolved and the Ministry of Health saw the formation of ten divisions and two departments of Ayurved and Drug Administration. July 1990 saw three different projects viz. FP/MCH, EPI and NMEO being also made into divisions under the Ministry of Health.

By this time the five development regions had Regional Directorates of Health Services, which were functioning. This was as per the objectives of the Decentralisation Act 1982 and the expectation was that the integrated health services would be functioning properly and that basic minimum health services would be available to all Nepalese by the year 2000.

The concept of 9 *ilaka* health posts in each of the 75 districts plus the additional static health posts with their quota of the middle and lower level workers were expected to provide this service. The direct responsibility for its functioning rested on the District Public Health Office (DPHO).

Because of the concept of community participation or sometimes because of political pressure, the health institutions were not properly sited. The health posts were in a poor state and did not function properly. Siting of health posts became emotional issues. In 1988 only 242 of the health posts had their own premises whilst the other 433 were in rented premises. One opinion voiced at the Community Health Resources and Priorities (CHRP) meetings was that if health institutions were to be in appropriate sites, and then the land for constructing the building must be purchased. The prevalent practice of using or involving local personnel in the actual construction also resulted in non-completion or sub-standard work. As far as the 114 static sub-health posts were concerned, the staff costs of one AHW and one female MCH worker were to be borne by the village panchayat or the community. This decision was never put into practice. In the case of community level work, the VHW would be responsible to provide the integrated health care package to the community with the aid of the ward level health volunteer residing nearby.

In all this it was envisaged that the Decentralisation Act of 1982 would be enforced and that the concept of inter-sectoral collaboration brought into play. Provision had been made in this for the formation of a District Health and Population Committee to look after the PHC activity at that level. This advocated the formation of what was referred to as *Seva Kendras*[2] or service centres with the following services: health, education, water supply & sanitation, agriculture and postal services. Some, like the ones at Sahare and Babiya Chaur in Surkhet District, were at times partially functioning. However such efforts of inter-sectoral cooperation at the *ilaka* level though it was tried out in a number of places, never really succeeded. This may have been due to half-hearted attempts, limited political commitment or lack of community participation. It is noteworthy that by this time some guidelines had been formulated for the establishment of new health posts, bearing in mind such criteria as:

- Walking distance
- Settlement and population density
- Population
- Accessibility.

In spite of all these guidelines, other considerations were followed when the final site decision was made.

This particular plan of action envisaged using Panchayat Based Health Worker (PBHW) plus malaria field worker and vaccinators to provide an integrated service at the then existing Village Panchayat level. It was in this frame work of health care delivery that the government decided to have the Community Health Volunteers (CHV), drawn from the community itself, on the basis of one from each ward of the village panchayat, to provide both preventive and curative primary health care services.

Post *Jana Andolan I* Health Services

Following the *Jana Andolan I* and the subsequent changes in government, major changes were apparently in the offing for the health services.

In 1990 Malaria Eradication Project, FP/MCH Project and EPI were made into one of three new divisions at the Ministry of Health (8).

The HFA 2000 Steering Committee was reconstituted and renamed Basic Minimum Needs and Health For All 2000 Steering Committee under the Honourable Member of the National Planning Commission. This denoted that Nepal's health policies were still in conformity to the

2. Service Centres

country's commitment to BMN and HFA strategies.

A process of restructuring of the health services was considered. This meant applying the concept of strengthening of the district health systems and WHO support was sought for this. What was agreed and done was that certain districts were identified for special attention with a view to monitoring the implementation of some special programmes for strengthening district health systems. That the situation was bad is exemplified by no less a person than the then Minister of Health saying, "The system doesn't work and hasn't worked for 30 years. We must find out how to make it work."

Eighth Plan Period, 1992-97

The Eighth (five years) Plan, which should have started in 1990, was delayed because of the *Jana Andolan I*. It was mid-1992 that saw the start of the Plan. The new objectives were those that had been stated in the National Health Policy of 1991 (see Annexure I).

With this implementation the intention was to (8):

- involve lower levels e.g. regional & district in the planning and delivery of health services including responsibilities of supervision and monitoring.
- give further impetus to the integration process, which was underway since 1987
- provide a combined preventive and curative package at the district level.
- bring about more efficient management by combining together functions of finance, logistics, and training, IEC & MIS.
- have a more compact working force by eliminating development staff positions.

The Annual Report of DoHS 1994/5 (2051/52 BS) stated that the four objectives from the health section of the Eighth Plan were to:

- improve the general health condition of the people in order to provide the health personnel for the country's development;
- extend basic and primary health services to villages to improve the health status of rural people;
- extend mother and child health services and family planning to the local level to make the population control programme more effective; and

- develop specialized health services in order to provide quality services throughout the country.

The budgetary allocation for the health sector in 1994/95 was a meagre 5%. The rallying cry of the National Health Policy and of the Eighth Plan was "Attainment of the highest possible level of health by the Nepalese people." The targets to reduce IMR to 50, the U5MR to 70 and measles deaths by 90% by 2000 AD were not attained.

The newly elected government took steps to (i) provide health care to the people and (ii) institute effective measures to try to contain the growth of the population. The people's expectations had increased for a more socially oriented society and with a more equitable distribution of resources. Budgetary provisions for the social sector had to increase.

By 1998 eight periodic plans had been implemented with the oft-repeated promises of improvements. The national budget allocation for health and nutrition during the seven fiscal years starting 1988/89 to 1994/95 varied between 3.61% and 5.57% of the national budget.

Review of the allocated annual budgets during the years 1998 to 2004 showed this to be 4.97% on average but how and on what basis the budgeted expenditure was utilised was not clear. Irrespective of the assurances of whichever was the party in power, the % of budget for health stayed around 5%.

What happened over the years was just the formulation of plan. But these plans were not implemented. Projection figures given for health in the year 2000 were not based on realities and target figures were not attained with the usual performance. A previous plan stated that large numbers of HRH were required by the year 2000 AD. However because of inadequate number of posts or non-advertisement of vacancies, posts were not filled. The people were told that health services couldn't be provided because of lack of manpower whilst the actual truth was that the expansion of the health services had not taken place as per the need, nor was there enough budgetary support for social services such as health. In 1991 the major political parties stated in their manifestos that they would improve the health facilities if elected. It was just a ploy to get the votes. The concept of "Health Rights" though talked about, was not being provided as promised at times of elections

In the planning of health matters it is necessary to include people outside of the MoH to get proper feedback. Concerned specialists from outside of government service or those who have retired should also be involved in the planning process. Due considerations should be given to their suggestions and a process be started by which on-going research in the various fields gives guidance for the future.

The GoN brought out the National Health Policy of 1991. In the process leading up to this and subsequently too, a large number of the health personnel were retired ostensibly to make the health services more efficient. The sudden termination of many temporary staff's contract too, led to difficulties in the delivery of services, especially the Expanded Programme of Immunisation (EPI).

The Nepal Medical Association, citing the argument that different provisions had been made for other sectors e.g. legal, customs and even postal services, made various representations to the Administrative Reform Commission for a separate Health Act. In the period just before the *Jana Andolan I*, the Health Services too had been put in the special category of essential services with emergency rules being enforced. The Health Act was passed and though officially put into operation, could not be implemented. A number of amendments even by ordinance did not make it workable. It has been further amended.

As for the health of the people, there was not much to show for it at the start of the nineties. The IMR and the U5MR were coming down, but the percentage of the many malnourished Nepalese as a result of the poverty that prevailed was a grim reminder that all was not well. Much more could have been achieved during the almost four decades after the end of Rana rule.

The new organogram came into being as the answer to the proper functioning and efficient health service delivery. A new organisational set up of the MoH came into effect on the 16th of July 1993 (1st Shrawan 2050 BS). The new hierarchical organisation structure of the MoH had under it the three different departments, - Health Services, Drug Administration and Ayurved. The facilities provided by the DoHS were as follows:

Central Level

- Central Hospitals

- Health Education, Information & Communication
- National Tuberculosis Centre
- AIDS and STD Control
- National Public Health Laboratory
- National Health Training Centre

The health services at the regional and lower levels were under the jurisdiction of the Directorate of Health Services in the region concerned and were as given below:

Regional Level

- Regional Hospitals
- Regional Training Centre
- Regional Laboratory
- Regional Tuberculosis Centre
- Regional Medical Store

Zonal Level

- Zonal Hospitals

District Level

- District Health Office under which is the District Hospital and the District Public Health Section.

In the electoral constituency were the Primary Health Care Centre, Health Posts at the Ilaka Level (The district was divided into 9 ilakas; a total of 675 integrated health posts plus additional 14 state health posts) and at the VDC level, the sub-health posts (SHP). One SHP was to be established in every VDC where there is no other health facility through community participation with a total of 3199 stated to be operational by 1998.

In April 1994 at Surkhet District where the objective of integrating the delivery of rural and hospital services by combining district public health and medical services under the DHO had not led to the desired result up to then. It had in fact created confusion about the roles and responsibilities between the DPHO and the DHO. At the grassroots level where proper implementation should have occurred, no proper supervisory and reporting linkages had taken place between the sub health post, primary health centre, health post and the district administration.

As has been already stated, the UML Government instituted various steps related to the Health Sector. The New Medicine Policy which had been passed some time earlier was put into practice from around 3rd April, 1995. The mentally ill patients who used to be kept in jail, as per previous recommendations, were no longer to be kept imprisoned from 2nd April, 1995. This same month of April saw newly reconstituted Nepal Health Research Council. Task forces and committees to solve problems in various areas were:

Special committee was set up to look at Post Graduate Medical Education in this country, with a view to forming an autonomous Post Graduate Institute at Kathmandu, using the facilities of the Valley Group of Hospitals. This superseded the committee formed by the previous Nepali Congress government.

The Organogram

The Organogram of 1993 was revised in 1995 and the restructuring that took place had been shown in the annual report of DoHS of 2003/4 as consisting of as follows:

The number of PHC centres, health posts and sub-health posts stated as being completed in the 9th Plan document were:

Primary Health Care Centres:	100
Sub-Health Posts:	3187

Stress was laid on the delivery of some essential health care to far-flung areas of the kingdom by way of mobile health camps for which budgetary provision was made.

In the period prior to the Ninth Plan, pronouncements were made by the Minister of Health that much more stress will be given to the Ayurvedic system of medicine during the course of this period.

Ninth Plan Period, 1997-2002

This Plan focused on the task of poverty alleviation and planned for the health sector to play a major role in its implementation (9). Having made specific and annual plans in the context of national needs, on the basis of priorities and by bringing about co-ordination between Government, NGO's and donor agencies, the Second Long Term Health Plan 1997-2017 was prepared by creating awareness and on the basis of community

Fig. 5.1 **Organogram[3] of Department of Health Services (DoHS)**

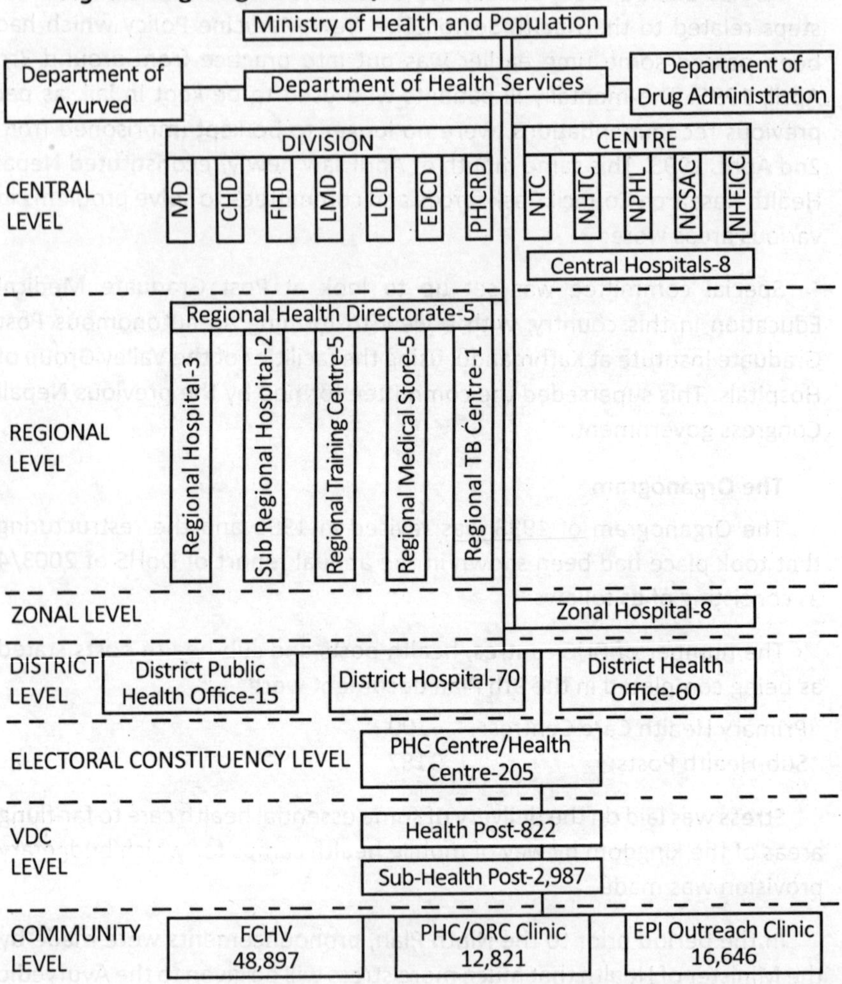

Source: DoHS, Annual Report 2068/69 (2011/12)

Acronyms

MD	Management Division
CHD	Child Health Division
FHD	Family Health Division
LMD	Logistics Management Division
LCD	Leprosy Control Division
EDCD	Epidemiology and Disease Control Division
PHCRD	Primary Health Care Revitalisation Division
NTC	National Tuberculosis Centre
NHTC	National Health Training Centre
NPHL	National Public Health Laboratory
NCASC	National Centre for AIDS and STD Control
NHEICC	National Health Education, Information and Communication Centre
FCHV	Female Community Health Volunteer
PHC/ORC	Primary Health Care Outreach Clinic
EPI	Expanded Programme on Immunisation

3. Replace reactivation by Revitalisation

participation. The objectives were of long-term for providing essential health services to:

- persons and communities not so serviced
- communities in dangerous situation
- women and children
- those living in rural and far flung areas
- backward and deprived sections

Policies, identified for implementation are:

- Essential Care Health Services (EHCS) at district level and below
- Strengthening District Health System (SDHS)
- Health care services beyond the district - Special forms of tertiary and specialised care
- Ancillary and support services (Laboratory & Blood Bank) at Regional, Zonal and District level. Also IEC for nutrition, environment and School Health Services
- Ayurvedic Services
- Other traditional systems of medicine - Homeopathy, Unani & Naturopathy
- Organisation and management of health services on the basis of decentralisation
- Health financing on the basis of internal and external resource mobilisation, health insurance and cost sharing or cost recovery schemes
- Increased role of Private and NGO sectors
- Coordination and inter-sectoral collaboration
- Health Research

Both the National Health Policy (NHP) 1991 and the SLTHP (1997-2017) had realised that to achieve the health sector objectives it was necessary to have a proper Health Sector Information System (HSIS).

The primary objective of the Nepal Health Sector Programme - Implementation Plan (NHSP-IP) covering the period 2004 - 2009 was to establish the Health Sector Information System (HSIS) which in turn was essential for the implementation of the Implementation of the Health Sector Strategy: An Agenda for Change, 2003.

Second Long Term Health Plan (SLTHP), 1997-2017

With the "vision of an integrated health system including public, NGO sectors in which there is equitable access to health care, self- -community participation, decentralisation, gender sensitivity and efficient management, resulting in improved health status of the population," GoN of Nepal brought out the draft of the SLTHP in April, 1997 (10).

In mid-July, 1997, a public notification asked the public to send suggestions for this Second Long Term Health Plan.

In late July, a draft of this Second Long Term Health Plan 1997-2017 was officially released. The hope was that this document when finalised would provide the guiding principles to tackle all health development issues over the coming 20 years. Whilst the SLTHP was not a final blue print for the functioning of the health sector, it was to be used as a rolling plan and resource document, which would be reviewed on a periodic basis and linked to on-going evaluations.

The scenario in the post *Jana Andolan I* period is that there have been a number of changes of government during this period. Changes in ministers entailed not only changes and transfers of administrative staff but also technical personnel leading to a disturbing effect on the delivery of health care in Nepal. A NGO document of 1995 went on record to state (11):

"Again, notwithstanding the limitations of the available information on health in Nepal, what the data made clear was that there has been hardly any significant change in the health status and health scenario of Nepal during the last five years (1991-95)."

Tenth Plan Period (2002 - 2007)

This plan too had been focussed for the task of poverty alleviation and covered the period from 2002 to 2007. It must be noted that though poverty reduction had been stressed from the time of the Sixth Plan (1980-1985), a lot still needed to be done. The overall poverty was expected to be reduced from 38% to 30% and literacy raised to 70%. With overall access to drinking water to 85 percent and GDP grown rate at 6.2%, the life expectancy was expected to go up to 62 years.

Following *Jana Andolan II* there were a number of incidents in which attacks were made on doctors following the deaths of patients. Because of these incidents the all hospital services except for emergencies came to a halt. Even private clinics were closed at this call of the NMA. Pressure was put on the MoHP and the GoN to enact the Health Professionals Protection Act.

In an effort to improve the lot of the Nepali people, the GoN had from 2000 encouraged young Nepalis to go for employment abroad. After 2005, the remittances sent by the Nepali workers abroad has gradually increased. It is this remittance which has helped to improve the living standards of a lot of the Nepali people. It has been estimated that as much as 80% of the remittance money is spent on daily consumption.

Eleventh Periodic Plan, Three Year Interim Plan (2008 – 2010)

"Health as a fundamental right of the people" was incorporated into the Interim Constitution of Nepal 2007. This periodic plan stressed on:

- Access to quality health services to all citizens, irrespective of geographic regions, class, gender, religion, political ideals and socio-economic status that they belong to.
- Community Drug Programme and Community Co-operative Clinic

The Interim Constitution directed for a Free Health Care policy. After the first republic budget of 19th Sept. 2008, GoN decided to make free health services up to 25 bedded district hospital, especially to the targeted people (9).

Table 5.2. Number of government health institutions by types in different regions of the country (12)

Region	Hospital	PHC Centres	Health Posts
Mountain	16	20	148
Hill	50	104	364
Terai	25	86	164
National	91	210	676

Twelfth Periodic Plan, Three Year Plan (2011-2013)

The direction for the provision of free basic health care services for all with special emphasis on the poor and disadvantaged was maintained. Also controlling and treating non-communicable diseases e.g. cancer, heart disease, hypertension, diabetes and mental health. The effort was to be done nationally.

Thirteenth Periodic Plan, Three Year Plan (2014-2016)

A blue print of this plan was prepared and passed following the intense activity of public consultations at both local and national levels. Politicians of various parties were also involved to assure of consensus and the subsequent implementation of this periodic plan. The major objective of this plan is to raise Nepal from its current least developed country status to developing country by the year 2022. The main target of the plan is to reduce the poverty line from the present 23.8% to 18% within this three years period. Education, energy, health and rural development have been stressed upon (12).

HOSPITAL SERVICES

From 1950, the health care of the people became the responsibility of the government. Though some health services were provided by NGOs and the private sector, health care delivery was by and large a government affair. Whilst the health services provided by the government were said to be free, it was only the doctor's services and the hospital bed that this was so. The patients had to pay for the medications or to procure them before they are used for treatment. Besides the western oriented type of modern medicine there were also many Ayurvedic institutions within the country. It was for promoting the indigenous system of medicine that the Ayurvedic Department started to function from 1982 as a separate entity.

Up to the mid-fifties the hospitals that were in existence were those under the government. Most of these were under the Ministry of Health, with the Tri-Chandra Military Hospital under the Defence Ministry being the exception. With the opening of hospitals and health posts by the missionaries' viz. the NGO's semi-private hospital came into being. This has led on to the establishment of nursing homes also. The early eighties saw the setting up of the hospital under other ministries. With the starting of the outpatient services in July 1983 and the inpatient services at the Tribhuvan University Teaching Hospital as from 7th March 1986, the Education Ministry too was involved in the provision of health services (13). The establishment of TUTH and initial support by the Japanese Government has been with the involvement of JICA.

Similarly, the Birendra Police Hospital started with a modest number of 25 beds in April 1984 (15) under the Home Ministry. This was subsequently expanded and is now becoming a 300 bedded.

Another category now are the hospitals, which are attached to the private medical colleges at Pokhara, Bharatpur, Nepalgunj, Bhairahawa, Birgunj, Palpa, Lalitpur and Kathmandu.

Thus the hospitals now existing in the country can be broadly categorised into three main groups:

1. Governmental
   a. Civil (General Population)
   b. For Service Personnel - Army. Police and Civil Servants
   c. Educational - Medical Schools
2. Non-Governmental, including mission and not for profit health institutions. Another category which has come up remarkably are the community initiated and supported hospitals and co-operatives. Almost all mission hospitals have been handed over to government or local organisations.
3. Private, for profit nursing homes/hospitals

Government Hospitals

a. Civil

On the civil side, the Bir Hospital, established as long ago as 1889 AD, has the pride of place as the first institution of the western medicine type, for health care. Because of its long history it has been shifted, added to and renovated periodically over the years. Following the end of Rana rule in 1951 major changes occurred in the different sectors. Renovation of Bir Hospital, construction of Surgical Block and nurse's residence with support of USAID started in 1965 and was completed in a few years. New OPD facilities with help from India, opened in November 1985. Following the 1986 decision to develop different super-specialities at the Bir Hospital, the ADRA Sydney Hospital Heart Project started there in 1987 as one such (14). Others are also now functioning. On 7th June 1997 the Indian Prime Minister Mr. I. K. Gujral during the course of his three-day visit unveiled the plaque for the construction of a 200-bedded Emergency and Trauma Centre to be built with the aid of the Indian government. The construction work started as late as 2006 and the hospital was finished in 2009. The sad part of all this is that though there is so much road traffic and other accidents, this institution had not till end Jan. 2014 started functioning.

In 2004 however, Bir Hospital was concurrently made into the National Academy of Medical Sciences and is responsible for PG training such as MD/ MS for medical doctors courses run in various hospitals in Kathmandu Valley. The MDS course for dental surgeons is also conducted. Beside these the PCL and BN courses are also done there.

A Civil Service Hospital for government employees had been discussed over the years and finally set up with the support of the Government of China. This hospital was officially opened by the then PM Madhav Kumar Nepal with the inauguration of the out-patient services on 2nd Feb. 2010. It has 132 beds and will be fully operational in five years' time.

b. For Service Personnel

As already described, the first and foremost of these is the Tri-Chandra Military Hospital, which had been built as a memorial for those who had died in the World War I. It was opened in 1926 with 64 beds including cabins. Gradually over the years various specialist services have been added. Following the opening of the Shree Birendra Hospital at Chhauni, this health facility was only providing outpatient facilities to some of the veterans or their families. The old military hospital had been developed as a diagnostic centre as from 2007.

Smaller army field hospitals exist in different parts of the country i.e. at Itahari, Siddhartha Nagar, Nepalgunj and Dhangadi.

The Shree Birendra Hospital at Chhauni was opened on 20th Dec. 1990. It was initially increased to 240 beds and in 1998 it had 300 beds. Besides looking after the service personnel it also provides emergency service plus serves as a trauma centre for use by the general public. The Nursing School and Nepal Army Medical College have already been started and the Dental College is to start soon. The capacity of the hospital is also being increased by a 100 beds. There are plans to open a Veteran's Hospital too.

The Birendra Police Hospital was established in 1984 with a total of 25 beds. It has expanded over the years and has a total of 155 beds in 2013. Other smaller hospitals were opened in other parts of the country, the 15 bedded one at Dipayal being the first to start functioning as from mid-May, 1996 has been upgraded to 25 beds and another similar one is being established at Nepalgunj. The Police Hospital is also in the process of increasing capacity to 300 beds prior to opening its own medical college with an intake of 100. Future plans include the starting of a Dental and a Nursing School with intakes of 40 for both the BDS and BSc Nursing courses (15).

The new Armed Police Force has, since March 2006, its own 110 bedded Nepal APF Hospital at Balkhu that provides various medical services for personnel under its command.

c. Educational

The Tribhuvan University Teaching Hospital was the first. With periodic additions the TUTH is in 2013 the largest health institution in the country. A new expanded Emergency Section has been built by Mr. Meen Bahadur Gurung of Bhatbhateni Supermarket in memory of his parents.

The B. P. Koirala Institute of Health Sciences, an autonomous institution has a mandate for education, service and research activities was the second government institution for the training of doctors. It now has a total of 700 beds.

The Patan Academy of Health Sciences (PAHS) is the third governmental institution producing different grades of Human Resources of Health.

A fourth Governmental institution is the Karnali Academy of Health Sciences (KAHS) to be based at Jumla.

A fifth institution in the process of being set up is at Attaria, Geta and will function as a Teaching Hospital in the Far Western Region of Nepal.

Others, some of which are private, are in the process of being expanded further (see later). Speciality institutions for different areas of health e.g. cardiac, paediatric etc. with facilities for Post Graduate Education are in the process of being set up.

Other Hospitals and Health Facility

General Hospitals

The hospital situation as of 2008 with the different categories of institutions was as follows:

District Hospitals: Of the 75 districts in the country only 70 had a district hospital as such with a capacity of 15 to 25 beds. An additional 11 districts however had inpatient facilities being provided by the zonal or regional hospitals sited there.

Zonal Hospitals: The eight in this category were at Mahendranagar, Dhangadi, Nepalgunj, Butwal, Janakpur, Rajbiraj, Biratnagar and Chandragadhi.

Regional Hospitals: There were three in existence. The Western Regional continued functioning but the Eastern Regional at Dharan changed its identity to become the B P Koirala Institute of Health Sciences (BPKIHS). Some other hospital, most likely the Koshi Zonal Hospital was then to be categorised as the Regional Hospital. Similarly Hetauda Hospital is the Regional Hospital for the Central Region. The mid-West Regional Hospital was at Birendranagar in Surkhet.

With the establishment of new medical colleges outside of the capital more centres of tertiary health care will have been established at these places.

Central Hospitals: These were then at Kathmandu and Lalitpur. The total bed state of these five central hospitals added up to 1110 with the breakdown as given below:

Bir Hospital – NAMS	350
Kanti Children's Hospital	300
Paropakar Prasuti Griha (Maternity) Hospital	310
Shukra Raj Tropical & Infectious Disease Hospital	50
Mental Hospital	100

The above are referred to as the "Valley Group of Hospitals" and following the creation of National Academy of Medical Sciences by Ordinance in 2061 BS a number of Certificate, Bachelor and Post Graduate educational programmes for the health sector are being conducted there.

Table 5. 3 Number of Governmental Health Institutions by type as of 2008

Total Hospitals under Ministry of Health	**89**
Medical College Teaching Hospitals	2
Specialised Central Hospitals	5
Regional Hospitals	2
Regional / Sub regional Hospitals	3
Zonal Hospitals	8
District Hospitals	69
District Health Offices	75

Primary Health Care Centres (PHCC)	180
Health Centres	13
Health Posts (HP)	711
Sub Health Posts (SHP)	3,179
PHC Outreach Clinics	5,548

Source: National Symposium of Health. Oct. 2008

Hospitals attached to Teaching Hospitals of Universities

The current total number of eighteen, three of which are governmental, eight of which are attached to KU and seven to TU is expected to rise in the future. These hospitals are at varying stages of development in different parts of the country as has been described in the previous chapter.

The Tribhuvan University Teaching Hospital (TUTH) is at Kathmandu. Though originally of 250 it was increased subsequently to 401. Further increases were by way of a Ganesh Man Singh ENT & Head, Neck Surgery Centre and a Man Mohan Cardio-Thoracic Vascular and Transplant Centre and a special accident ward. TUTH has the distinction of having done the first successful kidney transplant in Nepal in 2008. A Child Health Unit and a Obstetrics and Gynaecology unit have been opened and plans are afoot for a separate Orthopaedic Unit. There is already functioning the B P Koirala Lions Centre for Ophthalmic Studies. The total number of beds will finally increase to 802. The Nursing Campus at Maharajgunj is also in this same site.

The B P Koirala Institute of Health Sciences (BPKIHS) at Dharan has a deemed university status and conducts Medical, Dental and Nursing programs both at undergraduate and PG levels. It started a School of Public Health from the academic session 2005.

The Kathmandu University Medical School (KUMS) is the medical school of Kathmandu University. It presently comprises of the Dhulikhel Hospital of 300 beds. Basic Sciences Block is in an additional compound at Chaukot.

The Patan Academy of Health Sciences (PAHS) was established in 2008 as a deemed university and is using the Patan Hospital Complex for its teaching-learning activities. It took its third batch of MBBS in 2013. A tele-medicine service to 25 districts of Nepal is also conducted from there.

Specialised Hospitals

It must be noted that some of the Central Hospitals are also specialist ones viz:

- women's' hospitals for obstetrics and gynaecology
- children's' hospital
- infectious diseases hospital
- mental hospital

Eye Hospitals

The eye hospitals have come to occupy a pride of place in Nepal's health services and have furthered the cause of Ophthalmology. As of October 2013 there are a total of 17 eye hospitals within the country.

In tracing the origins of the eye hospitals one must remember that the first eye camp in Nepal was held at Butwal in 1947 with the aid of two eye surgeons from Sitapur Eye Hospital. At this same time, a free camp of about one-month duration was also held at the Shree Juddha Ghat at Tripureshwar, the place now occupied by the Nepal Eye Hospital building. This may be said to have ushered in the concept of eye care services in Nepal.

Dr. Yagya Man Baidya was the first eye surgeon in Nepal, who along with Dr. Nem Bahadur started eye care services in Nepal. Starting with eye departments at Bir Hospital, this specialisation has extended to major urban centres of Nepal. There are now no less than 17 NGO run eye hospitals with a capacity of over 1000 beds (16).

Tilganga Institute of Ophthalmology (TIO) is an institution established by the Nepal Eye Program. This NGO which is a not-for-profit, community based has a vision for the prevention and control of blindness in Nepal and beyond (17). TIO trains Ophthalmic Assistants and also conducts the MD in Ophthalmology residency programme. The NGO also runs the Hetauda Community Eye Hospital (HCEH) plus also eleven Community Eye Centres in various parts of the country.

Cancer Hospitals

Nepal government established the B P Koirala Memorial Cancer Hospital (BPKMCH) at Yagyapuri, Bharatpur in Chitwan in 1996. It was built with the assistance of the government of the People's Republic of China. The hospital began its day care services to the patients from October

1995, whereas full-fledged OPD services started from June 1999 and inpatient services one month later (July 1999). This hospital was officially inaugurated in Sept. 2000 has at present in 2011 a total of 162 beds but its total capacity is planned to be increased to 350 beds by April 2014. The hospital runs a 25 bedded day care facility and also a hospice and palliative care services. Because of its proximity to the East West Highway the hospital has good accessibility from all over the country (18).

In July 2013, the governing board of the hospital announced that they intended opening branches at Nepalgunj, Dharan and Patan (Lalitpur). They were also looking into the possibility of starting similar branches at Kathmandu, Janakpur and Pokhara.

The building of an institution started as Chandra Loke Dispensary on 17th Asar 1961 BS (1904) later became the Bhaktapur Cancer Hospital at Dudhpati, Bhaktapur. With the construction of a new building for the local hospital, dwellers of the town converted the old part into a Cancer Hospital with help from Rotarians of Nepali origin in various parts of the world. It started functioning in 1995 with 15 beds. It runs the OPD and day care patient service in the new building. It has currently 72 beds but the Nepal Cancer Relief Society is in the process of expanding it to 100 beds capacity (19).

Geriatric Hospital

The GoN was to build a Geriatric Hospital during the Three Years 12th Periodic Plan (2010-12). It did not materialise. The MoHP has recently announced that Patan Hospital Is building a geriatric ward as is also the National Ayurvedic Training & Research Centre at Kirtitur. Ten out of the 25 beds will be for geriatric patients. There are also plans to have a 10 bedded geriatric ward in all the regional and zonal hospitals as the percentage of the geriatric group continues to increase. Currently it constitutes 6.5% of the population.

Cardiac Care Hospitals

It was decided in 1995 to set up the Shahid Gangalal National Heart Centre. It was brought into operation initially with the aid of ADRA Nepal. As from Dec 1999 the outpatient services were started. There are presently 80 beds but a 100 beds are being added soon. Facilities for open-heart surgery are being provided presently.

...tute of Medicine opened a special wing known as the Man ...nikari Cardio-Thoracic Vascular and Transplant Centre opened by ... M Pushpa Kamal Dahal on 12th Baishakh 2065 BS.

Hospital and Rehabilitation Centre for Disabled Children (HRDC), Banepa

This hospital set up in 1985 was initially functioning as Terres des hommes at Jorpati. After a number of years it shifted to new premises at Jamsikhel and finally to its own building at Janagal, Kavre in 1997. This hospital looks mainly after children with orthopaedic disabilities. In 2011, the 72 bedded hospital was functioning at full capacity and providing both treatment and rehabilitation. Special mobile camps are conducted annually in different parts of the country. Plans are underway to increase the capacity to 100 beds in the future (20).

Nepal Orthopaedic Hospital

This hospital was started in 1998 with the joint efforts of Nepal Disabled Association and the Rotary Club of Patan. It served 631 patients during its first year of operation. During the course of the last twelve years the out-patient load has increased gradually and now stands at 27,270 (21).

Paediatric Hospitals

A Women's and Children Hospital, with community participation, has been set up at Bhaktapur since 1993. It is run by the Siddhi Memorial Foundation and currently has a 36 bed ward providing service to mothers and children. It has a birthing centre and provides dental service plus also a day care service. It has attached to it a hospice for elderly citizens.

The Siddhartha Children's & Women's Hospital was established at Butwal by AMDA- Nepal, a NGO working for the elevation of health situation in the country. The Japanese people and also Mainichi Newspapers have helped it. Initially started with 50 beds, the hospital hopes to increase its capacity gradually.

A National Children's Eye &Ear Hospital and Rehabilitation Centre has been set up by the B. P. Eye Foundation at Manohara in Thimi.

Ishan Children's Nursing and Maternity Home was started initially as a 15 bedded nursing home for children. It was increased to 25 beds in 2054 BS. Besides the two specialities in its title it has expanded to other fields and is in the process of expanding capacity to 55 beds.

Respiratory Diseases Centre: The GoN has announced that it plans to build a 100 bedded centre in honour of former PM late Girija Prasad Koirala. There is doubt about its location being either at Tanahun, Bhadrakali VDC or at the Seti Ganga Community Hospital site.

Central Jail Hospital: With the intention of giving service to all imprisoned within the country, this 25 bedded hospital is being constructed within the compound of the Central Jail at Kathmandu.

PHC Centres

A new category of health institution with treatment facilities that has been introduced is the PHC Centre. Though health centres with bed facilities had been introduced years ago and numbered 33 at the end of the Fourth Five Year Plan they had over the years been reduced to a figure of 18 by 1990 or at the end of the Seventh Five Year Plan. This was because the policy during Panchayat days had been to either upgrade them to district hospitals or to downgrade them to health posts. Now with the policy of upgrading health posts or building a primary health care centre in each of the 205 election constituencies, providing the services of a doctor, it seems that we have come full circle.

Thus it was that mid-1992 saw the start of the Eighth Plan.

The plan regarding PHC Centres was that 1993 saw the building of new or upgraded health posts so that a figure of 20 was reached. Getting doctors to man these was a problem but the DoHS tried to solve it by appointing some of the Bachelor graduates of Ayurvedic medicine (BAMS) to man these PHC Centres. Some questions have been raised regarding the legality of post mortems being performed by ayurvedic physicians. The total number of PHC centres in 2010 was 209.

Besides the government and university hospitals (TUTH and BPKIHS) mentioned, a number of hospitals have come up under the private medical colleges. Though the total number of beds run by them and the nursing homes was claimed to be 13, 406 in October 2008 not all are functional.

The total number of beds, including the 65 ayurvedic and the six homeopathic beds, in the country come to 12,589 as shown below in Table 5.2:

Table 5.2 Number of available hospital beds by types of institutions - government, private and NGO

Institution types	Number of hospital beds
Government hospitals (allopathic)	3,397
Government teaching hospitals	1,200
NGO run Eye hospital	973
Service personnel hospitals	346
Community hospitals	30
Private hospitals	722
Private teaching hospital	5,850
Ayurved hospital	65
Homeopathy hospital	6
Total number of hospital beds	**12,589**

Ayurved and other health institutions

The ayurvedic institutions had been started with the objective of providing health services to the people on the basis of the traditional cures, which used both herbs and other ingredients such as precious metals etc. The ayurved department thus came into being. The hospital was established in 1916 (1873 BS) as a social organisation and started inpatient services with four beds the following year. To meet with the requirement of the people it was envisaged that besides the Central Hospital at Kathmandu, there will be other hospitals and dispensaries in different parts of the country. Thus it came about that besides the Ayurved Training School, there were also the *Vaidyakhana* and the various hospitals and dispensaries established over the years.

Following the introduction of NESP the production of Ayurved health personnel became the responsibility of the IoM which conducted classes for the Certificate and Bachelor levels of training at the Naradevi Ayurved Hospital under the MoHP. The capacity of this hospital was increased to 100 beds. Subsequently IoM shifted its campus and built an Ayurved Hospital at Kirtipur. Nepal Government with the support of the Chinese government, constructed its own Ayurvedic Hospital and Research Centre at Balkhu adjoining the Tribhuvan University site too. This hospital has not been fully functional as in 2013 only OPD services were being provided.

It was as late as 1982 (2039 BS) that GoN started a separate department of Ayurved in the MoHP. In most areas of Nepal it is now accepted that the Ayurved system of medicine is best for the treatment of jaundice. Because sanitation in Kathmandu is poor it comes as no surprise that viral hepatitis due to faeco-oral route of infection is very prevalent. Many of the cases of jaundice recover as a result of the treatment provided by the ayurvedic physicians or baidyas. The current thinking is that there is no specific treatment for viral hepatitis. Nepal government has given importance to Ayurved treatment by formulating the National Ayurved Policy 2052 BS.

Table 5.4 Number of health facilities - Ayurved and other systems of medicine

Types of health facilities	Number
Ayurved hospital	2
Vaidyakhana	1
Anchal Ayurved Aushadhalaya	14
District Ayurved Swasthya Kendra	55
Ayurved Aushadhalaya	216
Homeopathic hospital	1
Yunani Chikitsalaya	1

Source: Website of MoHP. www.mohp.gov.np

A thirty-bedded ayurved hospital located at Bijauri, Dang in the Central Region is now functioning, as is also the 25 District Swyastha Kendras. A medicine production unit exists in the form of the Singha Durbar *Vaidyakhana* also at Kathmandu. Much stress has been laid during the last few years on Ayurved. It is the government's policy to have an ayurvedic health centre in each of the 75 districts and an ayurvedic clinic for each of 5 VDCs.

In the meantime the University Grants Commission had submitted a report in May 2010 stating that the Sanskrit University should also set up an Ayurved Campus for teaching / learning activities. It is in the process of constructing a 100 bedded hospital at Beljhundi in Dang and has started the Doctorate course in Aurved.

On 3rd April 2011 a National Ayurved Research and Training Centre (NARTC) which had been constructed with Chinese aid was formally opened. The intention is to conduct activities and programmes of health care services, research and training. It has still to function properly and though OPD services are being run, there is vagueness about the objective and functioning of this institution. It has a capacity of 30 beds and the local papers have reported that there would be 10 beds for geriatric patients (22).

Homeopathic Medicine

Homeopathy had been introduced into India by a French doctor John Martin Honiberger when he first visited India in 1810. On a subsequent visit to India in 1839 he treated the then ruler of the Punjab Maharajah Ranjit Singh. The spread of Homeopathic medicine occurred after this time.

Homeopathic medicine was introduced into Nepal at a time when Chandra Shumsher was prime minister and during which time there was cholera pandemic. Because of its success in controlling this pandemic the then C-in-C Rudra Shumsher is said to have been instrumental in popularising homeopathy by helping to print a publication "Paribarik Chikitsa".

In 2007 BS, a homeopathic dispensary was opened at Ramghat, Pashupati during the time that Mohan Shumsher was prime minister of Nepal. Though three other homeopathic centres were opened at Palpa, Gulmi and Dhankuta, all of them soon closed down due to lack of funds. Later the Pashupati Homeo Hospital was opened in BS 2010 during King Tribhuvan's reign. Subsequently, this hospital was upgraded to 25 beds and shifted to its own building at the Harihar Bhawan surroundings. There is a move to also have a homeopathic hospital in each of the five regions of the country.

Table. 5.5 Region-wise distribution of hospital beds by types of institutions

Region	Government		Service personnel		NGO	Total beds
	General	Teaching	Army	Police	Eye	
Eastern	537	700	6	-	56	1,299
Central	1,912	500	178	410	553	3,553
Western	508	-	6	-	83	597
MidWest	235	-	6	-	133	374
FarWest	205	-	25	-	148	378
Total	**3,397**	**1,200**	**221**	**410**	**973**	**6,201**

Hospitals through Media Eyes

The health services as provided by the government are to a certain extent always under scrutiny. The need for the services is ever there and demands are ever increasing. In short it is a never-ending spiral. One has only to recall newspaper headlines and photographs about services provided by the hospitals to realise that all is not well. There is much dissatisfaction in the public sector of the health delivery system. This applies to nursing homes or even hospitals in the private sector too. Whilst it is but natural that some complaints are always present regarding charges for the services provided, what is apparent is that the services provided are not always up to the standards expected. There are reasons also for complaining and the Nepal Medical Council should be more involved in seeing that the public is protected.

Urban Health Centres

The National Urban Health Policy had been introduced from July 2010 with the object of providing free primary health services to poor people in the 58 municipalities all over Nepal. MoHP and the Ministry of Local Development will be responsible . Health Units will be set up as per the need and the plan is to have one Urban Health Volunteer for every 1,000 population, As per the free health service policy, 40 medicinal drugs at the District Hospital, 35 at PHC centres and 25 at sub-health posts will be free of cost. This is in keeping with the Interim Constitution 2007 which declared health as a fundamental right, as a result of which every citizen is entitled to receive basic health care from the state. The Prlmary Health Care Revitalisation Division under DoHS is seeing to this.

In June 2013 the Ministry of Local Development had announced the formation of 41 new municipalities in the country. This has not been implemented still. The new proposal before the cabinet is still for the 41 new municipalities to be created. There are 80 applicants. To be eligible to become a municipality there must be at least 20,000 population in the Terai and bigger valleys and 10,000 in the hilly and Himalayan region, infrastructure development etc. The above action has been taken in accordance with the Local Self Governance Act. With the worldwide increasing trend of urbanisation these new municipalities will soon come into being.

The Future

In an attempt to improve the standard of hospital services in the capital, Nepal Government had formed on 15th May, 1996 a 18 member Valley Hospitals Development and Management Co-ordination Committee under the chairmanship of the Health Minister. Besides the directors of the various hospitals in Kathmandu Valley the Committee also had representation of social workers and the mayors of the municipalities of Kathmandu Valley on a rotating basis, starting first with the Mayor of Kathmandu.

Though the Health Ministry has the largest number of employees, a point always propagated in the past was that there were not enough health workers of different categories to provide the health services. What is a reality is that there is always some headline in the papers about the non-availability of one grade of staff or another at the institution where there should be. One reads that the country faces a shortage of HRH though it produces substantial numbers of all grades. However the Second Nepal Health Sector Programme Implementation Plan (NHSP - IP II) noted that though the population increased by 35% since 1991 the workforce increased only by 3% and of this almost 25% was unskilled. No wonder therefore that it is always the peon who has to cater to the patients at the districts! In terms of health personnel a WHO document brought out in 2008 but based on figures of 2005 stated that there were 14.9 health workers of all grades for a population of 10,000. In comparison India had 25.0 and North Korea 113.0.

It was stated in Feb. 2013 that the MoHP however has a plan under the NHSP-IP (2010-2015) to get 14,932 workers soon. The MDGs Needs Assessment 2010 had stated that Nepal requires additionally 2,448 medical doctors, 3,418 nurses and 9,202 paramedical staff.

The expansion of the health services both in the government and the private sector is little compared to the increase of the population. The GoN proposes to encourage private institutions and has recently put out a draft document regarding 'State Non State Partnership (SNP) or Public-Private Partnership (PPP),' as a realistic way for delivering services in the health sector of Nepal. The New Health Policy II which is in the offing is expected to extend this further.

The outline of the policy gives ground for optimism. The stated aim is to provide a doctor in each of the 205 electoral constituencies that exist. It was planned to do this through the medium of the primary health care centres. This would be justified for people in the rural areas for the current ratio between urban to rural populations is 17:83. This will lead to services in the rural areas improving. The supervision by the District Health Office and the services by the doctors there, will meet the local demands so that people do not have to go further afield. The existing and proposed Regional and Zonal Hospitals will widen and improve their services so that people living along our border areas do not have to go outside the country or even to the central hospitals unless absolutely necessary. The new private medical schools will also help towards that end. With this taking place, the load at the centre should decrease. The central hospitals too will improve and expand the health services offered so that people do not have to go out of Nepal, thus saving both Indian and other foreign exchange. This means also that units like the new cancer and cardiac units at Bir Hospital must not be allowed to get run down and have to continue to provide service of high standard. With a satisfactory "on site", fully supervised health service and a functioning referral system it should lead to a "Health service that works." This presumption simply means that :-

i. People know about it.
ii. People are educated about how/when to use it.
iii. People have confidence in it and trust it.
iv. People see that the staffing is committed.
v. People see that the drugs and equipment are there and available for use by the people.

In an effort to extend services Nepal government with aid from external NGOs is trying to extend tele-medicine facilities in twenty five districts of the country. The existing state however can be exemplified by the case of the very accessible 15-bedded Baglung District Hospital the first phase of the construction of which has not in Oct. 2013, been completed in four years. Such are the realities.

PARTNERS FOR DEVELOPMENT IN HEALTH

The Annual Report of Department of Health Services, 2011-12 lists partners in the health sector as:

A. Multilateral Organisations: UNFPA, UNICEF, World Bank, World Food Programme (WFP) and WHO, etc.

B. Bilateral organisations: AusAID, Department for International Development (DFID), Deutsche Gesellschaft fur Internationale Zusammenarbeit (GIZ), Swiss Agency for Development and Co-operation and USAID etc.

C. INGOs involved in the field of health

D. NGOs working actively with the DoHS in the health sector

A description of some of these organisations are given in this Chapter.

A. MULTILATERAL ORGANISATIONS

United Nations Population Fund (UNFPA)

UNFPA, the United Nations Population Fund established in 1969, is an international development agency that promotes the right of every woman, man and young people to enjoy a life of health and equal opportunity and started its assistance to Government of Nepal (GoN) from the beginning. UNFPA has a two-pronged country programme as: a) At the national level, it supports development/update of RH policy/strategies, protocols, manuals and national standards and coordination, and b) At the district level, it support implementation of the national policy on decentralization in accordance with the Local Self-Governance Act (LSGA), 1999.

The major programme focus are on:

- Reproductive health;
- Population and development
- Gender
- Support development/update of policy/ strategies, protocols, manuals, national standards

The geographic coverage is nationwide with specific programs in 18 districts.

United Nations Children's Fund (UNICEF)

UNICEF supports the Government of Nepal with health and nutrition initiatives to further accelerate the attainment of MDGs 1, 4 and 5 in a sustainable manner.

UNICEF's work focuses on the most disadvantaged and on reducing inequity. Apart from supporting the government in strengthening ongoing health and nutrition programmes, interventions and institutional frameworks at policy and planning level, UNICEF has a very strong presence in the field and supports the piloting of new, innovative interventions and community-based approaches, such as the Community Based Management of Acute Malnutrition (CMAM), the Newborn Care Package (CB-NCP), low-dose vitamin A for newborns etc., through partnership with district line agencies, NGOs, and community-based organizations.

It strongly advocates and supports the sector-wide approach (SWAp) and supports in the area of child health and nutrition, maternal and neo-natal child health, immunisation, water sanitation and hygiene (WASH) and HIV/AIDS.

World Bank

The World Bank has prepared an Interim Strategy Note covering fiscal years 2012 and 2013. It proposes development programs that are consistent with the government of Nepal's Three-Year Plan.

Supporting the government of Nepal's overarching goal to build a peaceful, prosperous and just Nepal, the strategy is organized around three "pillars" which are: to enhance connectivity and productivity for growth; reducing vulnerabilities and improving resilience, and promoting access to better-quality services. Governance, accountability, gender equality, and social inclusion are themes that run across all three pillars.

The Community Action for Nutrition Project (1000 Golden Days "Sunaula Hazar Din") for Nepal is to improve attitudes and practices known to improve nutritional outcomes of women of reproductive age and children under the age of two. The budget comes from a trust fund (SAFANSI/SUNITA) supported by AusAID/DfID.

World Food Programme (WFP)

WFP's work in Nepal primarily targets the most food insecure and hard to reach districts of the Mid-and Far-Western Hills and Mountains. In 2013, WFP starts a new five-year Country Programme through actively supporting the Government of Nepal in tackling food insecurity, focusing on social safety nets in the areas of nutrition, education and rural livelihoods support. The interventions concentrate on the most vulnerable populations of the 9 districts: Dadeldhura, Baitadi, Darchula, Bajhang, Doti, Achham, Bajura, Salyan, and Solukhumbu in the mid- and far-west hills and mountain regions. where the most food-insecure people live.

World Health Organisation (WHO)

WHO is an inter-governmental specialized agency of the United Nations System, and has its objective as the attainment by all peoples of the highest possible level of health. WHO's collaborative work in Nepal are:

- Strengthening health system planning and management - health policy and health systems, and district health systems
- Control and prevention of diseases and disability -neglected tropical diseases, non-communicable diseases, oral health and mental Health
- Improving human resource development
- Child, adolescent and reproductive health - immunization, maternal and child health, and nutrition
- Emergency preparedness and response - epidemiological surveillance and disease prevention, TB, Malaria, and HIV
- Other areas include: blood safety, promoting healthy lifestyles, provisions of essential drugs, biological and environmental health and health related academic and public health Institutions and networks.

B. BILATERAL ORGANISATIONS

Australian Agency for International Development (AusAID)

Australia started providing assistance to Nepal as early as the 1960s. The Australian Government's Development Cooperation with Nepal supports peace building; governance, and issues associated with poverty and discrimination, including against women, dalits and janajatis. Australia also supports sustainable livelihood activities and activities that promote improved service delivery, particularly in health (HIV, child health and water and sanitation). The strategy was to adpot Sector-wide Approach (SWAp) for access; equity ; quality; and good governance in health. In terms of coverage, AusAID is one of the five pooling donors to NHSP II, hence AusAID's contributions is attributable to every program covering all 75 districts.

Department for International Development (DFID)

The Department for International Development's (DFID) strategy, in line with the principles of the Paris Declaration and International Health Partnership, is to support the GoN and other national partners to deliver health and HIV prevention and treatment services by providing flexible funding and engaging in national policy dialogue. DFID promotes a particular focus on:

- maternal, newborn and reproductive health,
- nutrition,
- HIV/AIDS,
- gender equity and social inclusion,
- governance and accountability,
- health policy and planning and health systems, and
- strengthening at national level and specific programs at sub-national level.

The objective of DFID's programme is the elimination of poverty in poorer countries. It is in this line that DFID is supporting to GoN, local NGOs and private partners in the above mentioned areas.

Deutsche Gesellschaft Für Internationale Zusammenarbeit (GIZ)

The Health Sector Support Programme (HSSP) - a joint programme of the Ministry of Health and Population (MoHP) and German International Cooperation (GIZ) is executed under the overall coordination of the MoHP. The overall objective of HSSP is to improve the access to effective health care services in particular for disadvantaged population groups of Nepal. The programme has three components: decentralization and quality improvement; improved access to health care services - social health protection and health financing; and sexual and reproductive health and rights with focus on young people.

HSSP works in the following 11 districts: Achham, Baitadi, Banke, Bardiya, Dadeldhura, Dailekh, Dang, Dhading, Doti, Jumla, Kailali, and Surkhet. Through policy advice to MoHP and central level partner institutions, the extent of HSSP's coverage is the population at large. The current focus are on areas of decentralization and quality improvement; fair financing and social health protection; promotion of sexual and reproductive health and rights with a focus on young people. Further it has harm reduction programme to access qualitative Opioid Substitution Therapy (OST) and HIV services for injecting drug users nationwide.

Indian Co-operation Mission (ICM)

The aid from India has been coming to Nepal from the fifties of the last century. Starting with the Tribhuvan Raj Path it has been in all sectors. In the health field India has been associated with the construction and expansion work in the cause of the under mentioned hospitals:

a. Paropakar Maternity & Womens' Diseases Hospital
b. Bir Hospital, now the National Academy of Medical Sciences set-up
c. Birendra Police Hospital

India has been assisting in Goitre Control through the supply of iodised salt.

The major work in the health sector now has been in the setting up of the deemed university B P Koirala Institute of Health Sciences at Dharan. The Trauma Centre at Bir Hospital is completed but still to start functioning. The ICM has however been helping many hospitals and committees by its donations of a number of ambulances every year.

Japan International Cooperation Agency (JICA)

Since 1950 there has been some collaboration between Japan and Nepal in the health field. Whilst Japan helped Nepal to establish the Tribhuban University Teaching Hospital it has also been interested in 2 major areas:

i. Promotion of public health activities especially in MCH and Community.
ii. Promotion of health / medical service delivery (1).

Swiss Agency for Development and Cooperation (SDC)

Rural Health Development Project (RHDP), a bilateral project of the Government of Nepal and the Swiss Agency for Development and Cooperation (SDC), aims at achieving the overall strategic objective of enhancing the status of disadvantaged groups by empowering them to exercise their rights and improving their capacity to claim better access to, and enjoy their rightful share of, national health services. RHDP began in Dolakha district in 1990 as the Primary Health Care, Mothers and Child Health and Family Planning Project, which eventually became the Rural Health Development Project in 1997. RHDP's coverage grew to Ramechhap (in 1996) and Okhaldhunga (in 2006) and currently focusses on Social inclusion; Empowerment; Primary health care; Family planning; and Health information.

United States Agency for International Development (USAID)

The United States Agency for International Development (USAID) has worked with the Government of Nepal (GoN)'s health programs for almost 60 years.

USAID works closely with the GoN and other stakeholders to advance remarkable progress to reduce maternal and child mortality and increase access to voluntary family planning and HIV/AIDS services. USAID's assistance aims to build the capacity of host country systems to improve the survival and quality of life of Nepalis through equitable and well-governed health systems that focus on five major areas in the fiscal year 2011/12:

- Family Planning/Reproductive Health (FP/RH) - reducing fertility by increasing access to and use of family planning services and commodities through the public and private sectors covering nationwide plus focused program in 51 districts.

- Maternal, Newborn and Child Health (MNCH) - reducing maternal, neonatal, infant and child mortality by increasing access to and use of key maternal, newborn and child health care services and commodities, and improving key household behaviours covering nationwide plus focused program in 24 districts.

- Nutrition – addressing under-nutrition among pregnant women, mothers, and children under two by promoting good nutritional practices and micronutrient intake in 28 districts.

- HIV and AIDS - preventing the further transmission of HIV and other sexually transmitted infections (STIs) among most-at-risk populations; building national capacity in strategic information, communications and program management; increasing access to quality care, support and treatment services through public and NGO sectors; and supporting national coordination of Nepal's multi-sectoral HIV program in 33 districts.

- Other Public Health Threats - controlling infectious and neglected tropical diseases and improving surveillance systems, including immunisation of preventable diseases on a nationwide scale. To provide clean water, sanitation and hygiene, it has worked in Achham, Surkhet plus 20 districts of Suaahara project. For rehabilitation physically to people living with disabilities it has covered seven districts namely, Banke, Dang, Kanchanpur, Kathmandu, Morang, Sarlahi, and Surkhet.

In addition, USAID provides technical assistance in service delivery, training, behaviour change communications, and logistics management and supply chain management for health commodities. It has also supported the targeted and national population based surveys, data analysis, assessments, and capacity building. The Agency has always concentrated on infrastructure building and overall development.

POINTS TO PONDER

The health services have increased markedly within the last twenty years because of the increased facilities not only in the capital but also in the different urban centres. The government has also tried to provide free treatment, inclusive of medicines at the District level according to the Primary Health Care facilities. As health is now constitutional right the responsibility are great. Hopefully health delivery and care will be vastly improved in the future.

References

1. Annual Reports of DoHS, 1994-95 to 2011-12
2. Country Health Profile Nepal. PPM&SD, MoH, June 1988.
3. Four Decades of Development - The History of U.S. Assistance to Nepal 1951-1991. CA Skerry, K Moran, KM Calavan, USAID, Kathmandu, 1991.
4. Long Term Health Plan, 1975-90. MoH, Pachali, Kathmandu.
5. Chhetri T, Nursing Services in Nepal, J Nep Med Assoc 1974; 12(5,6): 77-88.
6. Karki BB, Primary Health Care Development in Nepal, J Nep Med Assoc 1977; 15(4), 16-24
7. Evaluating the Strategies for Health For All by the Year 2000. PPM&SD, MoH/WHO, 1990.
8. Health Section of 9th Plan, National Planning Commission, 1998
9. Second Long Term Health Plan (1997-2017), PPFA&MD, MoH, 1999
10. Health in Nepal. Realities and Challenges. Ed. Mathura P Shrestha, Shanta L Mulmi, RECPHEC, Kathmandu, 1997
11. Nepal Population Report 2011.MoHP, Population Division.
12. Ghimire, P. No plan Holiday Now. The New Spotlight, 9th August, 2013.
13. TUTH Opening - Souvenir, 1986. & 31st Souvenir
14. Bir Hospital Centenary Souvenir, 1990 & 2011.
15. Birendra Police Hospital Bulletin, 2050 BS & 2068 BS.
16. Pokharel, Ram Prasad. From Darkness to Light (Nepali) , 2010.
17. Tilganga Eye Hospital - Annual Report, 2012

18. B.P. Koirala Memorial Cancer Hospital Souv.
19. Bhaktapur Cancer Hospital Bulletin. March 2013.
20. Hospital and Rehabilitation Centre for Disabled Children. Annual Report 2011.
21. Health Situation in South-East Asia Region 2001-2007. WHO, New Delhi, 2008

6.

PRIVATE AND PUBLIC MIX

PRIVATE MEDICINE AND HEALTH INSURANCE

Private medicine of some sort has been present from the early days of Rana rule in Nepal. The concept of the fee for service was started by no less a person than Jung Bahadur when he utilised the service of the British legation doctor for vaccination. Then later, during the subsequent periods of Bir Shumsher and Chandra Shumsher's premiership, a number of doctors, mostly from India were employed in the health sector by the civil and military authorities. As the scale of pay was meagre the personnel were allowed to practice with a "Fee for service" (FFS) concept. But even then the fees were not exorbitant as the population at large was very poor. Coupled with this, some health workers were brought into the country from British India on short visits and it was customary too, to pay for their services.

During the time that the British were in India a number of missionary groups were working on the borders of Nepal. From there some went inwards to the western parts of Nepal, such as Dandeldhura whilst others went northwards from the Nautanwa area in southern Nepal. At the time of the last days of Rana rule in 1951, the United Mission to Nepal was officially able to enter Nepal. This involvement had all begun following a six-month trip by Dr. Robert Fleming who was accompanied by his wife Dr. Bethel and Dr. Carl Taylor to study birds in Nepal (1).

Over the course of the years, as the standard of the living increased, a substantial percentage of the population opted for the private facilities that had gradually come into being in the capital. WHO came up also with the concept of public and private mix. Access to both public and private facilities varies considerably by income group with the wealthier having higher utilisation of both public and private facilities. The private hospitals and nursing homes are increasing day by day. The current concept has become PPP or private-public partnership.

Group Practice to Polyclinic concepts

Sajha Swasthya Seva was a offshoot of the co-operative movement that had been introduced into Nepal in the sixties. The idea was to have in the major towns, chemist shops within the hospital compound or nearby it with the object of selling medicines at reasonable prices. The reason for this was that people at that time were being overcharged, if not forced to pay exorbitant prices for life saving drugs, which were in effect the final arbitrator of life and death. Over the course of the years, another body known as the Chemists and Druggists Association came into being and attempted to try to standardise services and prices.

The main Sajha medicine shop tried to provide services during the hours that the hospital outpatient services were not functioning. Thus some young doctors of Bir and other hospitals provided almost 24-hour consultation service and the specialists provided service for a consultative fee during the afternoon or evening at the Sajha clinic. This was the start of group practice concept at Kathmandu. Following this, others such as Siddhi Polyclinic and Hargaans were also started. Up to this time some surgeons had some inpatient and operating facilities in their clinics. The pioneer in the development of admitting facilities and private medicine was the Kathmandu Nursing Home, established in 1986.

As more applications were made for the registration, availability of facilities and running of nursing homes, the Ministry of Health constituted in mid 2043 BS a special committee under the chairmanship of the Chief of the Planning Division. Contacts were made with institutions in Bangladesh, India and Thailand with the idea of framing Rules and Regulations concerning nursing homes and their functioning. This activity, started on ad-hoc basis, was not sustained and it was not until 1994 that some regulations were framed.

In the succeeding years many new doctors did not opt for government service and the development of nursing homes was more rapid. Many doctors, on retiring from government service became more active in private medicine whilst other even opted for it, leaving government or semi-government jobs. From July 1984 the TU Teaching Hospital started having both morning and afternoon sessions, and some fifteen months later there was notice of "no private practice" at TUTH. Some of the medical faculty therefore opted out and started working in the various private medicine facilities that had sprung up in the capital.

It was with the realism that the government in the developing countries would not be able to provide the desired or even the required health facilities that the concept of private medicine was put forward and encouraged. Whilst the developed countries had safeguards for the protection of the public, such facilities were however minimal. The Nepal Medical Council, though formed in 1964 has never been very active in this regard. It was much later that being conscious of these rules and their own responsibilities that the Department of Health Services sent out inspection teams to find out what the situation was.

In the meantime other nursing homes sprouted up in the capital and other urban centres in the country such as Biratnagar, Janakpur, Birgunj, Bharatpur and Nepalgunj. Some other privately run hospitals also came into being such as the Model Hospital at Bagh Bazaar. A small district hospital, Bajrabarahi People's Hospital, was started at Makwanpur during 1994 and by Feb. 1997 was running 25 beds inclusive of maternity services. A further trend was that more recently the various Nursing Homes have been converted into "Hospitals & Research Centres".

The 20 bedded Lunkarandas-Gangadevi Chaudhari Charity Hospital at Duhabi was inaugurated in December 1995. This hospital built and to be supported by an industrial house was the first of its kind from two different angles. Whilst it was the first hospital in the country to be run by an industrial house it was also one, which as per the name, was run on a charitable basis and not for profit. Such categories were:

a. Public sector: All government provided health institutions
b. Not-for-profit sector: Voluntary, Missions, Community and / or Trusts run health institutions
c. Organised Private sector: Nursing Homes, Private Hospitals, Co-operatives and care provided by fee for service practitioners
d. Private informal sector: Care provided by traditional healers such as *dhamis, jhankris, jharphuks* and others who have not had any formal training

The National Health Policy 1991, states that there will be increasing opportunities for the private sector and the NGOs in the delivery of the health services. The suggestion has been made that, "we also need to strengthen existing public medical hospitals so that people are not forced to go to private institutions due to lack of choice." Rules and regulations for Nursing Homes had been made in 2006 (2061 BS) but had still to be implemented. Only effective rules will guarantee proper functioning.

The criteria set so far are on the basis of the facilities being extended by the nursing homes and the party concerned must accept these before registration can be done.

Criteria for hospitals / nursing homes are dependent on whether they are for:

a. Fifteen to twenty-five beds
b. Twenty-six to fifty beds
c. Fifty-one to hundred beds
d. Hundred to two hundred beds.

The basic requirements for diagnosis are a laboratory and also a X-ray Department. On the curative side, a 24 hours emergency service must be provided including a minor theatre, major theatre, operation room and isolation room. Three essentials free services, which must be catered, for and for which related material will be supplied by the health ministry are:

1. Rehydration services
2. Family Planning & MCH services
3. Health Education services

It is obligatory to have one free bed for poor patients for every fifteen beds being run by the hospital or nursing home. These rules are however being flouted for there are no provisions for effective implementation.

This registration for functioning is done by the Department of Cottage Industries *(Gharelu Udyog)* on the basis of recommendation by the Health Ministry. The permission is usually given on a temporary basis for one year and there is no provision for making this either permanent or cancelling it.

There is no disputing the fact that the Nursing Homes have been responsible for the development of diagnostic facilities. Whereas tertiary care facilities of the government or the University for that matter did not do kidney transplant pleading the non-existence of a Human Organ Transplantation Act, the private medicine sector went ahead with and such an operation was performed for the first time in Nepal at the Everest

Nursing Home on 27th May, 1995. It was not a success. It was the rush to do such operations at other places, with patients and donors from outside of the country that made the government constitute a special committee in the first week of July 1995 to look into all aspects of renal transplants. The Human Organ Transplantation Act took over four years to be enacted.

The Association of Private Health Institutions Nepal (APHIN) was established in 1998 and has periodically held seminars and meetings with a view to improving the facilities offered to the public (2). Newspapers have quoted the MoHP stating that "it is necessary to have legal provision for the setting up of nursing homes. However though some criteria have been set up for nursing homes to be opened by the Nepalese, nothing has been laid down for starting nursing homes with foreign investment."

Private Nursing Homes and Hospitals

The period of more investment in private medicine in Nepal was the starting in 1996 of two parties from India viz the Escorts and the Apollo Group setting up of diagnostic and later inpatient facilities in Nepal.

Because of increasing demand for better health care facilities a number of nursing homes too were started by Nepali doctors. After a few years, to avail of increased facilities given by the government, some nursing homes changed their names to hospitals and research centres. With the concept of Private / Public Mix being accepted quite a number of nursing homes started in the urban centres of the country. This trend has been most marked in the capital as there has been over the years a marked increase in the population. The shifting of people from the rural areas to towns or urban centres of Nepal has resulted in a similar trend elsewhere.

The MoHP, considers non-state partnership as a long-term sustainable strategy for improving the health status of the people of Nepal, especially women, children and under-served sections of the population. They issued in Sept. 2012 a draft for consultation. Whist big hospitals are being built, the MoHP hasn't been able to lay down standards for health care institutions above 100 beds. The important point to be noted is that whatever criteria are laid down, these must be followed by both the public and private institutions. Many of the existing institutions are in residential houses converted for use as hospitals. There is doubt about the safety of patients at times of disasters such as fire and earthquakes. The GoN in

2011 had issued a directive for hospital buildings to be as per the Building Code 2003 and Building Bye-laws of April 2013 (3).

Eastern Region

Birat Nursing Home: This institution has been in existence for some years. It was part of a teaching hospital at one stage and is in the process of becoming one again. It provides services in various specialities.

Central region: The maximum number of these are functioning in the capital are:

Alka Hospital: This institution was started at Jwalakhel as Alka Pharmacy in 2052 BS, became Alka Polyclinic in 2057 and finally into a hospital in 2063. Though started with only 15 beds it is now being increased to 100 bed capacity. It has recently expanded its services and is functioning in the same area. It is also running a Bachelor course – BN for nurses.

Annapurna Neuro Hospital: This is mainly an institution for neurological cases but also caters to patients with other problems.

B & B Nursing Home: This hospital in Lalitpur has been providing specialized health services to the people of the capital since 1997. It now has 300 beds, to provide various speciality services and is forming cardiac and cancer centres. It also has the B & B Institute that trains nurses.

Bharosa Hospital: This hospital at Baneshwar provides both in and out patient service.

Binayak Hospital & Maternity Home: Currently this hospital is located at Samakhusi Chowk in Kathmandu. Started originally at Chabahil in 2052 BS, this hospital is directed towards serving the middle and lower middle class of Kathmandu residents. It provides services in many specialities. Started originally with 25 beds, it now has 55 and is in the process of increasing capacity to 100.

Blue Cross Hospital: This hospital at Tripureshwar was started in 1992 with CT facilities and a Polyclinic. It became first the Blue Cross Nursing Home and then the 30 bedded Blue Cross Hospital with an additional 7 ICU beds in 2010.

Dr. Iwamura Memorial Hospital: This hospital at Sallaghari, Bhaktapur was built in 1998 as a private institute and is functioning as such. Noboro

Iwamura, who was 10 at the time of the bombing of Hiroshima & Nagasaki developed blood dyscrasia but went on to study medicine. Dr. Noboro Iwamura who worked for over twenty years in Nepal and had served part of the time in Bhaktapur working in the fight against tuberculosis. Japanese Rotarians of International District 2640 and also 2680 helped in the setting up and the running of the hospital. It has 51 beds and is being upgraded into a 100 bedded hospital. It also trains various grades of middle level HRH at the Iwamura College of Health Sciences that it runs.

Everest Hospital: This hospital started its work as the Everest Nursing home in 2044 BS as the 25 bedded Everest Nursing Home providing specialist services. It is now 100 bedded and also runs a training institute for producing middle level HRH.

Grande International Hospital: This hospital, with the collaboration of the Samitivej Hospital of Bangkok, has been established at Dhapasi, Kathmandu. It has a capacity of 234 beds with state of the art technology and following a soft opening in Jan. 2013, started providing it services to the public.

Himal Hospital: This institution was started in 2044 BS as a Nursing Home & Research Centre. It now provides specialist service in many areas.

Hospital for Advanced Medicine & Surgery Pvt. Ltd. (HAMS): This institution was started at New Baneshwar in 1998 with 50 beds in the form of ICU, NICU, PICU and general ward. Its mission is to provide quality health service with the help of modern and cost effective techniques.

Janatrantrik Hospital: Apollo Health Care and Research Centre Ltd was registered in Nepal and ran a 100-bedded hospital at Balaju for some years. This hospital was initially known as Siddhartha Apollo Hospital. As from the middle of 2008 it is under a new management supported by the CPM (Maoists). It is now Janatantrik Hospital under a new management and this hospital group is in the process of setting up the Ayushman Medical College.

Kantipur Hospital: This hospital established in 2054 BS has been providing multi-speciality service in the Baneshwar area for a number of years. It has both in and out-patient service. There are 100 beds out of which 6 are in ICU.

Kathmandu Hospital Pvt. Ltd.: Originally started in 1986 as the

Kathmandu Nursing Home it continued as hospital from 1997 initially with 50 beds with the intention of increasing it in due course to 100. It provides service in various specialities.

Medicare National Hospital & Research Centre Ltd: Was established in 1990 by its parent organisation Medicare Nepal as the Medicare Nursing Home with 10 beds which were increased by stages to 30, 75 and now 100. It now provides various services at its permanent building at Chabahil.

Model Hospital: This is situated in the vicinity of the Exhibition Road in the centre of Kathmandu and is providing much needed service to Kathmandu dwellers. It is also trying to start a medical college.

National Dental Hospital: Established in 2054 BS and provides various services in dental specialities. It has a separate wing which conducts free dental camps in different parts of the country.

National Institute of Neurological Science & Allied Sciences: Better known as the **Neuro Hospital.** This private institution providing facilities for neurological and other services. It has been conducting a neurological academic programme under the aegis of the Kathmandu University.

Nobel Hospital: This is a newly opened hospital at Sinamangal, Kathmandu is offering multi- speciality services.

Norvic International Hospital: The first phase in 1997 was the starting of a Heart Centre by the Norvic Health Care and Research Centre at Thapathali, Kathmandu. It has expanded in the last fifteen years and is becoming a 200 bedded entity soon. Plans are afoot also to upgrade it into an academic institution.

Om Hospital & Research Centre: It was originally established in 1990 as Om Nursing Home is now at Chabahil, Kathmandu. This hospital came into prominence by helping infertile couples to have children by way of the 'in-vitro fertilisation' or 'test tube' babies. It offers various speciality service and now has a capacity of 175 beds.

Sarvanga Swasthya Sewa Sadan: This hospital was started in 1992 in Lalitpur. Special facilities are available for women's' health and urology. It conducts free health camps periodically.

Shankarapur Hospital: This hospital at Narayantar in Jorpati was established in 2064 BS with 50 beds and has expanded over the years to

100 beds. It has ICU beds and also trains HRH such as health assistants, nurses and laboratory technicians (4).

Sumeru Hospital: This 100 bedded hospital at Dhapakhel, Lalitpur is well equipped and is in the process of increasing its capacity by hundred beds more.

The Kidney Centre: This centre has been functioning since last ten years and providing dialysis to a number of patients of not only the capital but from different parts of the country. It is helping to start such facilities at Nepalgunj.

Vayodha Hospital: This is a new hospital recently established at Balkhu near the Ring Road, with state of the art facilities. It has currently 50 beds for inpatients and has multi-speciality services.

Venus International Hospital: This is the new set up of the original Nepal-China Boda Hospital that had been inaugurated in the urban area of New Baneshwar by the Health Minister in June 2009. It has both in and out-patient facilities.

Thus Kathmandu has over the last decade seen a number of hospitals coming up in different parts of the valley. A recent survey of 252 samples which was done found that choice for treatment varied because of certain factors. These were proximity, faith in the doctor or institution, hearsay or recommendation etc. and is as follows:

Table 6. 1 Reasons for choosing institution for treatment

Reasons	Number
Doctor working at the Institution	139
Recommendation from friend	33
Cost consideration (Expensive)	25
Hospital facilities, amenities	42
Others (Proximity etc.)	13

The article by Ms. Cilla Khatry stated that there were now 99 registered hospitals in the valley. Kathmandu patients prefer to go to India or elsewhere as they feel that the hospitals here are not reliable. Some always go to the extent of getting their tests done at different hospitals to see if they are credible and match or not (5).

The government in turn does not have standards for hospitals with over 100 beds and the sad part is that whilst it expects the private sector caretakers to maintain these standards the hospitals of GoN have also got to be functioning as per the rules. The standards sent out in 2004 in the Building Code have to be updated, and all other factors pertaining to environment have to be considered. Facilities for value added tax (VAT), tax rebate or facilities for starting health care should be clearly spelt out. It should not be necessary to call a hospital a 'research centre' just to get tax free facilities for import of equipment or vehicles in the name of ambulances. In fact it would be 'unethical' to do research on patients who are admitted there without the informed consent of the patient concerned. As far as the teaching medical colleges are concerned, the Nepal Medical Council is supposed to look after these matters rather than just counting the number of beds as is done at present (6).

Western Region

Unity Hospital: The 'Unity Conglomerate' had started various services as a co-operative organisation in 2007. Most of this organisation collapsed in 2010 but the hospital at Pokhara continues to function.

Crimson Hospital: It is at Butwal and is a private hospital with 50 beds. An additional 200 is being added soon.

Mid-Western Region

Rapti Life Care Hospital Pvt. Ltd: This hospital at Tulsipur, Dang has been set up to help women and children and disadvantaged individuals. It is an institution with 55 beds. It also runs the Health Science Nursing Institute.

Far Western Region

Bayalpata Hospital: This hospital which is the result of collaborative effort between the NGO Nyaya Health and the MoHP is already serving the people at Badelgada, Achham.

Amisha Hospital: Even Bajhang has a private hospital which opened its doors in 2010. A news item in August 2013 however stated that as the District Hospital at Bajhang was not functioning due to lack of doctors, it had been run for some years with MDGPs supported by Nick Simons Institute.

Community Hospitals

The first organisation in this category may be said to be the **People's Jana**

Chikitsalaya, which was started at Chhetrapati years ago. It was officially registered as a social organisation in 2045 BS. It receives support from locals and from NGOs and individuals from different parts of the world. It also provides dental services and has facilities for admission.

People, having realised the difficulty of getting health services from the government have also tried to avail of services by their own efforts when nursing homes came up in different parts of Nepal. This process has been going on for two or three decades but more so since the nineties when a general awakening occurred in the country.

The **Kali Gandaki Hospital (KGH)** was an example of a community-based health care. KGH as an institution was started in 1989 at Rampur, Keladi, Palpa by a group of social workers with their own resources and providing PHC services to a remote population. The 15-bedded hospital was similar to the District Hospital set up of GoN. As from mid-August 1993 it has been shifted to Kawasoti, Nawalparasi and steps are being taken to make it 51 bedded.

The foundation stone was laid on 30th Jan. 1998 of the **Hetauda People's Hospital** to be constructed by the community. Though there was initial enthusiasm periodic newspaper reports have suggested that the enthusiasm has flagged and not much has occurred since.

Mid Sept. 1998 saw the foundation laying of **Satya Sai Hospital** at Kirtipur. It is still to function properly. A Kirtipur Hospital is being run by the Model Hospital group.

Other recent efforts by different people with community participation have also been attempted in this direction. One reads of *mahayagya* being held to collect funds to set up a school, or a health clinic or even a hospital.

Bearing in mind the load at the Bharatpur Hospital the community is collecting funds to build a public hospital at Ratnanagar Municipality area in the Terai.

The transfer of the District Hospital to representatives of the local community at Lamjung led to the institution being much better managed and functioning better.

In May 2005, a Swiss citizen, paralysed during the course of climbing has very generously funded the setting up of a **Pasang Lhamu Nicole**

Hospital of 13 beds with a community oriented health service set up at Chaurikhark in the Solu area. This is the third hospital in the Solu area the other two being at Khunde and Phaplu. Besides the locals they will also cater to the needs of the trekkers and mountaineers.

The **Star Hospital** is a 50 bedded Community Hospital based at Sanepa Chowk, Lalitpur. It was established in 2006 by 43 promoters. Its objective is to provide service to middle and lower middle class.

A 50-bedded community hospital is also being run at Pharping in the Dakshinkali area. The VDC is taking active part in setting it up with the aid of two NGOs - New Cedel and Himalayan Height.

The 60 **Nagarik Community Teaching Hospital** at Gatthaghar Bhaktapur was set up in 2008 with the backing of 560 shareholders. It is now functioning as a 100 bedded general hospital and has 10 ICU beds.

A **Phul Kumari Mahato Memorial Hospital** with 24 beds was opened by President Dr. Ram Baran Yadav at Siraha in May 2012 to serve the community there.

A **Mahendra Narayan Nidhi Memorial Hospital** was set up in the capital. As it sited near the Pashupatinath it is hoped that it will provide services to pilgrims coming to the holy site.

A 30 bedded **Worker's Care Hospital** is in the process of being constructed at Sonapur in Siraha on the initiative of the Workers Savings & Lending Co-operative.

The local community at Khotang started a 15 bedded community hospital providing maternity, child care and orthopaedic services in October 2013.

State of Hospital Beds

The state of hospital beds in the country has varied over the years. At the end of the Seventh Five Year Plan period there were 12 districts without any hospital or health centre where there were facilities for admission. The number of hospitals - governmental, non-governmental and private at the end of 1990 was 123, with a total bed capacity of 4,717 beds. (This figure of hospitals number was subsequently corrected, as many were never opened or functioning). In terms of a population of 19 millions it worked out to just 2.4 beds for every 10,000 population.

At the end of 2004 the number of hospital beds in the country had gone to 12,889 for a total population of 25,151,423. This works out to about one bed for 1951 population or 5.1 beds for every 10,000 of the population. This statistic compares very poorly with the figures for other SAARC countries.

Table 6.2 State of hospital beds in 2013

Types of Hospitals	Number of hospitals	Number of beds
Government hospitals	113	8,160
Medical College Teaching Hospitals	14	8,776
Private hospitals	141	6,338
Other hospitals	10	677
Eye hospitals	17	1,415
Total	**295**	**25,366**

Source: Based on Table in Dr. Sitaram Adhikary's "Chikitsha Shikshama Fadko" 2013. (7)

NB: New guidelines of NMC have reduced the number of beds required in that a medical college with intake of 50 must have 405 beds, that with 100 intake needs 535 and that with 150 must have 750. The new figure for the 14 private medical schools is therefore around 10,000. What must be remembered is that not all of the required beds of the medical colleges are functional.

It is stated that a figure of one bed for one thousand population is a minimum one. On the basis of this Nepal would in 2013 require a minimum of 26,000 beds. However as we do have about 26,000 estimated beds, the ratio of hospital beds to a population comes to 1 bed for 1,000 population. This is the recommended state.

Health Insurance

With the intention of providing free health services to the disadvantaged, the government is also in the process of starting health insurance.

To this effect, the MoHP announced that it was implementing the National Social Heath Insurance Scheme in the first phase in five districts (Ilam, Sarlahi, Banke, Kaski and Baglung) as from 1st March 2013; the idea is to increase people's access to health care. The GoN has completed a draft of Social Health Insurance Policy to provide universal health coverage to people.

SOCIAL SERVICE NATIONAL CO-ORDINATION COUNCIL (SSNCC)

The Social Service Co-ordination Council (SSNCC) was formed to regulate the various social service organisations that were coming into the country to do welfare work. Most of the agencies were interested in working in areas, which were easily accessible from the capital where their central office was situated. Failing that, it was in areas, which were near urban centres or tourist attracting spots. It led, thus to an influx of such agencies in certain areas and none in others. There was a question that some of the organisations may be involved in using funds for making religious conversion financially attractive. Last but not least were the requests to do such work in areas, which were politically sensitive. The fact was that social service work within the country needed to be regulated. It was this background that led to the formation of the Social Services National Coordination Council in 2034 BS with late Queen Aishwarya as the Chairperson. The work involved was divided into six main areas:

1. Health Services Coordination Committee (HSCC)
2. Child Welfare Coordination Committee (CWCC)
3. Disabled Welfare Coordination Committee (DWCC)
4. Women Services Coordination Committee (WSCC)
5. Community Services Coordination Committee (CSCC)
6. Youth Activities Coordination Committee (YACC)

Following the government decision, a number of the International NGOs decided that they had their commitment to the people who had provided them funds and so were not in a position to betray that trust by acting in the manner that was being demanded of them. They also desired more transparency in the method of working and so a number of the INGOs decided to quit Nepal. This objection has been maintained over the years.

After the first five years of working and experience it was decided to combine the activities of the DWCC with that of the HSCC and form a new sixth coordination committee viz: Hindu Religion Services Coordination Committee (HRSCC).

In the health field a substantial amount of work was done by some of the agencies that were in the HSCC. Whist the Nepal Netra Jyoti Sangh (NNJS) was involved in setting up Eye Hospitals and providing eye care, the Save the Children Fund of the different countries such as UK, USA, Norway and Japan were involved in activities related to children or the community.

Following the political changes in 1990 this Council functioned under the chairmanship of the Hon. Minister for Labour and Social Service. The registration of NGOs and INGOs has been simplified leading to a surge of activity in the social field. The number of NGOs and INGOs working in Nepal increased appreciably after 1990.

Those who operate at a local level and are not Western *mukhi*[1] can be registered with the local administration or the District Administration Office. There has been a lot of criticism in the local press in that many of the NGOs are not what they appear to be and have individual interests. The charge is that many have been raking off the dollars meant for social service for the disadvantaged.

In 1992, the Social Welfare Act 2049 BS was passed and a new Social Welfare Council was constituted. It had the Minister for Social Welfare as Chairperson and representation from Parliament, National Planning Commission and from six related ministries. Representatives from NGOs doing social service of which one at least should be female plus individuals doing social work were nominated to the Council.

The new Act made it a special point not to limit the activities of the Non-Governmental Social Service Organisations to just social welfare and rehabilitation but also involve in developmental activities. The new executive body did not come into being immediately and took almost one year to be formed.

In 2046 BS, there were said to be just 300 plus registered NGOs. By the end of Asar 2055 BS or mid July 1998, there are said to be a total of 7,389 NGOs registered with the SWC for working in this country. There are also some others registered with the CDOs at the local level and these have not been included in these figures. The breakdown of the NGOs working in the districts of the five development regions of the country in 1998 and 2005 is as given in Table 6.3.

1. Mukhi meaning influenced, Western oriented

Table 6.3 Number of NGOs by Development Regions in 1998 and 2005

Regions	Number of NGOs in 1998	Number of NGOs in 2005
Eastern	825	1,968
Central	4,588	10,216
Western	1,104	2,208
Mid-Western	544	1,122
Far-Western	328	911
Total	**7,389**	**16,425**

The NGOs registered with the SWC have also been categorised by their related activity into the ten different areas as given in Table 6.4 below. At the end of 2061 BS or mid April, 2005 the total number of NGOs had reached 16,425.

The particulars of the ten areas into which the NGOs were categorised are as follows:

Table 6.4 No of NGOs registered with SWC by areas in different years

S.No.	Areas of Work	1998	2005	2012
1	AIDS & Abuse Control	32	55	88
2	Child Welfare	164	508	951
3	Community & Rural Development	3,641	9,147	18,625
4	Educational Development	63	198	492
5	Environmental Development	470	972	1,318
6	Handicapped & Disabled	203	342	597
7	Health Services	177	375	703
8	Moral Development	197	442	876
9	Women Services	723	1,457	2,305
10	Youth Services	1,619	2,929	4,321
	Total number of NGOs	**7,389**	**16,425**	**30,276**

- This is the total number of NGOs who have been given registration over the 33 years period of 2034-2067 BS.

Number of NGOs given registration in 2068/69 BS was 568.

Number of NGOs given registration in 2069/70 BS was 572.

What was soon realised was that this division could not be watertight. For example, some NGOs dealing with deafness, blindness or even leprosy have been registered in the health group whilst others were in the handicapped/disabled one. Furthermore the fact that one NGO was registered with one group did not mean that it could not work in another area. Most worked in many areas/sectors and so the involvement was actually multi-sectoral.

Though it is stressed that most of the NGOs should be rural oriented the agency concerned might go to an area for one of various reasons such as accessibility, donor visibility, political patronage etc. As an example, the Sindhupalchowk area, which came into prominence because of the flesh trade and AIDS susceptibility, has many NGOs working in this area. In such a situation the question arises as to who should get credit for in reality it was almost a combined effort of all the NGOs working in the area.

In November 2008, the Social Welfare Council (SWC) was suddenly dissolved citing irregularities in its functioning. It has now been reorganised and continues to function but not without political influence from time to time.

With the frequent change in governments, there is great difficulty in proper functioning of the SWC. One general complaint is that executive officers continue to run the SWC without any reference to the other members. It is doubtful as to how much has been achieved as no real assessment of work is done and publicly reported.

NON GOVERNMENT ORGANISATIONS (NGOs)

The member secretary of Social Welfare Council (SWC) while being questioned about NGOs and INGOs in the country remarked that there were in mid 2013 a total of 37,400 NGOs and 175 INGOs affiliated with the SWC. Of this number however, he felt that only about 10% of NGOs are actively working (8). It is a known fact that about a quarter of the INGOs are yet to co-ordinate with the local bodies while carrying out their development projects. Another feeling about them is that most are working in areas which are quite near and accessible. There are a lot of complaints about transparency plus duplication and the charge is made that the same data is reused by a number of them.

Association for the Welfare of the Mentally Retarded (AWMR)

Founded in 1981 during the observance of the International Year of

Disabled Persons (IYDP). It was registered with the SSNCC in 1985 and subsequently with the Social Welfare Council (SWC). The aims and objectives of the AWMR are to better meet the individual needs of people with mental retardation within the complexities of modern society. Besides the central offices there are a number of branches outside the capital.

A brief description of major NGOs working in the health field are agiven below:

B P Health Foundation

The B P Health Foundation was established in 1991 with the objective of improving the eye health of the Nepalese population. It is estimated that 1.56% of the population suffer from low vision and blindness in one or both eyes. Cataract account as cause of two thirds of the blindness. Vitamin A deficiency, injury, trachoma, glaucoma and diabetic retinopathy are other causes (9).

Besides providing eye health services and doing research, the foundation is involved in the production of manpower at the National Eye Health Manpower Training Centre at Kathmandu in collaboration with Tribhuvan University, Lions Club and Sight First programmes. It has recently set up the Nepal Children's Eye and Ear Hospital and Rehabilitation Services (CHEERS) at Manohara, Kathmandu. The foundation also conducts eye camps in various parts of Nepal.

Family Planning Association of Nepal (FPAN)

This association was established at Kathmandu in 1958 with the initiative of the Nepal Medical Association and the Pathfinder Fund. The first woman Asst. Health Minister Mrs. Dwarika Devi Thakurani was its president. It celebrates 18th September as FP Day. It became a member of the International Planned Parenthood Federation (IPPF) in 1960. In the seventies many branches were opened and there was a lot of activity. Later in 1992 it was providing about 25% of the family planning services plus supplementing those of the government. By mid-1997, the Association had extended its activities in 33 districts, 771 Village Development Committees (VDC) and provides services to nearly 1 million married women of reproductive age (MWRA) (10). The activities of FPAN comprise educational programmes, natural family planning programmes and sterilisation programmes that are conducted through its clinics and the rural family health projects. It is estimated that 21% of married women practise contraception. Female sterilization is more popular than that of males. The method mix of FP acceptors in 2002 showed that Depo Provera was most popular method (48%) followed by condom (27%) and pills. FPAN has been playing an active role for the liberalisation of abortion laws. As a result of this, new provisions have been made in the Eleventh Amendment of the Muluki Ain. It has currently 3 static clinics and also runs mobile ones in five districts every year. FPAN also has activities to improve women's status and is running training programmes for income-generating skills. FPAN's mission statement is for promoting and providing quality sexual and reproductive health services to women, men and youth and to support the government in meeting the demand for these services throughout the country. Combating gender based violence is one of the most important programmes implemented by FPAN (11).

Friends of the Disabled

Since 1985 this NGO has been providing comprehensive rehabilitation care to underprivileged physically disabled children of Nepal. This organisation has been working with the support of the Terres des hommes that has its headquarters in Switzerland. Following shifting from its initial site at Jorpati it ran a hospital and rehabilitation centre for disabled children in a rented facility at Dhobighat, Jawalakhel. King Birendra formally inaugurated the permanent facility of the Hospital and Rehabilitation Centre for Disabled Children (HRDC), near Banepa on 17th April 1998. This hospital has a total of 72 beds for inpatients and rehabilitation services. The plans are to increase its capacity to 100 beds (12).

In Dec. 2011 Dr. Ashok Banskota, Chief of the institution received the "World of Children Health Award" for the work that HRDC has been doing for the cause of disabled children for last 27 years.

Grace Hospital

In November 2009 the Grace Hospital supported by the Christian Community opened its doors at Chuchepati, Chabahil. It was inaugurated by the then PM Mr. Madhav Kumar Nepal.

Heart Foundation

This was founded in 1978 and has been active in making people aware about heart disease. It is also involved in anti-smoking campaign.

Himalaya Health Care

This NGO was started in 1992, which is supported by many well-wishers in the travel trade. Besides conducting various medical and dental camps it helps in educational and income generating activities.

Lions Club

A branch of Lions International was formed on 7th May 1971. The first Lions Club was that of Kathmandu which came into being in 1972. It is a separate entity in Nepal, and referred to as District No. 325. The Lion movement then gradually increased in the country. The many clubs are involved in running a number of health clinics, plus periodic eye and ear camps in various parts of the country. The clinic at Naya Baneshwar, Kathmandu also has adjoining 15 bedded facilities. Increased stress is being laid on eye care too by this NGO.

On 11th Feb. 1995, Mr. Man Mohan Adhikari, then prime minister laid the foundation stone of the B. P. Koirala Lions Centre for Ophthalmic Studies (BPKLCOS) in the Teaching Hospital Complex at Maharajgunj. This started functioning in 1996 and has been doing eye surgery on outpatient basis.

Currently worried that the literacy rate of the country is not going up as planned by the government, Lions Club International District 325A has started an endowment fund of ten million rupees, the interest from which will be utilized for scholarship to students from far flung areas.

Marwari Welfare Committee

Started in 2010 BS after a public collection of Rs. 459/-, this organisation was officially inaugurated by King Tribhuvan on Basanta Panchami of that same year. In 2014 BS it started functioning from its own premises at Phasikeba in the heart of Kathmandu. The organisation also runs a hostel for children of leprosy-afflicted persons. It celebrated its fifty years of existence by starting a Homeopathic Hospital at its central site. It is always involved in setting up First Aid Health Camps to help devotees at times of religious functions such as during *Shivaratri*.

Maryknoll Nepal

This organisation has been working in Nepal for many years in the field of providing help to the mentally retarded. It has been running a rehabilitation centre near Sundarijal. Under an agreement signed with JICA in Jan. 1998, Maryknoll Nepal will construct a 2 storey Mental Hospital at Nayapati, Kathmandu. There will also be facilities to treat the ill on an outpatient's basis by providing services such as occupational therapy and vocational activities.

MIREST / Nepal

In the absence of local bodies organisations such as Media Initiative for Rights, Equity and Social Transportation (MIREST / Nepal) have evolved a way to make those in charge at the VDC more transparent and socially accountable. MIREST / Nepal has been working with programmes that are running in seven district headquarters, three municipalities and 21 VDCs in the country.

Mrigendra Samjhana Medical Trust

Dr. Mrigendra Raj Pandey, a physician and a social worker established Mrigendra Medical Trust in 1975 as a local NGO. Its work is devoted to promotion of health services and social welfare activities in the backward rural areas of Nepal. Besides medical care the Trust also provides education, drinking water and income and employment generating facilities. It has been working in Sundarijal, Pharping, Dakshinkali and Jumla areas. It has been actively involved in anti-smoking campaign. The present name of the Trust has been in use since 1994.

Nepal Anti Tuberculosis Association (NATA)

This organisation came into being as a result of the efforts of its ten founding members in July 1953. It was initially known as Nepal Tuberculosis Association and had the then PM Matrika P. Koirala as its founder President. However its official inauguration by late King Mahendra only took place on 13th Mangsir, 2020 BS. Since then the association has observing this day as 'Anti TB Day'. The Central Chest Clinic services were first started in 1966 at Kalimati and expanded over the years subsequently to Biratnagar, Birgunj and Palpa. A sanatorium with 25 beds had been opened at Kalimati, but now it has been converted into the Kalimati Chest Hospital. A total of 283 patients were treated there in 2068/69 BS.

Since 1983 the Aid Medical et Sanatoria (AMS) has been providing aid to 2 districts in Western Nepal. From 1986 the German aided project GENETUP has been helping with a TB clinic within the association premises. From 1995 Norway's Lung & Heart Association (LHL) has been helping in training and supervision of the association activities.

NATA is affiliated with the Social Welfare Council and currently has 34 district branches in the country (13). It conducts activities reaching to the grassroots level and plays an important role in controlling TB by providing treatment services and health education activities.

Nepal Cancer Relief Society

This Society was formed on 31st Bhadra, 2039 BS (1982) with the four objectives of providing promotive, preventive, curative and rehabilitative services to the patients liable to suffer or suffering from cancer. In practical terms it means creating awareness in the people about cancer, its early detection and information about existing facilities for treatment plus rehabilitation.

As smoking has been a major cause of cancer, the society is also active in the anti-smoking campaign. Immediately after the *Janaandolan I*, it was involved in the renovation of the old building of Bhaktapur Hospital. This was converted into the Bhaktapur Cancer Hospital in collaboration with Government of Nepal and with aid from community and Rotary International since 1982. It is also planned to start Hospice facilities for cancer patients at Banepa (14).

NCRS has, besides its central office in Kathmandu and as of August 2013 a total of 43 branches scattered in different parts of the country with as many as 10,000 volunteers. To bring about more awareness about cancer, it has started celebrating 4th February as World Cancer Day as from 2006.

Nepal CRS Company

This organisation was started in 1978 as a pilot project of GoN Nepal by the FP/MCH with the objective of strengthening the FP and PHC programmes. In August 1963, CRS was given corporate status when it became a non-profit, private limited company. It is being supported by USAID and the German Development Bank (Kreditanstalt fur Aufbau i.e. KfA). Social marketing activities for family planning products, rehydration salts and home delivery kits are undertaken by it.

Nepal Disabled Association

In 1969 the Nepal Disabled and Blind Association started institutional rehabilitation services at its "New Life Centre", which in the course of time led to the starting of a rehabilitation centre at Jorpati. Later a separate building for disabled children was constructed and opened in the same compound with the support of SOS International.

In April of 1996 the construction of the Orthopaedic Hospital was completed with support of the Rotary International District 7090, World Community Service and Patan Rotary Club. The 20 bedded hospital is officially functioning since mid-1998.

Nepal Epilepsy Association

The Korean Epilepsy Association "Rose Club", based at Seoul, helped in the founding of the *Soon Pate* Club on 26th Sept. 1986 with the object of providing treatment facilities for epilepsy. About two and half years later it was registered with the SSNCC as Nepal Epilepsy Association. Currently it is running the Gauri Shankar General Hospital at Dolakha Bazaar. In 2004 this organisation withdrew from its services commitment and handed this hospital to the local people. This hospital has recently come under the management of the Model Hospital at Kathmandu.

Nepal Leprosy Relief Association

This organisation which came into being in 2026 BS is responsible for looking after plus running the Syanja based Malunga Leprosarium since 2033 BS and the Khokana Leprosarium since 2041 BS (1985). It has been looking after the children of leprosy patients from the very beginning and besides hostel facilities also gives stipends for study. Last but not least are the objectives of relocating former patients back in the community from which they initially came.

Nepal Netra Jyoti Sangh (NNJS)

The formation of this organisation was preceded by the setting up of the Nepal Eye Hospital in 1965 with a total of 12 beds. This capacity was however increased to 54 about a decade later when it was registered as an NGO to allow proper functioning. The NNJS came into being in 1977 the following year with a view to manage the Nepal Eye Hospital plus also to conduct all eye related activities. It was with the initiative of the members of this NGO together with GoN and WHO that the Nepal Blindness Programme was started in 1979 (15). This whole programme was turned over to NNJS for implementation.

A Nepal Blindness Survey was done in 1981 with the help of the

Netherlands. The resulting estimate was that there were 117,623 blind in Nepal. It is with the active involvement of this organisation that an extensive eye care programme has been developed over the length and breadth of Nepal. The **NNJS** has branches in 23 districts and has activities in 13 of the 14 zones of Nepal.

The NNJS runs eye hospitals, Primary Eye Care Centres and speciality clinics in different parts of the country A Ram Prasad Pokhrel Eye Hospital is being set up at Dhankuta.

The NNJS and its two eye hospitals Eastern Regional Eye Care Program (Sagarmatha Choudhary Eye Hospital) and Lumbini Eye Institute received the Antonio Champalimaud Vision Award from the President of the Portuguese Republic in Sept. 2013.

Nepal Red Cross Society (NRCS)

The Nepal Red Cross Society was founded on 4th Sept. 1963, exactly a hundred years after Jean Henry Dunant had started the parent body in Geneva. Initially an ad-hoc committee under the Chairmanship of the late Princess Princep Shah was functioning. The following year the executive committee was elected and on 1st October 1964, the Nepal Red Cross was officially given recognition by the International Committee of the Red Cross (ICRC). On the next day, i.e. 2nd Oct. the NRC became a member of the League of Red Cross Societies.

Whilst the initial work was with the Tibetan refugees, the Nepal Red Cross started within two years the first Blood Bank service in Kathmandu valley. Over the course of the years the Red Cross has opened District Chapters or branches in all the 75 districts of the Kingdom and other 2,777 units such as sub branches, cooperation committees. The Junior Red Cross Programme which was started in 1965 as an youth movement has expanded tremendously and had in 1994 as many as 1700 Junior Red Cross (JRC) Circles working mainly in the rural areas. These younger members of JRC are very active. The NRCS is also providing ambulance service plus relief at times of national disasters.

The Society completed its First Development Plan from 1984-90 and in the process built up an effective service delivery in the areas of Primary Health Care, Community Health and Disaster Relief Programmes. The Second Development Plan from 1992-1997 focussed on three inter-related and important issues for country viz. Disaster Preparedness, Health and

Community Services. The Society states that in Oct. 2004 it had a total of 8.5 lacs members of which 7.5 lacs were Junior Red Cross and others adult (17).

The Society is currently expanding its Blood Transfusion Service (BTS) which provides blood, free except for service charge, to needy patients. Currently it is running a campaign to expand this service.

Nepali Technical Assistance Group (NTAG)

The Technical Assistance Group (TAG) established in 1993 as a caveat of National Vitamin A Programme to provide technical support during implementation of the programme, has been registered as an NGO in 1996 as The Nepali Technical Assistance Group (NTAG) in 1996. The major activities are in the areas of maternal and child nutrition; training to health workers and FCHVs; research and surveys; and promotion and advocacy in all 75 districts of thecountry.

Paropakar

This organisation was founded initially as *"Paropakar Aushadhalaya"* on Asoj 10th, 2004 BS (1948) by Mr. Dayabir Singh Kansakar. In course of time an orphanage and school were also started. The efforts of this organisation led to the foundation stone lying of a maternity hospital in April 1954. The Shree Panch Indra Rajya Laxmi Prasuti Griha, as it subsequently became known started functioning with 40 beds in 1959 (2016 BS). It has expanded gradually over the years first with the addition of gynaecological beds and baby unit in 1968. Subsequently the baby unit was expanded in 1980. It is now the main centre for maternity care in the country and is currently functioning in 1994 as a 250 bedded maternity hospital (17). After *Jananaandolan II* the name of the hospital was changed to Paropakar Maternity & Womens' Diseases Hospital.

Pasang Lhamu Nicole Hospital

In 2005 was set up a third one at Chaurikhark VDC in the Solo region known as the Pasang Lhamu Nicole Hospital.

Rotary International

Following the inauguration of its central branch at Thapathali, it has over the years opened a number of branches. In the health field, this INGO's has through its many branches, been actively involved in social work in many different fields such as the immunisation campaign, especially polio, eye care and rehabilitation work.

Sonja Kill Memorial Hospice

A recent trend has been the starting of Hospices for long term care of patients. The Sonja Kill Memorial Hospice was inaugurated in Jan. 2006 and is being run by Maiti Nepal.

Sushma Koirala Memorial Trust

The Sushma Memorial Plastic and Reconstructive Surgery Hospital, a complex at Sankhu, Lalambutar, was established with the aid of Interplast-Germany, and inaugurated in Nov.1997. Its objective is to provide free service to repair cleft lips and to correct post-accident and burn deformities in the poor and helpless Nepali patients.

TEAM Hospital

The Evangical Alliance Mission (TEAM) group have opened hospitals at Doti and Dadeldhura and are building a third at Jajarkot. It is reported that they have in 2013 handed over the institution to local people. There are also other some hospitals, which were built and subsequently handed over to the government by the INGOs.

Vajra International

The Vajra Foundation was started in 1998 by a Dutch national to work in the Sindupalchowk area. Besides helping the schools, the organisation has been helping in drinking water and sewage disposal projects. It has also been involved with medical colleges for the holding of regular health camps with surgery on site and at a later date, at the teaching hospitals itself.

OTHER INGOs INVOLVED IN THE FIELD OF HEALTH

Any INGO wanting to work in Nepal is required to submit an application to the Social Welfare Council for permission prior to commencement of work. The number of INGOs working in Nepal in mid 2013 was 175 and came from 19 countries.

Action Aid International Nepal (AAIN)

Working in Nepal since 1982, it has involved communities on its integrated programmes to address health care, education, agriculture, infrastructure and income generation. During the last 30 years it has worked in partnership with 250 civil society organisations in altogether 42 districts. As per its Country Strategy Paper IV (2012-2017), AAIN is now directing its campaign against poverty and injustice with a Human Rights Based Approach (HRBA). Its area of involvement is in the agricultural, health, education and water sectors.

Adventists Development Relief Agency (ADRA)

This missionary group, as the Seventh Day Adventists went to Banepa in 1957 and opened a small hospital. This has over the years developed into the Scheer Memorial Hospital.

Later the ADRA - Nepal started work in this country in 1987. One year later a heart surgery team from Sydney Adventists Hospital, Australia and following an official agreement, the organisation extended help in setting up the Cardio Thoracic Unit at Bir Hospital with the object of developing heart surgery in Nepal. The first open heart surgery was done at Bir Hospital in 1989 with the aid of the ADRA team. From 1991, ADRA - Nepal has been helping the TU Teaching Hospital at Maharajgunj to set up a similar unit.

ADRA's priority now is to support the development of efficient local capacity and partnerships with government and civil society at all levels. It focuses for reproductive health, economic development, basic education, women empowerment and disaster relief. It also involved in the implementation of various health projects such as Safe Motherhood. ADRA Nepal's work is based on the theme of community in 18 of the 75 districts of Nepal.

Association of Medical Doctors of Asia (AMDA)

This association with its base in Japan is involved in health work in different countries. The local AMDA-Nepal, established in 1990, has now a team of 30 committed medical doctors working in and outside of Nepal. It had been working with AMDA-Japan for the welfare of the Bhutanese refugees in Eastern Nepal. The Referral Health Centre it has been running in Damak of Jhapa district since 1992, was upgraded to a 30 bedded hospital in Jan. 1996. Bed capacity has now been increased. The slogan under which AMDA works is "Better Quality of Life for a Better Future."

Currently AMDA Nepal runs three hospitals, academic programmes for health related courses, health and nutrition services to Bhutanese refugees, AMDA ASHA project and community related PHC programmes.

AMS Nepal: French Medical and Sanitary Aid in Nepal

This NGO has been working in Nepal since 1983 with the Nepal Red Cross Society. Its main work in the community health sector are in the districts of Myagdi and Parbat in the Dhaulagiri zone. It helps to improve the health conditions by way of conducting training for community health workers and also providing support for health care facilities.

Britain Nepal Medical Trust (BNMT)

The BNMT was established in 1967 with the object to assist with the health problems of Nepal. This INGO, initially based at Biratnagar, started functioning in May 1968 and had been involved in providing health services by way of the health posts in sixteen districts in Eastern Nepal. The main programme areas had been drug supply, TB and leprosy control, the training and supervision of community health workers. The BNMT played an important role in the establishment of the National TB Programme and has been actively supporting the NTC in achieving the goals of the National Tuberculosis Programme (NTP) for the implementation of the TB Control and prevention activities. BNMT is the sub-recipient of The Global Fund National Strategic Application (NSA) and has been active in 34 districts of Nepal, where the fund is being utilised.

Since Feb. 2003, BNMT through its integrated Health Improvement Programme (HIP) with its five major components viz.

- infectious diseases
- reproductive health
- TB
- HIV / AIDS / STD
- Essential drugs.

Co-operative for Assistance & Relief Everywhere (CARE)

This INGO started work in Nepal in 1978 as CARE - Medico and stress was on the training of paramedical workers. Subsequently, however, efforts shifted to building suspension bridges and agro-forestry. Further work was on a community basis with stress on infrastructure development, community involvement and mobilising of the same in an attempt to meet the community felt needs. In 1991 it also started PHC activities in 2 districts of Nepal. The involvement of this INGO is in eight districts of Nepal. CARE Nepal is working to alleviate the causes of poverty and social injustice. The three themes that it is currently stressing on are: (i) empowering women,

(ii) securing livelihood & managing natural resources and (iii) addressing equity and social justice.

CARE Nepal's health programmes are focussed on maternal and child health, HIV AIDS, health education, disease control, strengthening health and management systems especially in remote districts.

Centre for Development & Population Activities (CEDPA)

This is a women-focused organisation founded in 1975 and has been working with local NGOs in Nepal since 1988. CEDPA / Nepal has been mainly involved with family planning, literacy and education activities. Its mission is to empower women at all levels of society to be full partners in development.

FHI 360 Nepal

Since 1993, through financial support from United States Agency for International Development (USAID), FHI Nepal implemented four main HIV/AIDS programs. The last project was : on managing Advancing Surveillance, Policies, Prevention, Care and Support to Fight HIV/AIDS (ASHA Project) which ended in 2011.

From the fiscal year 2011/12, FHI has been converted to FHI 360 to manage USAID-funded Saath-Saath Project which covered 33 districts of the country in the areas of HIV prevention to care, support and treatment services; integrated family planning (FP)/HIV services; community and home based care; surveillance & research; and capacity strengthening of SSP's partners in close partnership with the GoN, civil society groups, NGOs, INGOs, UN agencies, and donors.

Helen Keller International

Since 1989, Helen Keller International has worked in Nepal with national partners since 1989. The current programs include:

Vitamin A Supplementation: HKI works in Kathmandu, Kirtipur, Lalitpur, Madhyapur, and Bhaktapur to sustain vitamin A distribution coverage for 90% of children between 6-59 months.

Action Against Malnutrition through Agriculture (AAMA): HKI's four-year AAMA program, which began in October 2008, expands on the Homestead Food Production model to deliver a package of Essential Nutrition Actions (ENA) to the most vulnerable communities and populations in Kailali, Baitadi, Bajura and Kanchanpur.

School Health Project (SHP): The SHP project in Nepal is mainly focused on trachoma elimination. The program will promote increased face-washing among school children.

Helping Hands

Helping Hands Nepal may be said to have been started in 1988 by a Health Trek NGO. It was officially registered in 1990 in Boulder City, Colorado. Similarly registered at Kathmandu in 2051 BS the organisation has been involved in health care work in the Sankhuwasabha district in Eastern Nepal. It has a number of branches in different parts of the country and together with health personnel especially brought from abroad. It has been holding health camps in the rural areas. Helping Hands Nepal has also established three permanent health clinics – one at Khandbari and two in Kathmandu valley.

HELVETAS - Swiss Intercooperation

Initially the health aspects of aid were handled by the Swiss Association for Technical Assistance. This started in the form of help at Jiri, which took the form of a hospital, an ANM training school, and help to the health posts of Dolakha district. This later became SATA/Helvetas. Whilst SATA is coordinating all this technical work in Nepal, Helvetas is responsible for co-ordinating NGO's activity. Now however the SDC, through its Rural Health Development Project (RHDP) helps HMG to empower the 'women, children, adolescent and men' to enhance their health conditions by way of improved local health facilities. Currently it is working in five areas.

International Nepal Fellowship (INF)

The International Nepal Fellowship started working in Nepal in 1952. Following permission to Dr. Lily O'Hanlon, the INF had initially opened a clinic at Ramghat in Nov. 1952. Hospital services were started the following year 1953 with the Shining Hospital, so named as the original prefabricated aluminium roofs shone brightly in the sun. Five years later saw permission being given for "new building at the existing hospital a TB Sanatorium and a Leper Asylum." The Green Pastures Leprosarium was subsequently established in 1957.

The International Nepal Fellowship (INF) mission had started working in Nepal with the opening of the hospital at Pokhara under the very descriptive name of the Shining Hospital way back in 1953. It was later incorporated into the Gandaki Zonal Hospital.

The Shining Hospital functioned at the original site from 1957 to 1978 when in-patients and maternity cases were no longer admitted there. As per agreement with GoN, the beds of this were amalgamated into the Gandaki Zonal Hospital, which in course of time became the Western Regional Hospital. Consequently, between 1978 and 1992 there has been considerable input into this institution. The Shining bit continued as an outpatient clinic and became the Shining Community Health Centre. Current plans are for the INF to be involved in district health services by way of the hospital at Beni. Besides the curative services, INF's work has been broadened from just disease prevention and control to include areas of health promotion, health related development and training for health personnel. Activities centre on the community health project especially in areas of tuberculosis and leprosy in the western part of the country.

From Nov. '94 the INF co-operated in the development of district health facilities by its involvement in the management of the Myagdi District Hospital at Beni Bazaar. Four other hospitals in the mid-Western region viz. Bheri Zonal, and the District Hospitals of Surkhet, Dang and Jumla have been targeted for upgradation and development in the coming years. This was in line with the current and INF's own thinking of making the "District Hospital the fulcrum of the health care delivery system for the population in the rural areas". After restructuring in 2004 INF started working in a bifurcated manner – INF/Worldwide and INF/Nepal.

In 2005/6 the INF was registered at both the local and national level as a Nepali Christian NGO. The Green Pastures Hospital, which is a part of the INF family was established in Kaski in 1957 and celebrated 50 years of operation in 2007. Besides offering both in and outpatient services for leprosy patients the hospital also provides a comprehensive rehabilitation programme for its clients. With the decline in leprosy cases the major part of the work is with disabled patients specially those requiring spinal cord injury rehabilitation. The institution also provides training to health care providers.

The INF Banke (TB Regional Centre) had been established in 1996 to provide both inpatient and out patient services. During the course of 2011-12 as many as 39,000 patients were served in the Mid-Western region of Nepal.

INF Nepal has its central office at Pokhara and runs six programmes at its branches at Baglung, Bajura, Banke, Dang, Jumla, Kapilbastu, Mugu and Surkhet districts.

Ipas Nepal

Ipas/Nepal is a non-political, non-profit making, public welfare social organization dedicated to protecting women's health and advancing women's reproductive rights. The main focus of this organization in the fiscal year in 2011/12 was in the areas of safe abortion care, family planning and reproductive health services in selected PHCCs and HPs in 16 districts.

Lutheran World Service/Nepal

This INGO started working in Nepal in 1984 starting with relief and rehabilitation operations. Initially its work concentrated on community development. It has been involved in looking after the Bhutanese refugees of Nepalese origin in the refugee camps of Eastern Nepal. With an office at Damak, Jhapa it is the implementing partner for the United Nations High Commissioner for Refugees (UNHCR). It adopts empowerment, human rights based integrated and collaborative approach whilst implementing humanitarian development programmes.

Netherlands Leprosy Relief Association (NSL)

This INGO's work in Nepal started in 1985. The initial major function was to help with the establishment of the Eastern Leprosy Control Project in Eastern Nepal. The groundwork for this started in 1980, although the project started functioning in 1982. It has built a number of district hospitals and handed them over to the government for running. Its objective is to help the government to reduce the total prevalence of leprosy so that it is no longer a major health problem. From 1991 this INGO's activates has been extended to the Far-Western Region, where it is also involved in TB control (14).

Marie Stopes International (MSI)

This is an INGO providing services related to the Sexual and Reproductive Health fields. Its local working partner is the Sunaulo Parivar Nepal (SPN), which has been functioning since 1994. The overall objective of MSI /SPN is to provide services to Nepali men, women and adolescents for sexual and reproductive health (SRH). Their mission is children by choice not chance.

OXFAM

OXFAM has been working in Nepal since the 1980s, The INGO is working to reduce poverty in Nepal with a view to improving the lot of the disadvantaged people of the country. The areas that it worked in the past were in community development, adult literacy, income generation etc. The focus now is on: (i) promoting gender justice (ii) partnering with local civil society and (iii) empowering communities.

PLAN International Nepal

This INGO initially started working in Nepal as Foster Parents from 1978 in collaboration with the then existing SSNCC at Sitapaila on the outskirts of Kathmandu. It has an overall objective of human development with a focus on children, their families and their community. From this small beginning, PLAN Nepal has expanded its activities to a number of different sites in 25 districts through NGO partners and is thereby giving benefit to many families and communities in many parts of Nepal. Its current focus is on six districts: Sunsari, Morang, Bara, Rautahat, Makwanpur and Banke.

Save the Children

Save the Children's work in Nepal focuses its effort on education, especially early childhood development and primary education, as well as basic health, including maternal child health and HIV and AIDS prevention and care. Special attention is paid to ensure that members of particularly disadvantaged groups such as "dalits" and other ethnic minorities are reached by these programs.

Save the Children Nepal unified country program is governed by a country leadership group (CLG). SC is one of the humanitarian and leading organizations in emergencies which provide child-centered disaster risk reduction, preparedness and emergency response. The main aim/ objectives of SC is to address fundamental violation of children's rights and accomplish lasting positive change for a large number of children. During SC Country Strategy Plan (2010 -2013) period, SC worked in the neediest 20 districts out of 54 existing working districts of Nepal with quality, comprehensive and holistic programming, and integrating key interventions of the thematic areas like education, health and Nutrition, Livelihood, , HIV/AID and Emergency. SC formed committee on adolescent sexual and reproductive health (ARSH) and strengthen collaboration with government and other partners to operationalize the National Strategy

(2000) and implementation guideline 2007 on ARSH. (See also Chapter 3)

Scheer Memorial Hospital

In 1957 a Seventh Day Adventist Mission from the States opened a small hospital at Banepa, known as the Scheer Memorial. It has increased in size over the years and is currently running a BSc Nursing course in affiliation with KU. Up to 2013 it is the only one of 22 mission hospitals that has not come under the government fold. Presently there are difficulties in running it.

The Himalayan Trust

This Trust was formed over a quarter century ago by Sir Edmund Hillary. The first hospital in the Solu region was thought about in 1964 and finally started functioning at the edge of a small Sherpa village of Khunde. Initially referred by Edmund Hillary as a 'New Zealand Hospital for Sherpas' it was later referred to in 1967 as 'Kunde Hospital' and finally as Khunde Hospital. The second hospital to be built in the region in 1976 was the 29 bedded Phaplu Hospital. After five years it was in 1980 handed over to GoN to function as the district hospital of Solokhumbu. Besides this, the Trust is helping to run 25 schools in the Solu region and is also involved in reforestation work (18).

The Mission to Lepers (UK)

In 1956, the Mission to Lepers (UK) was given permission by the government of Nepal to open a hospital, known as Anandaban at the edge of Kathmandu valley. The hospital was started in 1957. Currently a total of 125 beds i.e. 100 for leprosy and the other 25 for general patients. The institution is providing regional level leprosy and some PHC services to the surrounding areas. Laboratory research has been going on during this time, and many papers have been published on immunology and drug resistance. The hospital operates on the basis of 5-year agreements with the GoN. Comprehensive leprosy care, including Multi Drug Therapy is provided. There has been considerable research work done at this institution, including work on leprosy vaccine.

The Green Pastures Leprosy Hospital is at Pokhara is supported by a German mission. It started with outpatient facilities in 1957 but was officially opened with inpatients in 1972. Another INGO has built recently a leprosy hospital on the outskirts of Kathmandu at Sankhu. Yet another leprosy hospital has been built at Janakpur recently.

In 2010 it was stated that elimination of leprosy had been achieved at national level and this was so declared. This means that the incidence is less than 1 per 10,000 population. It was stated in 2011/2012 that elimination was now sustained in the country as national strategy.

A dispensary for those infected with leprosy was opened at Dandeldhura in 1960 and later expanded into a hospital run by another mission group in 1968. As the group concerned is The Evangelical Alliance Mission this is sometimes referred to as the TEAM Hospital.

United Mission to Nepal (UMN)

The work of the United Mission to Nepal started a number of women's and children clinics in the Kathmandu valley and had permission to start a Hospital at Tansen (1). The hospital at Tansen was started by Dr. Carl Friedericks and his helpers on 15th June, 1954.

UMN was one of the early Non-Governmental Organisations (NGOs) coming from outside to work in Nepal. The UMN, founded in 1954, is a joint effort by 26 member bodies from 17 countries and some affiliated organisations that work with GoN, local NGOs and individuals in Nepal. It is because of its diverse origin that led it to being called UMN. Its work in this country started with the starting of the five women's and children's clinic in Kathmandu valley. The first of these was at Bhaktapur or Bhadgaon as it was also more commonly known then. The second clinic, or rather a fifteen bedded hospital started in half of the premises of the Cholera Hospital in February 1954 on the 3rd anniversary of the attainment of democracy in Nepal (1). The opening was done by the then Prime Minister Matrika P. Koirala. One of the first workers of UMN at the Cholera Hospital stated "the hospital was shared with the maternity patients who would flee when there was an outbreak of cholera".

The maternity clinics in the Kathmandu valley became popular and overcrowded. The shared premises of the existing Cholera Hospital were not suitable to function on a more permanent basis. Ultimately in the following year, the maternity clinic, which was being unmanageable, was shifted to an old Rana palace at Jawalakhel and became Shanta Bhawan Hospital. Subsequent to this, some work started in 1957 with the object of starting a hospital at Bhadgaon on a wooded hillside known as Surya Binayak. This was to be a health institution looking specifically at the patient with tuberculosis. However with the building of a new government hospital at Bhadgaon, and with the object of keeping to the principle of not having duplication of services, the government asked the Mission to close its establishment at Surya Binayak. In the light of this government decision, both the government facilities at Tansen and Patan were closed and the mission institutions were given the task of providing the general services. The old government general hospital at Patan was made into the Mental Hospital and the Shanta Bhawan Hospital became the new Patan/ Lalitpur Hospital run by the United Mission to Nepal. The Mission hospital at Tansen continues to function but the old government hospital has been reopened and functions as a result of popular demand.

In course of time it was felt that the siting of the mission hospital in a section of the Cholera Hospital was inappropriate. By January 1956 a bigger hospital was started in a former Rana palace, and retaining its original name came to be known as the Shanta Bhawan Hospital. It was in this building, of the 1950's that the American Drs. Edgar and Elizabeth Miller came to work and thus were able to sensitise the local doctors with and about the modern curative medicine practised in the States. It was from this building and the nearby house of Surendra Bhawan where the maternity unit was sited, that the UMN continued to provide health services.

The thought of building a new facility originated in 1963 and agreement to this effect was done in 1974 after much deliberation. This project was completed only when they shifted to the site of the new Patan Hospital at Lagankhel on 9th November, 1982.

At about the same time that the hospital was started in Kathmandu, a dispensary was started in Tansen in June 1954 with the objective of upgrading it into a hospital at a later date. It was the families of Drs. Robert & Bethel Fleming and that of Dr. Carl Friedericks who with the help of other organisations set up a functioning hospital at Tansen. From its single room origin the hospital has grown to an institution with 131 beds (19).

The Mission Hospital at Amp Pipal in Gorkha district started as a rural community programme, then became a dispensary and finally a hospital.

Dr. James Dick was the pioneer and founder of the hospital at Okhaldhunga. Initially a dispensary functioned as such until 1972 when an agreement was signed with HMG to run a 25-bedded hospital on a joint basis. At the present time the hospital there is being run by a NGO – the Human Development and Community Services (HDCS), which will ultimately take it over and manage it. The bed strengths of these various institutions at the end of 1994 were Patan Hospital (138), Tansen Hospital (129), Amp Pipal Hospital (Gorkha) 53 and Okhaldhunga UMN Hospital was 32 (19). By 2002 the Patan Hospital had a total of 318 beds.

The UMN, over the course of the years opened a total of five hospitals. Four are still functioning but the initial attempt at Bhaktapur had to close down when the upgraded facilities of GoN started functioning there. In 1988, the UMN Health Services Department supported activities in 12 districts of Nepal.

During the 1970s and 1980s UMN's work focussed on development projects that had direct impact on communities. Besides the specific curative aspects of health, the UMN has also been involved in community development projects in various parts of Nepal. These community development projects are creating awareness and are teaching problem solving skills so that motivation, self-reliance are brought about in the people. At these grassroots levels, it has been involved in the training of *dhamis* and *jhankris* in childhood malnutrition, oral rehydration for diarrhoeal diseases and in various other aspects of public health and hygiene. The hope is that the projects will continue even when the external input stops.

With increasing number of hospital deliveries and the ever-present shortage of beds, the Patan Hospital had, as from January 1998 started what is termed the "Birthing Centre." This new innovation was started by renovation of its former *dharmashala*[2]. The idea was that women with normal obstetrical histories and experiencing routine antenatal care can be delivered in such places under the supervision of trained midwives. The UMN has also helped train basic health manpower such as ANMs and also AHWs at Tansen. It is currently running two nursing schools and helping to meet the great shortage of nurses that exists within the country.

In April 2001 a special children's ward of 82 beds named after Sahu Ganesh Lal was inaugurated by Sir Edmund Hillary.

As from November 2000, the UMN and GoN have been signing an agreement for 5 year periods with the objective of having Nepali owned

2. Inn providing lodgings

and managed services. In May 2003, the Health Service Department of UMN ceased to exist and the programmes were handed over to other transitional set ups. A number of new NGOs have been set up to carry on the work of some UNM programmes in different parts of the country.

The policy of UMN now is in transition by which is meant shifting of the ownership, governance and management of certain projects, programmes or institutions from UMN to local institutions or NGOs. Currently because of some difficulties, the local NGO for running Amp Pipal Hospital has not been able to do so. Following the consent of GoN in December 2003, the work of UMN has now been transferred to what is now referred to as clusters. The clusters planned are at Mugu, Sunsari, Kathmandu, Rukum and Dhading. (Rupendehi has also been accepted as an alternative cluster). The Mugu and Sunsari clusters were started in 2004.

The Patan Hospital now a teaching institution is known as Patan Academy of Health Sciences (PAHS).

POINTS TO PONDER

There are a large number of NGOs in this country. Some are genuine and some may have 'hidden agendas'. The attempt to oversee them is difficult. The rise of the private sector is heartening but many undesirable activities have crept in. Unnecessary repetition of tests, and 'fee splitting' are examples. The Nepal Medical Council is failing in its duty to protect the public.

References

1. Nepal and the Gospel of God. Jonathan Lindell, UMN, 1979
2. APHIN Souvenir 2068 BS (2011)
3. Awale Sujata. When hospitals are a safety hazard. The Himalayan Times Perspective, Jan. 2013
4. Shankarapur Hospital – Souvenir 2068 BS
5. Khatry Cilla. Mushrooming hospitals in the week, Republica, 21st June, 2013
6. Guidelines
7. Adhikary Sitaram. Chikitsa Shikshama Fadko, 2013
8. Rabendra Kumar. SWC will streamline INGOs. The New Spotlight , 12th July, 2013
9. BP Health Foundation website

10. Karki BB. Primary Health Care Development in Nepal. J. Nep Med Assoc 1977; 15(4), 16-24
11. FPAN Annual Report, 2012
12. Hospital and Rehabilitation Centre for Disabled Children. Annual Report 2011
13. Nepal Tuberculosis Programme. Annual Report, 2011-12
14. Bhaktapur Cancer Hospital Bulletin. March 2013
15. A study of present status and future prospects. Nepal Netra Jyoti Sangh. 1994.
16. Nepal Red Cross Movement – A short introduction. 2004.
17. Paropakar Maternity & Womens' Diseases Hospital – 54th Anniversary Souvenir. 2013
18. Modern Medicine and International Aid. Susan Hayden. Orient Black Swan 2009
19. Friedericks CW, Over Thirty, 1986, UMN, Kathmandu

7.

PLANS, POLICIES AND THEIR IMPLICATIONS

Following the ushering in of democracy in Nepal, after 104 years of Rana rule in 1951, some development started to take place. A national planning agency – Planning Commission was constituted in Nepal in 1956 under the Chairmanship of the Prime Minister. At the time of the introduction of the Panchayat political system in 1960 a Rastriya Yojana Parishad (National Planning Council) was formed under the Chairmanship of the King. Presently there is a National Planning Commission (NPC) under the Chairmanship of the Prime Minister.

In the early days of health planning in Nepal a number of plans were made. However, there was a tendency for part of the plans to be suddenly and periodically changed by ministers and secretaries. With change in individuals, the priorities were sometimes so drastically altered that it became difficult to work. It was in that setting that the need was felt to have a Long Term Health Plan or even just a Plan, which could not be arbitrarily changed.

Long Term Health Plan (1975-1990)

Twenty-five years after the ushering in of democracy in Nepal it was felt that the infrastructure for proper delivery of health care was in place. It was felt to be the opportune moment to think in terms of a Long Term Health Plan. An initial draft was made by a group of three doctors at the Ministry of Health.

With the blessings of the then Minister of Health, an eight-member committee with five doctors and three baidyas was formed to formulate an overall health plan for the whole country. The five doctors involved were:

Dr. Lakshmi N. Prasad

Dr. Narendra B. Rana

Dr. Manindra R. Baral
Dr. Sundar Mani A. Dixit
Dr. Nagendra Dhoj Joshi

This team travelled to various parts of the country with the objective of making a twenty-five year plan. Following initial discussions at the Ministry some other doctors were added to the committee. The question of whether the posts at the government hospitals should be "non-practising" or "practising" was discussed.

After further deliberations at the *Janch Bujh Kendra*[1] of those days, this plan was modified and ultimately resulted in to the Long Term Health Plan 1975-90 (1). This time frame included the Fifth, Sixth and Seventh Plan periods with the idea that what was achieved in one plan period would be dovetailed into another. The inference at that time was that the future health policies, strategies and activities were to be according to this. The main emphasis in this LTHP was the provision of basic health services to a large majority of the people. This was an honest attempt by the authorities to get things moving in the health field.

This document recorded the state of the health services existing, and the long-term aspects. Primary health care, hospital services, family planning and management aspects were also looked at. The annexure gave the criteria of service and manpower allocations to various grades of health institutions.

In course of time it was soon apparent that things were not going on as per the plan. The general complaint was that when people asked for activities listed, the excuse was lack of budgetary resources and that it would be done in due course. What was not in the plan could not be considered. The end result as per the gossip circulating around that only facilities for the doctors working in the ministry were carried out and everything else was held in abeyance!

It was the mid-term review of the first of the three plan periods i.e. 1975-1980, which had been done over the period from March 1978 to June 1979 by a special team with the help of New ERA for the collection of data (2). For the sake of accuracy the authors:

"undertook a sample survey of a variety of health institutions and of population with differing access to health services. In all, thirty-one of the

1. Investigation Bureau

seventy-five districts were included in this survey, providing representation of all four development regions as well as both hill and Terai areas. Over 150 separate health facilities were visited, and interviews were conducted in nearly 3,700 households in eighty panchayats."

Even before 1990 came, the general complaint was that whenever one went to the Health Ministry with a proposal, the first reaction as to its feasibility was whether it was in the Plan or not. If it was not in the plan, there was no possibility of getting it done. If it was in the plan, the authorities would consider it, but in all probability it would not be done because of lack of funds etc. As a result of all this, ad hoc decisions on the basis of political expediency were the order of the day. At times when offers simply came out of the blue e.g. that of a teaching hospital by the Japanese, then there were grounds for such action. Just as the Teaching Hospital came into existence in the eighties without really having been fully planned earlier so also the BP Koirala Institute of Health Sciences (BPKIHS) also came out of the blue in the post *Jana Andolan I* period of the nineties.

All said and done this mid-term review report was ready by June 1979, but as it was thought to be fairly critical of the state of health and its affairs and so was not distributed. The observations were categorised into two groups viz. those regarding policy and those related to management. Some of these, which were critical, are given below:

On Policy Issues

- District Hospital role in preventive care delivery, training and supervision largely not being discharged.
- Leprosy and tuberculosis follow-up programmes were largely not being implemented.
- Government health services had low geographic accessibility, extremely limited outreach facility, and as a consequence low use.
- VHWs visited more households than PBWs but both much less than MFWs. The PHW-VHW difference was greatest in Terai. More VHWs than other field staff felt the number of houses to be visited to be a serious constraint to effectiveness.
- District Health Committees seldom had representation from projects or are even known to project staff other than ICHP.
- Supply shortages existed in all projects except Malaria.

- Most post level units did not have their own water supply. At best only half the post units have latrines with Ayurvedic clinics being the least well served.
- For over half the staff at district and health post units no housing was provided. To a small extent this was compensated for by some free accommodation provided by the community.
- A fixed programme of refresher training was not offered by any project. The need for further training among field worker was most felt by PBWs.

On Management Issues

- Community awareness and use of family planning and maternal and child health services, and facilities was low. Understanding was low even among the aware population in areas where FP and MCH services and facilities were available.
- Many workers were unclear about role in preventive tasks prescribed by central organisation.
- Most health committees at both district and health post were inactive. Few people in HP areas knew of the existence of health committees.
- Few community leaders had been involved with the selection of local health worker; those who had been involved were mainly in the VHW selection.
- Critical shortages in disease prevention vaccines in all units, which may severely inhibited preventive programmes, particularly in hospitals.
- The majority of all units never received operating funds either development or regular on time. The situation improved with each quarter of the fiscal year.
- There was a shortage of written guidelines for supervision in all projects but primarily in ICHP.

Country Health Resources & Priorities (CHRP)

This exercise may be said to have been done to review what had been achieved in the Seventh Five Year Plan period and at the same time to help the National Planning Commission to lay down guidelines for the Eighth Plan 1990-95.

The first phase consisted of a 5-day preparatory workshop, which looked at various issues on hand. This was followed by a second phase of 14 days where four groups of between 5 to 10 members each looked at the under mentioned four areas:

a. National Health Policy
b. Development of Health Services and Institutions
c. Minimizing Risk Factors
d. Prevention and Control of Diseases

A fifth working group worked further and made a CHRP working document which the organising committee then improved and sent as the second draft to various HMG officials plus various agencies for comments and suggestions. The final version of the document was brought out in January 1990 but was never distributed thereafter (3). During the one-year period of the Interim Government it was not referred to. The National Planning Commission went on a so-called "one year Plan holiday" which in fact turned out to be two. Thus the schedule of the Eighth Plan period came to be 1992-1997.

The World Bank, too, did a survey and came out with suggestions for a reorganisation (4).

Situation analysis for the re-structuring of the health services was done over a six month period during end of 1990 and early 1991 (5). Taking the commitment of Basic Minimum Needs Programme of GoN, it brought into focus the fact that previous studies had shown that the existing health system was not, "both quantitatively and qualitatively geared up to achieve the BMN goals". Following the period of study, certain macro recommendations were made for the re-structuring of health services. These were:

a. Strengthening outreach services i.e. health posts and below
b. Strengthening district health system
c. Development of appropriate, effective and efficient regional and national (central) health organisations
d. Development of strategic national perspective plan
e. Manpower planning and development

Following elections of 1991 the Nepali Congress formed the government and the PM took the portfolio of the Health Ministry. It was at this juncture that a delegation of the Nepal Medical Association met him and requested a White Paper on Health. This was agreed to and a committee was formed under the Secretary of Health to think about the matter and proceed accordingly.

Before any firm decisions were taken, a medical doctor became the new Minister of Health. GoN in Sept 1991 formed a committee and subsequently a number of other subcommittees to draw up a plan of action with appropriate strategies to provide health services up to the village level as per the guidelines of the contemplated National Health Policy 1991. The new group looked at various aspects of health and their reports were submitted by the deadline of Nov. 1991. In hindsight, it may have been a strategy to keep people occupied, and to create a state of "make believe" that something is happening. The first reaction is that this report is now shelved and unlikely to see the light of day.

National Health Policy - 1991

The National Health Policy of 1991 focused on two broad areas for singling out and may be categorised as follows:

Preventive Health Services

Family Planning (FP), Safe Motherhood, Expanded Programme for Immunisation (EPI), Control of Diarrhoeal Diseases (CDD), Acute Respiratory Infections (ARI), and Malaria.

Promotive Health Services

Health Education, Nutrition and Environmental Health.

Strengthening of the District Health Systems

Special efforts were made to prepare plans and strategies for the strengthening of the health service delivery at the district levels.

But all said and done one has to look for a delivery of health care, which one can afford. A Global Research Project conducted by SCF (UK) looked at the sustainability of the health sector in Nepal during the course of 1991/92 (6). Some of the comments in its executive summary are:

- At approximately $ 1.30 per capita, the expenditure on health by the Ministry of Health is very low, even for a developing country, although the share of government expenditure on health (about 4% in recent years) is about average for less developed countries.
- The period between 1951-74 was characterised by the entry into Nepal of INGOs for direct health service delivery and the establishment of vertical disease control programmes by major donors.
- The period between 1975-90 was characterised by greater attention

to planning for the health sector for meeting national and global goals.

- Nevertheless, the health sector infrastructure and numbers of staff continued to expand rapidly, most due to donor initiatives and funding, while the capacity to manage these new resources tended to lag behind.

It was in this context too that a special consultation was done towards the end of 1993 to look into ways and means of strengthening the district health systems. Task forces were created with a view to tackle the problems. It was felt that some of the district hospitals could be made into models to show it's functioning to be mutually supportive with the district health systems. To ensure that HRH personnel function effectively to deal with the health problems of the society, this particular report makes a plea for training and research to be located in the settings and systems in which the health workers are most needed. Quoting from a Round Table discussion article entitled "Educating Tomorrow's Doctors" in World Health Forum, it goes on to say:

"The consensus is becoming firm in both developed and developing countries that academic health centres should associate themselves with defined populations, where they focus teaching and research related to the health of the population and the effectiveness of the health care system."

The recommendation is that the universities should be encouraged to collaborate with the government in the development of district health systems for the purposes of education and research. Such thinking is very pertinent in view of the fact that a number of teaching institutions have been established over the last decade in different parts of Nepal.

In this same vein it is worthwhile remembering that just prior to starting of the MBBS course at the Institute of Medicine a number of district health surveys were done at Tanahu, Bara, Dhankuta and Nuwakot. A later survey was at Surkhet. Repeat survey was done at Dhankuta. Such research identified the existing situation, the health service demands and the needs. During the course of the eighties foreign medical graduates did a number of health studies with accompanying Nepalese medical students and sometimes faculty in other areas of Nepal. A regular feature of the community oriented MBBS programme of the IoM is that each batch of medical students have spent time in the community and done a report of that study. A recent report by Tiwari (7), which drew on some of these studies, stated that "there is generally poor response by the majority of the people to the available health services particularly in the rural areas." This report of April 1994 stated that the primary health services in the country were inadequate and that the existing health institutions are not functioning properly due to the lack of trained manpower, medicines and equipment.

The year 2052 BS (mid-April '95 to mid-April '96) may be taken as the policy-making year for during this one year a number of policy documents were made public. These were:

National Policy for AIDS & STD Control - 2052 BS
National Ayurvedic Health Policy - 2052 BS
National Safe Motherhood Policy - 1998

Logistic Management Division

The division was started in the Department of Health Services in 1993. This attempt to systematise health care logistics was started then and is continuing to this day. An efficient logistic management of health care commodities (essential medicine, vaccines, contraceptives, medical equipments / instruments, HMIS / LMIS forms etc) involves technical, managerial and administrative expertise, which has to be maintained at all, times.

Nepal Multiple Indicator Surveillance (NMIS)

The NMIS was designed as an ongoing monitoring scheme to produce information useful for planning at national, district, and community and household levels. Started with a multisectoral baseline survey in early 1995 the NMIS process comprised of repeated cycles of data collection, analysis, interpretation and communication of results with and objective of stimulating action (8). Each cycle focuses on a priority set of issues as given below:

Cycle 1. Information about malnutrition and feeding practices among young children. Indicated need for more information
Cycle 2. Primary Education (in Spring/Summer 1995)
Cycle 3. Diarrhoea, Water and Sanitation (in first half of 1996)
Cycle 4. Early Childhood Feeding, Nutrition and Development (in second half 1996)
Cycle 5. Care during Pregnancy and Delivery

Second Long-term Health Plan (1997-2017)

The specific purpose of the Second Long Term Health Plan (SLTHP) is to provide a guiding framework to:

- Build successive periodic and annual health plans that would lead to improvement in the health status of the population.
- Develop appropriate strategies, programmes and action plans that: reflect the national health needs and priorities; are affordable and consistent with available resources.
- Establish co-ordination among public, private sectors (including NGOs) and donor partners (9).

Based on the demographic and disease profile an "Essential Health Care Services (EHCS)" of highly cost effective public health measures and essential clinical services for traditional and other systems of medicine is proposed. The EHCS is to address the essential health needs of the population at the district level and below during the course of the next twenty years.

To effectively implement the EHCS the health sector must:

1. redirect resources from high-cost low-impact interventions to those that could substantially reduce morbidity, mortality and disability without increasing expenditures;
2. address the issues which limit the effective utilization of scarce human and financial resources; and
3. adopt alternative financing mechanisms, which seek to mobilize non-governmental funds to support health care and increase the public-private mix in terms of financing and provision of services.

Within this context, the Second Long Term Health Plan defines the EHCS and identifies the key issues and policy options necessary for:

1. improving the efficiency and effectiveness of the health care system;
2. improving inter- and intra-sectoral coordination and providing the necessary conditions and support for effective decentralisation;
3. overcoming management and organizational constraints for effective public health sector service delivery;
4. ensuring that appropriate numbers, types and distribution of technically competent and socially responsible health personnel are available to provide quality health care to all the people of Nepal, particularly those living in rural areas;

5. ensuring that the health care system provides care that is effective in producing positive health outcomes as defined by health care professionals and in which the community is satisfied that their needs are being met;
6. providing the requisite data, analysis and interpretation necessary for informed decision-making and
7. addressing the changing trends of communicable and non-communicable diseases and emerging health issues.

Strategic analysis of the health sector was done in the presence of External Development Partners (EDP), NGOs and the private sector in Sept / Oct. 1999. The purpose was to map out future action with the objective of operationalisation of the strategies for the improvement of the health services (10).

While the concept and stress on working through NGOs is a good idea, the crucial first step is to separate the wheat from the chaff. In the long range, the SLTHP may turn out to be a document of good intentions, liberal rhetoric but short in action!

DIFFERENT POLICY

a. NATIONAL HEALTH POLICY – 1991

The Nepali Congress Government committed itself to creating a socioeconomic environment to allow all Nepali citizens to lead a healthy life in conformity with the saying "Health is Life." Highest priority was given to upgrading the health standard of the ninety-three percent of the Nepali people who live in rural areas using a Primary Health care approach. Particular attention is being paid to availability of family planning and MCH services, preventive health services, and easily accessible referral. In pursuit of the goal of improved health, the Government wanted to establish one sub-health post in each village development committee and 205 primary health care centres throughout Nepal.

The health system in Nepal has suffered from a number of problems in the past, including a lack of village orientation, weakness in implementation of plans, weakness in monitoring and evaluation, centralization of resources, and unfilled posts. The new health policy of the Nepalese government hoped to resolve these problems, and will strive, towards the targets of reducing infant mortality from 107 per thousand to 50 per thousand, reducing mortality of children under five from 197 per thousand to 70 per thousand, reducing total fertility from 5.8 to 4, reducing maternal mortality from 8.5 per thousand to 4 per thousand, and increasing life expectancy from 53 to 65 years.

The basic government plan for attacking the health problems of the Nepalese people was to have the following components:

1. Preventive health service to concentrate on family planning and MCH, including safe motherhood; expanded immunization; diarrhoea and acute respiratory infection control; and prevention and control of communicable and non-communicable diseases.
2. Promotive health services including health education and information for increased awareness of health matters; promotion of breast-feeding, use of iron, iodine and Vitamin A supplementation; and personal and environmental hygiene.
3. Curative health services to be expanded to provide sub-health posts, health posts and primary health care centres in the rural areas and district, regional and central hospitals for referral services.
4. Basic primary health care services to be based on the sub-health posts and 205 primary health care centres.
5. Community participation in health care to involve women volunteers, TBAs, and local leaders at every level.
6. Organization and management improvements to be made, including decentralized management, improved supervision, improved management information and improved logistics and supply arrangements.
7. Improved manpower development and management policies for HRH to be implemented, including increased cooperation between service and training, and improved policies posting, transfer and promotion.
8. Private, non-government and inter-sectoral coordination with the government system to be encouraged.
9. The ayurvedic and other traditional systems to be developed in a gradual manner to assist in the improvement of health in those areas where they are appropriate.
10. The quality and availability of drugs at the village level to be increased and effective funding mechanisms will be developed.
11. Every effort to be made to mobilize all government and external resources possible in a coordinated manner.
12. Health systems research to improve all aspects of service delivery and effectiveness attainment is encouraged.

13. The regionalization and decentralization process to be strengthened, district level health organizations to be given a more prominent role and micro-planning procedures to be adopted at the village level with special effort to reach the least privileged groups.
14. Nepal Red Cross Society to be authorised to conduct all programmes related to blood transfusion services, the practice of buying, selling and depositing of blood to be prohibited.

As the policy was over 20 years old, a two month review was done at the end of 2011 and early 2012 to identify issues and options for a new health policy (10). It was found that a total of 15 sub sector health policies, four health strategies and three overall plans had been introduced and implemented for the health sector. Considering these and the constitutional provision given in 2007 for access to basic health care, a new health policy is necessary.

b. NATIONAL DRUG POLICY - 1995

This drug policy has been promulgated in accordance with the objective of the National Health Policy 1991, to fulfil the commitment of GoN to provide "health for all" and to improve and manage by establishing co-ordination among governmental, NGOs and private organizations involved in the activities related to drug production, import, export, storage, supply, sales, distribution, quality assessment, regulatory control, rational use and information flow.

Besides the preamble other sections are:

- Main policy
- Objectives
- Policy Strategies including:
  - Drug Management
  - Quality Assurance & Regulatory Control Measures
  - Rational Drug Use & its Information
  - Manpower Development
  - National Drug Industry
  - Traditional Medicines
- Research and Development
- Technical Co-operation
- Monitoring and Evaluation

c. NATIONAL POLICY FOR CONTROL OF AIDS & STDs - 2052 BS

This policy has been promulgated with the objective of controlling the problems related to AIDS and STDs. This is being done as noted below:

- Policy
- National Executive & District Co-ordination Committee
- Co-ordination with NGOs
- Integrated Programme
- Blood Examination
- Reporting on AIDS and STD patients
- Maintenance of confidentiality
- Non-discrimination
- Stress on Safe Sex behaviour education
- Sterilization of equipment
- Middle level executive committee
- District level AIDS co-ordination committee

d. NATIONAL AYURVED HEALTH POLICY - 2052 BS

Passed by GoN on 14th Falgun, 2052 BS / February, 1996, it is divided into the under mentioned sections:

- Justification
- Objectives
- Organisation of Ayurvedic health services
- Mobilization of Inter Institutional and Community Participation
- Cultivation of herbs, production of medicines and profession
- Ayurvedic education and manpower development
- Ayurvedic manpower management
- Research in Ayurved
- Provision for resource mobilisation
- Nepal Ayurvedic Council
- Duties of District Ayurvedic Health Centre
- Responsibility of Ayurvedic Aushadhalaya

e. NATIONAL SAFE MOTHERHOOD POLICY – 1998

Under the umbrella of the Safe Motherhood programme, which is a component of PHC, the stress in the coming years will be on improving maternity care services, including family planning, at all levels of the Health Care Delivery System, even the community. This policy document has been arranged as:

- Policy Directive
- Policy Objectives
    - General
    - Specific
    - Strategies
- Maternity Care
    - Definition
    - Component
- Family Level
- Community Level
- Sub Health Post (SHP) Level
- Health Post (HP) Level
- Primary Health Care Centre (PHCC) Level
- District Level
- Zonal / Regional Level
- Central Level
- Referral System
- Institutional Arrangements
- Targets

f. NATIONAL HEALTH COMMUNICATION POLICY - 2012

This policy was endorsed and implemented with a view to making health related communication activities organised, transparent and people friendly. It is hoped that this policy will be effective in disseminating quality health messages or information to all Nepalis. The hope is to maintain the quality, correctness and appropriateness of the messages.

g. Other Efforts

Health Sector Strategy: An Agenda for Reform - 2003

Aware that health care facilities are not uniformly distributed in the country, GoN is trying to make it more equitable. After much deliberation, MoH came to the conclusion that it should focus and deal with those health problems, which are disproportionately and maximally contributing to the highest level of mortality and burden of diseases.

This is the rationale of the health care reform that is underway with the involvement of policy makers, NGOs, INGOs, private sectors and community in workshops, meetings etc, and a document was prepared in

2002. This was subsequently endorsed by the Council of Ministers in 2003. Key issues to be addressed by this strategy include (12):

- better value for the money that the public spends from its own resources
- strategy for better access of essential health care services (EHCS) to the poor and vulnerable. This comprises of safe motherhood & family planning, child health, control of communicable diseases and OPD services
- running of existing public services by GoN in a more efficient manner
- access to facilities of essential health care services provided by GoN
- better monitoring of health sector performance.

This reform will be over a 15 years period, which extends to the end of the Second Long Term Health Plan. There will however be an attempt to have realistic outputs at the end of the first five years.

The emphasis is on outputs and health outcomes. For this it is envisaged that there will be better Sector Management, which includes planning, programming, budgeting, and financing and performance management within the Ministry of Health.

It must be noted that the Health Sector Reform and is implementation is in the light of the National Health Policy 1991 and Second Long Term Health Plan (13).

The Nepal Health Sector Programme-Implementation Plan (2004-2009) was later extended to 2010, the Three year Interim Plan going on as scheduled to 2010.

Nepal Health Sector Programme 2004-10 & 2010-2015

The NHSP is a sector wide programme focussed on performance acts and health policy reforms implemented under a Sector Wide Approach (SWAp). Of the eight NHSP outputs 3 are for strengthening service delivery and 5 are for improving institutional capacity and management. The objective of NHSP is to improve health outcomes by expanding access to and increasing the use of Essential Health Care Services (EHCS) on a national basis with attention on the poor and disadvantaged.

The overall feeling was that Nepal has made some improvement in quality of access during the first NHSP. Planning exceeded nearly all outcomes and service output targets and is on track to meet the child and maternal mortality, MDGs. The current plan NHSP – 2 represents a continuation of earlier plans and policies. However expenditure in health remained low at 5.3% of GDP.

In NHSP – II there is stress on increased coverage and quality. It is hoped to give added impetus with the revitalisation of the PHC programme. The objective and targets are as below:

- Availability of basic health services as a health right as laid down in the Interim Constitution of Nepal
- Quality health services to be provided
- Easy accessibility to all Nepali citizens
- Implementation of health insurance
- Monitoring, supervision and evaluation of health care services
- Urban PHC facilities for urban disadvantaged population
- Implementation of sanitation and environmental programmes for healthy living.

20/20 Initiative

This was originally proposed by 5 UN organisations in response to the time-bound goals for social development and poverty reduction.

Following the initial meeting at Oslo in April 1996 to consider ways for universal access to basic social services a number of other steps have been taken.

The initiative called for the restructuring of government budgets and official development assistance (ODA) in favour of basic social services. The suggestion is that final allocation to such services be increased to 20% of the total government budget and that 20% of ODA be allocated to support these same services.

In connection with this a follow-up meeting was suggested in two years. In preparation of this a meeting for the process of restructuring and implementation of these suggestions was held in July, 1998.

As from Nov. 1999 Nepal committed itself to Vision 20/20: The Right to Sight. This is an international campaign to create awareness and mobilise additional resources for preventing and treating blindness. This global initiative is to tackle avoidable (preventable and curable) blindness by the year 2020. Whereas previously the thrust had been from hospital to community, it is now moving towards households and individuals. (14).

Hopefully this 'Sight for All by 2000' will achieve a lot for the Nepali people.

NATIONAL HEALTH POLICY II (Pending)

The National Health Policy II has been in the news for a number of years but because of the political uncertainties of the country has not been implemented so far. The vision is a healthy community where one and all have the opportunity to lead a prosperous life. Various targets have been set and the objective is to attain these by the year 2025. The components of the policy are in four broad areas:

1. Promotive services
2. Preventive services
3. Curative services
4. Rehabilitative services.

Millennium Development Goals

These goals were adopted by the United Nations in 2000 with the objective of initiating concerted action for global Health. In Sept. 2000 representatives from 189 countries, including 147 heads of state met at the Millennium Summit in New York to adopt the United Nations Millennium Declaration. Commitment has been made in seven areas: peace, security and disarmament; development & poverty eradication; protecting our common environment; human rights, democracy & good governance; protecting the vulnerable, meeting the special needs of Africa and strengthening the UN (15).

There is also a Road Map, which has established the goals and targets to be reached by 2015 in each of the seven areas. The goals in the area of development and poverty eradication are referred to Millennium Development Goals (MDG). This means that governments worldwide are obliged to do more to reduce poverty and hunger, tackle ill health, gender equality, lack of education, lack of access to clean water and environmental degradation.

- Eradicate extreme hunger and poverty
- Achieve universal primary education
- Provide gender equity and empower women
- Reduce child mortality
- Improve maternal health
- Combat HIV / AIDS, malaria and other diseases
- Ensure environmental sustainability
- Develop a global partnership for development

Three of the eight goals are directly health related; all of the others have important indirect effects on health without commitment from all the developed and developing countries the goals will not be met globally.

It is a matter of satisfaction for Nepal that we are not too badly placed as far as these objectives are concerned. The results that we attain are not only dependent on the on the aid that we finally receive but what efforts we ourselves make to attain these objectives.

Bill Gates, in writing about the Millennium Development Goals (MDG) in his annual letter of 2013 said:

- "The United Nations is starting to map out new goals for the years following the 2015 expiration of the current MDGs"
- "The MDGs were coherent because they focussed on helping the poorest people in the world."

As of September 2013 a report stated that since the MDGs were started in 2000, Nepal has managed to reduce poverty level by 2.5% per year, the IMR is 36 per 1,000 births, the U5MR is at 54 per 1,000 births and the Maternal Mortality Rate is down to 213 per 100,000 live births. This is all creditable for these were due to be attained by 2015 but have been achieved now.

This same report also stated that the contraceptive usage rate has to be raised from the 43.2% to 67.0% and that the supply of the retroviral combination needs to rise from the current 28.7% to a desirable 80.0%.

Multi Sector Nutrition Plan 2013-2017

The GoN has launched the 2013-2017 Multi Sector Nutrition Plan to improve maternal and child nutrition and thus save newborn lives. This drive known as 'Everyone Campaign' is involving a number of NGOs, USAID, and German Government funded projects.

Three Ministries Comparison - Budget for Health, Education and Defence

In the decade 1996-2006, the trend was for the budgetary provision to be increased for the two social sectors – health and education. Because of ongoing conflict within the country, Nepal's expenditure on defence had been going up. The figures pertaining then to the ministries, both in Nepal and in the region is given below.

Table 7.1 Comparison of health, education and defence budget in SEA region

Country	Percentage of national budget in different sectors		
	Health	Eudcation	Defence
Bangladesh	5	11	10
Bhutan	11	17	0
India	2	2	15
Maldives	9	18	10
Myanmar	3	8	29
Nepal	5	18	8
Pakistan	1	1	18
Sri Lanka	6	10	18
Thailand	8	17	6

Source: State of the Worlds Children 2005 (16).

Human Development Index (HDI)

Most newspapers make a great show of the fact Nepal moves up or down the HDI. Whilst this is a form of assessment of what is happening in the country, it does not warrant the amount of hullabaloo that is being generated every year. Noting the fact that Nepal had been making "good progress" over 25 years (1975-2000), the UNDP ranked Nepal 129 out of 162 countries in 2001.

In 2002 Nepal moved to 142 out of 173 countries with HDI value of 0.490. It must be pointed out however that 11 new countries were created during the course of this year and as their position in the ranking was higher than that of Nepal, one finds our ranking has slipped. The HDI report of 2011 titled "Sustainability & Equity: A Better Future for All" shows that Nepal has slid down to 157 position and is just above Afghanistan in South Asia. This however at 0.458 in 2011 is an improvement on the index of the previous year. This HDI Report, which is brought out annually by UNDP, is based on various indications pertaining to the country (17).

Oxford Poverty and Human Development Initiative (OPHI)

A study incorporating 10 indicators of poverty conducted in 102 countries with the support of the UNDP by the above group, has given the rankings given below to our countries of South East Asia. The results were published in October 2010 - Sri Lanka is at the top in 32nd ranking with Pakistan (70), Bangladesh (73), India (74) and Nepal (82). This is very relevant in the context that our government has taken the policy of alleviation of poverty.

In this context it may also be noted that the Third Nepal Living Standard Survey (NLSS III) of 2010 had shown that poverty levels had reduced from 31.5% in 2003/04 to 13% in 2013. This figure is debatable as those earning less that Rs. 52 per day only have been classed as poor. The poverty was said to be 11% in Kathmandu and 42% in the mountainous areas of the country.

Comparison in South East Asian countries

The overall level of public expenditure on health remained at 1% though it varies among the different countries of South Asia. The public expenditure in health in terms of percentage of GDP shows that in 1998, Maldives spent the highest amount at 5.1% whereas India and Pakistan spent the lowest amount on health viz. 0.8% and 0.9% respectively (17).

Table 7.2 Expenditures on health in South East Asian Countries as % of GDP

Country	1990	1998
India	0.9	0.8
Pakistan	1.1	0.9
Bangladesh	0.7	1.7
Nepal	0.8	1.3
Maldives	4.9	5.1
Bhutan	1.7	3.2
Sri Lanka	1.5	1.4
South Asia	1.0	1.0

POINTS TO PONDER

It is fitting and proper that there should be plans and policies to give direction to implementation. In our part of the world whilst plans and policies are well drawn up, the implementation tends to be lacking. One hopes that with the increased literacy and awareness of rights, this will be reversed.

References

1. Long Term Health Plan, 1975-90. (2034 BS), MoH, Pachali, Kathmandu
2. Mid Term Health Review 2035 BS. June 1979, MoH, Kathmandu
3. Final Draft Report on Country Health Resources and Priorities 1990-1995. Jan.1990. GoN, MoHP, Kathmandu
4. World Bank Report
5. Restructuring of Health Services in Nepal, Situation - Analysis. Singh, H. 1991.
6. Sustainability in the Health Sector. Nepal Case Study. SCF(UK), March 1992.
7. The Practice of Health Delivery System of the Government Health Service Centres in Nepal. MN Tiwari, 1994.
8. Early Childhood Feeding, Nutrition & Development. GoN, National Planning Commission, 1997.
9. Second Long Term Health Plan 1997-2017, PPFA&MD, MoHP.
10. Shrestha, IB and Pathak LR. Review of National Health Policy 1991, MoHP/ NHSSP.
11. Strategic Analysis to Operationalise Second Long Term Health Plan (1997-2017), GoN, MoH, 2001.
12. Health Sector Strategy – An Agenda for Reform., 2003, HMG, MoH.
13. Nepal Health Sector Programme = Implementation Plan (NHSP-IP), 2004-2009. Oct. 2004, GoN, MoH.
14. Sight for all by 2000.
15. Annual Report of Dept of Health Services, 2011/2012.
16. State of the World Children 2004.
17. Human Development Index 2011.
18. Human Development in South Asia 2002, Mahbub ul Haq, Human Development Centre, Oxford University Press.

ANNEXURE

Health Legislations, Acts and Rules

COUNCILS SET UP BY LEGISLATION

The passing of the Poor Law Amendment Act in 1834 in the United Kingdom is said to be the start of the concept of public responsibility for the health of the individual citizen (1). As far as Nepal is concerned the early legal references to health matters may be said to be the codification of the Nepalese laws into what became known as the Muluki Ain, the first promulgation of which was on 5th January, 1854 AD (2). It has been suggested that further developments were brought about as a result of the observations of Jung Bahadur of both the English legal system and the French Code Napoleon during the course of his Belait Yatra in 1856 (3). The latest eleventh amendment of the Muluki Ain deals with matters pertaining to abortion.

Health Rights is something, which everyone is aware of. WHO has been advocating the use of health legislation to attain HFA 2000 and also at later date. It is accepted that more than half the world's population does not have health care (2). We too in Nepal talked of Health Rights in 1990 at 15th All Nepal Medical Conference at Biratnagar where the theme of the Presidential address was Health Rights (3).

Health legislation covers a number of subject areas in its entirety. The countries of SEARO have legislation pertaining to:

- general public health laws
- tobacco laws
- blood supply laws
- organ transplantation laws, and
- international health regulations and food safety.

Bearing all this in mind I have tried to put the legislations in the historical order together with some categorisation so that reference to these legislations will be easier.

HEALTH & RELATED LEGISLATIONS

These are divided into five arbitrary groups as detailed:

1. Historical & Administrative

a. Ilaz Garne Ko or On Medical Practice in Muluki Ain
b. Nepal Medical Council Act, 2020 BS (1954)
c. Disabled Protection & Welfare Act, 2039 BS (1982)
d. Nepal Ayurved Council Act, 2045 BS
e. Nepal Nursing Council Act, 2052 BS
f. Nepal Health Professional Council Act, 2053 BS
g. Nepal Health Services Act, 2053 BS
h. Nepal Pharmacy Council Act, 2057 BS
i. Health Workers & Health Institutions Security Act, 2066 BS

2. Government Acts for Law & Order

a. Police Act, 2012 BS (1956)
b. Jail Act, 2019 BS (1963)
c. Some Public Offence & Punishment Act, 2027 BS (1970)
d. Black Marketing & Other Social Offences Act, 2032 BS
e. Drug Abuse Control Act, 2033 BS (1976)
f. Government Prosecution Related Act, 2049 BS
g. Vehicular & Transport Act, 2049 BS
h. Compensation for Torture Act, 2053 BS
i. Domestic Violence (Offence & Punishment) Act, 2066 BS

3. Diseases Related

a. Smallpox Control Act, 2020 BS (1964)
b. Infectious Diseases Act, 2020 BS (1964)
c. Natural Disaster Rescue Act 2039 BS (1982)

4. Food & Consumer Items & Related.

a. Drug Act, 2035 BS (1978)
b. Pesticides Act, 2048 BS (1990)
c. Breast Milk Substitute Act, 2049 BS (!992)
d. Environment Protection Act, 2053 BS
e. Iodised Salt (Prod.& Dist.) Act, 2053 BS
f. Consumer Protection Act, 2054 BS
g. Tobacco Product Control & Regulatory Act, 2065 BS

5. Educational, Hospital Services & Research

a. CTEVT Act. 2045 BS
b. Nepal Health Research Council Act, 2047 BS.
c. BP Koirala Institute of Health Sciences Act, 2049 BS
d. BP Koirala Memorial Cancer Hospital Act, 2053 BS.
e. Human Organ Transplantation Act, 2055 BS
f. Saheed Ganga Lal National Heart Centre Act, 2057 BS
g. National Academy of Health Sciences Act, 2060 BS
h. Patan Academy of Health Sciences 2064 BS (2008)

1. Historical & Administrative

Following his visit to England and France, Jung Bahadur the first Rana Prime Minister had enforced the Muluki Ain in 1854. Some form of updating the various rules and regulations then existing was done by King Mahendra in the Muluki Ain (Law of the Land) or Civil Codes of 1963/64. This was divided up into 5 parts, which were in turn sub-divided into various Clauses or Mahals (4). The health related parts and clauses are as follows:

Part III	Clause 15	Pertaining to adoption
Part IV	Clause 9	Pertaining to assault
	Clause 10	Post mortem by hospital doctor. Also abortions
	Clause 12	On Medical Practice (See 1 below)
	Clause 13	Assault with intention to rape
	Clause 14	Rape of women under and over 16 years of age
	Clause 15	Incest
	Clause 16	Sex with animals
	Clause 17	Relating to marriage. Age at marriage, prohibition of marriages of minors - Medical reasons for divorce

1a. Ilaz Garne Ko or On Medical Practice in Muluki Ain (5)

This is divided into ten sections each one dealing with a certain aspect of treatment.

a. Criteria for practising medicine, which could be even for those who have learnt it as an apprenticeship.
b. Necessity of consent for operation and when it could be waived.
c. Liabilities of the practitioner when even poisonous substances have to be administered for the sake of treatment.
d. Consequences when patient who has been operated dies. Examination and testing of any remaining medication.
e. Forbiddance to sell intoxicants, poisons or other medicines except by prescription.
f. Treatment of the mentally ill.
g. Obligation of those who have sick servants or other ill persons in their charge.
h. Responsibility of those authorised to give treatment in the event of the patient dying or suffering disability.
i. Practise of medicine by those not authorised and the penalties for death or physical damage to those given treatment.

j. Death during treatment and if due to malicious intent, the filing of complaint within three months.

NB. Jung Bahadur complied in 1851 AD, the first Muluki Ain out of the numerous orders, Lal Mohurs[1] and Sanads, which had been promulgated up to that time. This version of the ilaz garne ko is from the section of the New Muluki Ain, which received a Lal Mohur on 30th Chaitra, 2019 BS and came into force from 1st Bhadra 2020 BS.

- The Civil Code (Muluki Ain, 1963)
    - Prohibits child marriage, marriage without consent or forced marriage.
- The Civil Code (Muluki Ain, 1976, Sixth amendment).
    - Makes intention to rape an offence. A man contacting a girl over the age 11, who is not his wife; with the intention of raping her may be fined up to Rs. 5000 or imprisoned for a year or both. Intercourse with a woman above 16 years of age, without her consent, by threat or by taking advantage of the circumstances, is considered rape. Persons convicted of raping a girl less than 14 years of age are liable to imprisonment for 6-10 years. Those guilty of raping girls above 14 years of age are liable for imprisonment for 3-5 years. Instigators and abettors are liable for 1-3 years imprisonment.
    - Does not hold a woman liable for her actions in protecting her virginity or if, following rape, she attacks and kills her rapist within one hour of the rape having been committed.
- The Civil Code (Muluki Ain, 2003. Eleventh amendment).
    - This amendment, which came into effect immediately, is concerned with safe abortion and a number of sections of the old Civil Code have been repealed. The new provisions allow for abortions under certain conditions.

There has been some indication in the press that Supreme Court has approved the government's move to replace the Muluki Ain with new civil and criminal codes for the country. The Ministry of Law and Justice is in the process of doing this.

1b. Nepal Medical Council Act, 2020 BS (1964)

Enacted as Law No. 35 of 2020 BS and published in Nepal Gazette Vol. 13 No. 29 (Extraordinary) of Falgun 16, 2020 BS.

1. Red Seal denoting official approval

After dealing with the establishment of the Council and the constitution of the same, the term of office of the Chairman and members plus reasons for disqualification are defined.

i. Nepal Medical Council Rules, 2024 BS

Published in the Nepal Gazette of Poush 17, 2024 BS

It dealt with:

i. Provisions for entering of doctor's names in the register
ii. Meeting of the Council and other matters
iii. Miscellaneous

a. Nepal Medical Council (First Amendment) Act, 2044 BS

Enacted as Law No. 14 of 2044 BS and published in Nepal Gazette Vol. 37 No. 31 of Asoj 9, 2044 BS

Main changes are in the composition, criteria, suitability and duration of membership of Council. Clauses numbers 22, 23 and 24 of the original act dealing with powers of Nepal Medical Council regarding:

a. Registration particulars of degree, diploma given by medical institutions,
b. Appointment of inspector
c. Removal of recognition.

Three clauses No. 22, 23 and 24 were however deleted during the final phase when the Act was being passed by then functioning Rastriya Panchayat. The thinking was that as the University was doing this function, it was not necessary to duplicate it. Representation regarding this was made immediately and the subsequent enactment made the reinstatement.

b. Nepal Medical Council (Second Amendment) Act, 2047 BS

Enacted as Law No. 14 of 2047 BS and published in Nepal Gazette Vol. 40 No. 44 of Aswin 27, 2047 BS.

The three clauses, which had been inadvertently removed in the First Amendment of 2044 BS, were reinstated.

The number of institutions recognised was revised.

i. Nepal Medical Council Act, (First Amendment) 2047 BS Rules

These were enacted to amend the Nepal Medical Council Rules 2024 BS.

Published in the Nepal Gazette Part 3, Vol.40, No.28 of Kartik 12, 2047 BS.

c. Nepal Medical Council Act, (Third Amendment) 2056. BS

Approved a Bill by both upper and lower House of Representatives during the thirteenth session.

Enacted as Law No. ... of 2054 BS and published in Nepal Gazette of .... the, 2055 BS.

This amendment deals with the under mentioned aspects which have been changed in this amendment.

- Provisional registration period to be of two years
- Prior concurrence of NMC necessary before starting medical college
- NMC given authority to institute/conduct licensing examination.

d) Amendment to some Health Acts 2058 BS

By this amendment was initially passed as an Ordinance and later passed by the House. It deals with the number of NMC members in the executive and pre-requisites for the same. It is:

- Total number of members to be 19 of which:
  - i. By HMG nomination - 8
  - ii. by election - 9
  - iii. Ex officio - 2
- Pre-requisites for nominations/election
  - i. Chairman - 15 years registration
  - ii. Vice-Chairman - 12 years registration
  - iii. Member - 5 years registration

1c. Disabled Protection and Welfare Act, 2039 BS (1982)

Enacted as Law No. 13 of 2039 BS and published in Nepal Gazette of 6th Mangsir, 2039 BS.

This Act was enacted mainly with the commitment made during the International Year of Disabled Persons (IYDP) 1981. This is a comprehensive Act, which has as many as twenty-five headings dealing with the political and socio-economic aspects and needs of the disabled. One who is physically and mentally unable to lead a normal life has been defined as a disabled person.

1d. Nepal Ayurved Council Act, 2045 BS

Enacted as Law No. 21 of 2045 BS and published in Nepal Gazette Part 2,

Vol.38, No.46 of 28th Kartik, 2045 BS

a) Nepal Ayurved Council (First Amendment) Act 2055 BS

b) Revision of some laws Act of Republican Set up 2066 BS

1e. Nepal Nursing Council Act, 2052 BS

Enacted as Law No. 15 of 2052 BS and published in Nepal Gazette Part 2, Vol.45, (Extraordinary) No.49 of 7th Chaitra, 2052 BS.

Following the short title, commencement, establishment of the Council and its composition, autonomy, the criteria, tenure and disqualification from membership, duties, functions and rights of the Council plus matters for effective working are stated. The Act goes on to state the duties of the Registrar and details for registration and re-registration.

A Nursing Council Act had been initially drafted as far back as 1965 but was never enacted. It was thus after years of efforts that this version was finally enacted in 1995.

a) Nepal Nursing Council (First Amendment) Act, 2058 BS

1f. Health Professionals Council Act, 2053 BS

Enacted as Law No. 20 of 2053 BS and published in Nepal Gazette Part 2, Vol 46, (Extraordinary) No. 56 of 13th Baisakh, 2053 BS.

The preamble of this Act states that it aims at providing in an organised and scientific way the services of health practitioners other than those who are eligible to be registered at the Nepal Medical Council, so as to make health services timely and effective.

Following the short title, commencement, establishment of the Council and its composition, autonomy of the Council, tenure, duties and functioning of the of the office bearers, the meetings and decisions of the Council, duties of the Registrar and the registration of the Health Practitioners.

1 g. Nepal Health Services Act, 2053 BS*

Enacted as Law No. 32 of 2053 BS and published in Nepal Gazette Part 2 Vol. 46, (Extraordinary) No 59, of 15th Falgun, 2053 BS. This Act has been passed with a view towards making health services available in the far-flung districts of Nepal. It has incorporated allopathic, ayurved and homeopathy to give equal opportunities to doctors and health workers to provide health services and receive facilities and benefits in return.

* The Health Act was implemented as from 27th May, 1997 (14th Jestha, 2054 BS).

a) Nepal Health Services (First Amendment) Act 2055 BS

Some changes effected pertained to the implementation of the act as from 14th Jestha 2054 BS (27th May, 1997) and in certain areas.

- Prohibition to employ personnel of daily wages
- Upward movement / promotions
- Temporary appointments, transfers
- Promotions.

b) Amendment to some Health Acts, 2058

c) Nepal Health Services (Second Amendment) Act, 2058

i. Nepal Health Service Rules, 2055 BS.

Printed in the Gazette No 48 (Extraordinary 62) of 14th Poush, 2055 BS.

The 132 rules are divided among the 14 (?16) Chapters that this set of rules comprises.

There is some discrepancy between the Act and the Rules e.g. Rule 28(5) states that one must have spent four years in one post before promotion is given, whilst the Health Services Act (first Amendment) 2054 states that an officer in the 9th grade can be promoted after 2 years of work.

1h. Nepal Pharmacy Council Act, 2057 BS

Enacted as Law No 14 of 2057 BS and given Royal consent on 2057/10/18. (Jan 31, 2001) Published in Nepal Gazette. GoN implemented the Act on 2058/06/08 by constituting the Council.

As per the Act, no one can practice the pharmacy profession without registering his/her name in the Council. Pharmacy profession means profession which certifies the production of drugs, quality assurance, inspection and recommendation for drug industries, storage of manufactured drugs, technology for supply, supervision of supply, registration of drugs, drug medication for its effectiveness and quality and safety and term also includes Hospital pharmacy.

The main functions of the Nepal Pharmacy Council are as follows:

- To prepare and implement policy, plan and programmes to run profession of pharmacy scientifically and systematically.

- To grant recognition to the educational institution and the certificate and degree awarded by such institutions, which provide pharmacy education.
- To determine the standards of curricula, condition for admission and examination system of the educational institution providing pharmacy education, and enquire whether standards so determined are maintained or not, and abrogate the certificate and degree awarded by the educational institution which do not comply with standards so determined after completing the procedures as prescribed.
- To determine the qualification and register the name of pharmacist and pharmacy assistant as prescribed in the Registration Book of the Council who has completed the qualification so determined.
- To remove the names of registered pharmacist and pharmacy assistant from the Registration Book after the completion of the procedures as prescribed if they are found to violate or not follow the professional code of conduct as prescribed.

1i. Health Workers & Health Institutions Security Act, 2066 BS

Enacted as Law No. 2 of 2066 BS and confirmed on 2066/1/21. This Act has been passed to deal with any sudden emergency or financial liability that may arise in connection with the reliable, appropriate and beneficial treatment that is being provided to the public.

Health Workers & Health Institutions Security Rules & Regulations, 2069 BS

2. Government Acts for Law & Order

2a. Police Act, 2012 BS (1956)

Enacted as Law No. 8 of 2012 BS and published in Nepal Gazette of Asoj 31, 2012 BS.

Deals with unclaimed dead bodies and states that following necessary investigations if the cause of death were natural, then the body may be handed over to the nearest medical college (6).

Necessity of doing post-mortem in cases of accidents, suicides and suspected murder.

2b. Jail Act, 2019 BS (1963)

Enacted as Law No.46 of 2019 BS and published in Nepal Gazette of Magh

23, 2019 BS.

Deals with:

- Obligations of state to health and treatment of inmates
- Death in custody.

2c. Some Public Offence & Punishment Act, 2027 BS (1970).

Enacted as Law No. 12 of 2027 BS and published in Nepal Gazette of Asoj 18th, 2027 BS.

The Act deals with the production of written and figurative material relating to health sciences or public health, which is not considered pornographic.

2d. Black Marketing & Other Social Offences Act, 2032 BS (1975).

Enacted as Law No.12 of 2032 BS and published in Nepal Gazette of Bhadra 20th, 2032 BS.

Also deals with adulteration of medicine and sale of it.

2e. Drug Abuse Control Act, 2033 BS (1976).

Enacted as Law No. 24 of 2033 BS and published in Nepal Gazette of Asoj 10th, 2033 BS.

Deals with:

- Selling of narcotic drugs by prescription
- Intimation to users about use of drug
- Responsibility of prescribing doctor
- Freedom from prosecution whilst undergoing treatment at authorised treatment centre.

2f. Govt. Prosecution Related Act, 2049 BS

Enacted as Law No. 43 of 2049 BS and published in Nepal Gazette of 8th Poush, 2049 BS.

- Post mortem if cause of death is not known
- Examination of blood and semen.

2g. Vehicular & Transport Act, 2049 BS

Enacted as Law No. 45 of 2049 BS and published in Nepal Gazette of 12th Poush, 2049 BS.

- Pertaining to medical examination for fitness to drive.
- Ban on smoking in public transport.

2h. Compensation for Torture Act, 2053 BS

Enacted as Law No. of 2053 BS and published in Nepal Gazette of 3rd Poush, 2053 BS.

Pertains to examination by physicians under government service or otherwise.

- application by relative of accused if torture whilst in detention is suspected.

2i. Domestic Violence (Offence & Punishment) Act, 2066 BS (2009)

Act No. 1 of the year 2066 BS (2009)

Makes provision to respect the right of every person to live in a secure and dignified life, to prevent and control violence occurring within the family and for matters connected therewith and incidental there to making such violence punishable, and for providing protection to the victims of violence.

3. Diseases Related

3a. Smallpox Control Act, 2020 BS (1964)

Enacted as Law No.27 of 2020 BS and published in Nepal Gazette Vol. 13 No. 29 (Extraordinary) of Falgun 16, 2020 BS.

i. Smallpox Control Rules, 2023 BS

Published in the Nepal Gazette of Baisakh 18, 2024 BS

ii. Smallpox Control (First Amendment) Rules, 2027 BS

Published in Nepal Gazette of Baisakh 1, 2028 BS

It deals with:

i. Area demarcation and vaccination provision
ii. Vaccine, recording and certificate for it
iii. Miscellaneous

3b. Infectious Diseases Act, 2020 BS (1964)

Enacted as Law No. 28 of 2020 BS and published in Nepal Gazette Vol. 13. No. 29 (Extraordinary) of Falgun 16, 2020 BS.

The Act deals with various aspects including the following:

- Power to make special arrangements

- Power to entertain and make decision of case
- Protection for bonafide action

3c. Natural Disaster (Rescue) Act, 2039 BS (1982)

Enacted as Law No. 20 of 2039 BS and published in Nepal Gazette Part of 8th Poush, 2039 BS

- Responsibility of local committees to take injured to nearby hospital or health institution.

4. Food & Consumer Items & Related

4a. Drug Act, 2035 BS (1978)

Enacted as Law No. 21 of 2035 BS and published in Nepal Gazette of Kartik 8, 2035 BS.

There are forty Sections in the Act arranged in Seven Chapters. Chapter one deals about the definitions and explanations of different terminology. Chapter two deals about formation of Drugs Consultative Council (DCC) and Drugs Advisory Committee (DAC). Third Chapter deals about research and control of drugs. Fourth Chapter deals with legal procedures and measures related to manufacture, export, import distribution and sale of drugs. Chapter five deals about the quality and standard of drugs. Sixth chapter deals about the enquiry and inspection of drugs for its standard quality. In chapter seven miscellaneous legal provisions are included from section 25 to 40 (7).

Section 3 of the Act is about the formation of Drugs Consultative Council (DCC) and section 4 about Drugs Advisory Committee (DAC). Section 5 of this Act has vested executive powers to the Department of Drug Administration (DDA) for the implementation of the Drugs Act, Drug Regulations and Codes. Section 40 of this Act has empowered GoN to make necessary Regulations for implementing it.

This act, which had defined a physician as one, registered under the Nepal Medical Council Act, 2020 BS led to difficulties regarding the practise of medicine by paramedicals who had been trained by the Institute of Medicine, established in 1972.

a. Regulations on constitution of Drug Consultative Council & Drug Advisory Committee 2037 BS (1979).

b. Drug Registration Regulations 2038 BS (1981).

This gives the procedures and requirements to manufacture drugs. As per these regulation letter of recommendation has to be obtained from the Department of Drug Administration (DDA) for the establishment of drug industries.

First Amendment to Regulations 2058 BS

A number of major changes have been made in the implementation of the regulations.

c. Drug Enquiry & Inspection Regulations 2040 BS (1983)
d. Regulations on Standards of Drugs 2043 BS (1986). Published in Nepal Gazette Vol. 36 No. 18 of 27th Shrawan, 2043 BS.

This deals with all aspects pertaining to the standards of medicines produced in the country.

A number of Codes were made under the Regulations or Rules and these were specifically in the fields of:

- Drug import
- Registration of retail shops/firms, industries and products
- Procedures of enquiry and investigation
- Quality and standards of drugs.

Failure to observe and abide by the Drugs Act and Regulations pertaining to it would make the concerned party liable to penalties as specified in the Act.

Code for Manufacture of Drugs. 2041 BS (1986)

This was passed and subsequently published in Nepal Gazette Vol. 34 No. 22 Kha (Extraordinary) of 11th Shrawan, 2041 BS.

Code for Sale and Distribution of Drugs

Code for Advertisement of Drugs

Enacted and published in Nepal Gazette Part 4. Vol.34 No.22 Kha. of Shrawan 11, 2041 BS.

National Drug Control Policy

This was formulated following the recommendations of a workshop in July 1995 and its existence made public on Feb 2nd. 1996. It was approved by the cabinet and subsequently incorporated in the Ninth Five Year

Plan. This national policy covers aspects like law enforcement, demand reduction, treatment and rehabilitation services, preventive programmes with regard to drug abuse and its control.

NB. It has been flashed in the lay press that the Department of Drug Administration is in the process of updating the Drug Act of 1978 to make it up to international standard.

4b. Pesticides Act, 2048 BS (1990)

The Pesticides Act was promulgated in 1990 (2048 BS) with the objective of controlling import, export, production, sale and use of insecticides. The Act has sixteen sections.

4c. Breast Milk Substitutes (Marketing Control) Act, 2049 BS (1992)

Enacted as Law No. 39 of 2049 BS and published in Nepal Gazette of 29th Mangsir, 2049 BS.

4d. Environment Protection Act, 2053 BS

Enacted as Law No. 24 of 2053 BS and published in Nepal Gazette Vol. 46 (................) of 17th Baisakh, 2053 BS

The preamble goes on to state that the Act has been passed to protect the human race, the flora and fauna from the effects of environmental degradation and to further protect the environment from destruction by use of existing resources in proper manner.

Clause 7 deals with stoppage and control of pollution. No one is entitled to disturb the environment by adding to it industrial hazards such as sound waves, heat and radiation rays that are harmful to living beings.

Details of inspection for control are also stated.

4e. Iodised Salt (production, sale & distribution) Act, 2053 BS

Enacted as Law No 16 of 2055 BS and given Royal Assent on 2055/10/1.

Approved a Bill by both upper and lower House of Representatives during the thirteenth session. Its objective is to ensure the supply of iodised salt all over the country.

4f. Consumer Protection Act, 2054 BS

Enacted as Law No. 20 of 2054 BS and published in Nepal Gazette Vol. 47 (Extraordinary 54) of 15th Magh, 2054 BS.

The preamble goes on to state that the Act has been passed to protect the health, facilities and financial interest of the consumer in respect of the quality of the substance or services, the results and costs and in keeping with the interest of the consumer.

Definition provides for various terms:

- Substandard consumer items which are harmful to health, stale, poisonous or one to which harmful ingredients or colouring has been added

Clause 6 deals with the rights and wellbeing of the consumer in respect of substances or service provided for a fee, which causes harm to body, life or health of the consumer.

Clause 10 forbids the production and use of substance or service likely to cause harm to the health of the consumer.

4g. Tobacco Product Control & Regulatory Act, 2065 BS

This was enforced by the Government as an act in Aug. 2011.

5. Educational, Hospital Services & Research

5a. Council for Technical Education and Vocational Training Act, 2045 BS

Enacted as Law No. 20 of 2045 BS and published in Nepal Gazette Vol. 38 No. 46 (Extraordinary) of Kartik 28th, 2045 BS.

The Act provides for the establishment of CTEVT, which was to be made responsible for the training of basic and middle level technical workers. After stating the composition of the Council it deals with the duties, functions and powers. The following aspects are also catered for :

- Formation of subcommittees and task force
- Income of Council
- Delegation of powers.

5b. Nepal Health Research Council Act, 2047 BS

Enacted as Law No. 29 of 2047 BS and published in Nepal Gazette Part 2, Vol.40, No. 67 of Chaitra 29, 2047 BS.

This Act was brought with a view to establishing the Nepal Health Research Council to make a study of the various problems in the field of health and do research to maintain the health status of the people.

5c. B.P.Koirala Institute of Health Sciences Act, 2049 BS

Enacted as Law No. 48 of 2049 BS and published in Nepal Gazette Part 2, Vol. 42, No. 55 of Magh 5, 2049 BS.

This act was passed with a view to setting up the B.P. Koirala Institute of Health Sciences at Dharan as a memorial to the late leader and with the objective of making Nepal self-reliant in the health sector, providing good health care to the ordinary people, doing high quality research and study and producing the necessary health manpower.

i. B.P.Koirala Institute of Health Sciences Rules, 2050 BS

It deals with matters pertaining to the Council, Executive Committee, and various other officials of the Institute, their appointments, terms of service such as Director, Rector, Senior Administrator, and various matters concerning their functioning.

Other sections deal with code of conduct of students, academic and research work and the granting of certificates and degrees.

a) B.P. Koirala Institute of Health Sciences (First Amendment) Act 2055 BS

This amendment has effected certain changes such as :

1. The Prime Minister becomes the Chancellor of the institution and a new post of Vice-Chancellor is created.
2. The Institute is able to conduct Certificate, Graduate and Post-Graduate levels of study in medicine, nursing and in the health field.

5d. B.P. Koirala Memorial Cancer Hospital Act, 2053 BS

Enacted as Law No. 34 of 2053 BS and published in Nepal Gazette Part 2 Vol 46, (Extraordinary) No 59, of 15th Falgun, 2053 BS. This Act has been passed with a view to keeping alive the memory of the people's leader late Bishweshwar Prasad Koirala by establishing a Cancer Hospital to provide facilities for the research, and also high standard treatment for cancer patients.

5e. Human Organ Transplantation (regular & prohibition) Act, 2055 BS (1998)

(In 1995, following the appearance of a news item of a first renal transplant done at a nursing home at Kathmandu on 26th April, 1995; a letter regarding this was printed in The Rising Nepal (6). It drew attention to the necessity of having an Organ Transplant Act, as soon as possible to prevent the possibility of having spurious dealings related to kidney transplantation done in this country. Both upper and lower House of Representatives passed the necessary Act during the thirteenth session).

Enacted as Law No. 20 of 2055 BS and given Royal assent on 2055/10/21. It was to be effectively on publication in Nepal Gazette.

a) Kidney Transplantation (Regular & Prohibitory) Rules, 2058

5f. Saheed Ganga Lal National Heart Centre Act, 2057 BS

Enacted as Law No 13 of 2057BS and given Royal aasent on 2057/10/4. Came into immediate effect.

This Act has been enacted to set up a National Heart Centre in memory of Saheed Ganga Lal. Its objectives as stated in the Act are to:

- reduce the incidence of heart disease
- diagnose, treat and rehabilitate patients with heart disease
- provide facilities and do research in this field.

5g. National Academy of Health Sciences Act, 2060

Brought as an Act by way of Ordinance No 2 of 2060 BS. See below.

5h. Patan Academy of Health Science Act 2064 BS

ORDINANCES

1. SPECIAL ORDINANCE FOR HEALTH 2057 BS

This was the first time ever that a special ordinance has been passed for health act amendments. It comprised of measures to deal with certain health acts, which needed to be amended viz.:

- Health Services Act
- Nepal Medical Council Act.

This ordinance was subsequently passed by the Parliament.

2. National Academy of Medical Sciences , 2060.

Ordinance No. 2 of 2060 BS as per Dhara 72 of the Constitution of Nepal 2047 BS. Royal assent given on 2060/2/12.

The preamble goes on to state that this ordinance was brought about to provide high quality services all over the kingdom of Nepal by setting up of an academy for the training of high quality manpower. This Academy will also be a National Centre for the conduction of research also.

The ordinance came into effect immediately an NAMS with its main office at Kathmandu but can also have branches elsewhere in the country. Made later into Law No. 26 of 2063 BS.

HEALTH ASPECTS IN LEGISLATION ABOUT FOOD

There is limited legislation about the standards of food for sale or offered to the public and the hygienic standards at eating-places has been felt. Requests for more specific legislation regarding these aspects have been made from time to time. The Consumer Protection Act 2054 BS will be able to deal with certain aspects of it.

In 1998 cases of "dropsy", brought about by international adulteration of mustard oil in various parts of India have highlighted the inadequacies of our laws against any form of adulteration. It is a known fact that items such as butter yellow, orthotricresyl phosphate, mineral, white, paraffin and even engine oils have been used to adulterate cooking oils.

The accidental/intentional adulteration of mustard oil by argemone mexicana is liable to occur in Nepal. Though legal requirements existed for oil produced in Nepal to be labelled by source, batch number and date of production, it turned out that the producers had not been following this code and were resisting its application. Furthermore the testing facilities and the rigorous implementation of the same have to be done by the Food Research Laboratories.

Colouring matter used in various mithais (sweets), meat of lime fed animals, polished dal or lentils and even sand or marble chips in cereals are all harmful when eaten.

Laws safeguarding what we eat, inclusive of food, beverages and medicines must be enacted and the regulations strictly enforced by reliable, competent and properly equipped authorities. Only then will it have any meaning.

A. Food Act, 2023 BS (1966)

Enacted as Law No. 8 of 2023 BS and published in Nepal Gazette of 24th Bhadra, 2023 BS.

Provision exists for the concerned officer to confiscate and to forbid the distribution of foodstuff concerned harmful.

Such foodstuff should be examined at a designated laboratory and the report obtained from the designated officer/s.

i. Madira Niyamharu. 2033 BS

B. Animal Slaughter House and Meat Examination Act, 2055 BS

Under discussion as Bill by both upper and lower House of Representatives during the thirteenth session. Yet to be approved.

HEALTH ASPECTS OF INDUSTRIAL LEGISLATION

Labour Act 2049 BS (1992). Act No 9 of 2049 BS, published in Nepal Gazette on 2nd Baisakh, 2049 BS.

Section 5 deals with Health and Protection. Clause no. 27 details various aspects amongst which there is provision to ban smoking in the whole or part of the working area. This act is being amended in a major fashion but this is delayed as the House is not in session.

LEGISLATION FOR THE WELFARE OF CHILDREN

Relevant laws and regulations concerning child welfare prior to ratification of the Convention on the Rights of the Child were (9):

ACTS

- Begging (Prohibition) Act in 1961.
- Birth and Death Registration Act in 1976.
- Drug Abuse (Control) Act in 1976.

REGULATIONS

- Suckling Baby (Maintenance) Rule, 1963.

Prohibition of child labour was made statutory on 20th Sept. 1990. The new government then also promulgated the new Labour Act, 1991 and the Children Rights Act, 1992. The gist of the new legislation is as below:

a. The Constitution, 1990
   - prohibited the employment of children in any occupation, which is hazardous to life

- prohibited the trafficking of human beings including children, slaves, and serfs and forced labour. It restricted the sale, trafficking and abduction of children

b. The Labour Act, 1992
   - prohibits the employment of children less than 14 years of age
   - requires the employees of more than 50 workers to provide supervised care and also time for mothers to breast feed their children
   - provides for initial check-up and medical treatment of employees

c. The Child Rights Act, 1992
   - right of the child to name and birth date
   - prohibits the employment of children under the age of 14
   - prohibits the employment of minors, aged 14 to 16, between the hours of 18.00 and 06.00
   - prohibits the employment of minors, aged 14 to 16, for more than six hours per day and more than 36 hours per week
   - prohibits the employment of children in work that is likely to be harmful to health or hazardous to life

c.i. Rules and regulations relating to Children - 2051 BS
   - Preamble
   - Provision in relation to Central Child Welfare Committee
   - Provision in relation to District Child Welfare Committee
   - Duties, Functions and Rights of Child Welfare Officer
   - Formation of Management Committee
   - Provision of Chief, Child Welfare Centre and its management
   - Arrangements for Child Welfare
   - Miscellaneous

Many children are trafficked to India for work, including circuses and are vulnerable to exploitation and sexual abuse. There were reports that in the conflict with the Maoists many children and youth were used. Many children themselves are in conflict with the law. Many are accused and arrested, and may be brought for trial without proper investigation. In the meantime however the government has opened a 'Children's Correction Home' where such accused children are supposed to be kept. Many underage children are being used by traffickers as 'mules' for being minors they are not liable to severe punishment.

Under the Children's Act (1992), children below 10 years are not criminally liable; those between 10 and 14 receive warnings if the offence is punishable by a fine, and are sentenced to a maximum of six months if it is punishable by imprisonment, and those between 14 and 16 if convicted to half the penalty imposed by law on an adult for that offence. Currently a recommendation has been made that the age for criminal liability be raised from 16 to 18 years.

Other Legislations

The Decentralisation Act, with the object of transferring administrative and financial authority from the centre to the districts was passed in 2039 BS. (1982). It covered also administrative matters regarding health care delivery. So also The District Development Committee Act, 2048 BS, The Village Development Act, 2048 BS and the Municipality Act 2048 BS also deal with this aspect. The Local Self Governance Bill, after years of discussion was passed by both Houses of Parliament only in 2055 BS (1998).

The Local Self-Governance Act of 1998 has contributed to put some check and balance to make local bodies accountable to the people. Once the tenure of the local bodies had expired in 2002 there was a lot of chaos. There had been measure of resources and irregularities after the dissolution of the local bodies in 2002.

LEGISLATED COUNCILS

Nepal Ayurved Council (NAC)

Though the Act to establish this Council was passed as long ago as 2045 BS, it has not really been implemented. Whilst provision was made for the traditional practitioners plus those trained up to 1972, the HRH in ayurvedic medicine after this period felt that provision for their registration had not properly been spelt out. Hence the delay. This Act too is in the process of being amended for the registration of graduate manpower in this field.

Nepal Health Research Council (NHRC)

Nepal Health Research Council was established as an autonomous government body on the 29th April, 1991 in accordance with the Nepal Health Research Council Act, 1991 published in the Nepal Gazette dated April 12, 1991. Prior to this date, health research was one of the activities of the Ministry of Health and then Nepal Medical Research Committee functioned as one of several committees chaired by the Secretary of Ministry of Health.

The main objectives of the NHRC are:

i. to provide information and consultancy services to make the study and research activities relating to health more useful, and
ii. to acquire information concerned with medical researches and on various activities relating to health around the world and to brief Government of Nepal from time to time on these issues.

Nepal Medical Council (NMC)

It was at the time of the First All Nepal Medical Conference in 1963 that the Nepal Medical Association (NMA) requested by way of a resolution to HMG/N that a Nepal Medical Council Act and a Drug Control Act be passed. The Nepal Medical Council Act was ultimately passed in February, 1964. A notification, which appeared in the Nepal Gazette of Bhadra 28th, 2022 BS stated:

Under the powers delegated by Sub clause (3) of Clause (1) of the Nepal Medical Council Act, 2020 BS, His Majesty's Government has enforced the following Clauses 2,3,4,5,6,7,8, 10,11,12, 31,32 and 33.

The Council consisted initially of nine members viz. four elected by the NMA, and three nominated. The President of NMA was ex-officio member and the Director of Health Services was the first Chairman. The same notification went on to state that Mr. Bimal Raj Basnyat, then a section officer in the Health Services was the Registrar of the Council.

The first amendment to the Act was in 2044 BS when the composition was enlarged to 17 members with Dean of the IoM being ex-officio member. It also had more elected members than nominated members with a nominated layperson as a member too. A second amendment to the Act was in 2047 BS. The Nepal Medical Council has passed a Code of Ethics which all doctors who register are required to sign and then subsequently keep as guidance for behaviour in their future practices. Proposal for further amendments to the Act in view of the increased number of medical schools and also because of the starting of postgraduate education is in process. Guidelines regarding the establishment of medical and dental colleges, schemes of internship, have been laid down.

The effectiveness of the Act and its composition was tested recently. An attempt was made to summarily replace Dr. M.R. Baral as Chairman of the NMC. He was given a letter that he had been replaced as of 20th Nov., 1993. He obtained a Stay Order from the Supreme Court and subsequently filed a lawsuit against the then Health Minister and the Health Ministry. Dr. M.R. Baral won his lawsuit on 2nd May, 1995 and was reinstated as Chairman of the NMC.

In celebrating the thirty years of its establishment, the NMC together with the NMA held on 13th & 14th Sept. '95, a two day seminar with the theme "Medical education for the coming century". On the subsequent two days a workshop on "Policy and the Development of Medical Education" was also conducted. A book entitled "Medical Education in Nepal" was brought out on the occasion. A third amendment of the Act increased the membership to twenty-five.

At the present moment both medical and dental personnel have to be registered under the Nepal Medical Council Act. There was an effort to make it into a "Medical & Dental Council Act". This apparently cannot be done and so the possibility of a setting up separate Dental Council has been pending for almost fifteen years.

Nepal Nursing Council (NNC)

An attempt to form the Nepal Nursing Council was made in the sixties but somehow it got delayed. The act was in the final stage of being enacted and with the presumption that this would be done, registration of nurses and subsequent issue of Certificates, with the signatures of the Chairman and the Secretary of the Nepal Nursing Council, was done. A specimen of such a certificate, dated 13th April, 1960 shows the then Director of the Health Services as Chairman of the NNC. Such certificates of registration were issued till 1972 and over this period of thirteen years a total of 147 certificates, so stamped with the NNC logo, were issued. Then catastrophe for the fire at the Singha Durbar destroyed all the papers then. It can be presumed that there was every intention of enacting the Nepal Nursing Council Act, but why the process was delayed for so long is anyone's guess. The Act has now been enacted. It had been an uphill task to try to get legislation passed for the formation of the Nepal Nursing Council.

Nepal Health Professionals Council

This Council was formed following the passage of the Nepal Health

Professionals Council Act in 2053 BS. The act states that the objective is to make provision for providing in an organised and scientific manner, the services of health practitioners other than of those registered with the Nepal Medical Council.

Nepal Pharmacy Council

This council as per the provision of the Nepal Pharmacy Council Act 2057 BS monitors the quality of educational institutions and registers pharmacy manpower. At present it is registering personnel as required by the Nepal Pharmacy Council Act.

To try to regularise the distribution and sales of medicines in Nepal it is bringing out a 'National Good Pharmacy Practice Guidelines'.

PENDING LEGISLATIONS

Voices have been raised for the formation of a Homeopathic Council but apparently there are not a large number of personnel practising in this field. A Medical Education Act is contemplated.

The Drug Act of 1978 is to be updated to bring it up to international standard. The new act is expected to enable the DDA to regulate and monitor the trade more effectively.

References

1. Nayak RK. Development of Health Legislation in Some Countries of WHO SEAR. Regional Health Forum, 2003, 7(2), 20-33.
2. Souvenir of the 15th All Nepal Medical Conference, Biratnagar.
3. Levitt R & Wall A. The Reorganised National Health Service. 3rd Ed. 1984 Croom Helm, London.
4. Whelpton J. Jung Bahadur in Europe. 1983, Sahayogi Press, Kathmandu.
5. Muluki Ain, HMG/N, Ministry of Law, Justice and Parliamentary Affairs.
6. Journal of the Nepal Medical Association 3, No. 3, Medical Legislation Number, 1965.
7. Acts related to Police Administration and some Discourses, Chautari Prakashan, 2053.
8. Nepalese Pharmaceutical Guide, 1993.
9. Drug Bulletin of Nepal 2013. Vol. 24 No. 3, Editorial . DDA, Kathmandu.
10. Nepal Niyam Sangraha, Khanda 8(ka), 2040, Ministry of Law & Justice, GoN, Kathmandu.
11. Nepal Ain Sangraha Khanda 8(kha) 2055, Ministry of Law & Justice, GoN, Kathmandu.

12. Collection of Health Related Acts and Regulations, 3rd Edition, 2060 BS. Makalu Books and Stationers, Kathmandu.
13. Health Services Related Acts and Rules. 2067. Narayan Shrestha. Pairavi Prakashan.
14. Health Related Acts & Rules Collection. 2070 BS KP Bhandari & Rajendra Bhattarai.

INDEX

About the Author

Dr Hemang Dixit is a Nepali born at Kathmandu in 1937. Following schooling at Sherwood College, Nainital and Bishop Cotton School, Shimla in India, he went to the UK to do his A-Levels. Starting his medical education at Charing Cross Hospital Medical School of London University in 1956, he completed the same in 1961 doing both the MBBS (ULond) and LRCP, MRCS of the Conjoint Board. After his year of internship at the Charing X Hospital at Strand, London, he went on to do DTM & H from London School of Hygiene & Tropical Medicine and the DCH from the Conjoint Board, London.

Returning back home to Nepal in 1965 he started work at the Bir Hospital at Kathmandu. Subsequently in 1970, he was posted to the newly established Kanti Children's Hospital. In 1975, after about 11 years he left government service. He was awarded the Coronation Medal in 1973 and later the Suprabal Gorkha Dakshin Bahu in Dec 1993. In Feb 1994, he was awarded a Gold Medal for "Development of Paediatrics in APSSEAR Countries" at the Paediatric Conference held in New Delhi. He was awarded the "Qualified Teacher Awarded" by the Dr. Bala Ram Joshi Gyan Bigyan Rastriya Puraskar Pratisthan in Oct. 2009.

Joining the Institute of Medicine (IoM) of Tribhuvan University as Reader in Child Health in 1977, he subsequently became in 1979, Dean of the IoM for almost four years. After his term as Dean, he later became in 1985 the Professor in Child Health. In that capacity he worked once again on deputation at the Kanti Children's Hospital. Being also director of the Health Learning Materials Centre of the IoM, he has been involved in the production of teaching/learning materials. From February 2001 to June 2013, he worked as Principal of Kathmandu Medical College. He survived an assassination attempt in May 2006. Currently, he is the Head of Department of Medical Education at KMC.

He was a President of both the Nepal Paediatric Society (1986/87) and the Nepal Medical Association (1990/91). He has been in the Nepal Medical Council for number of years, of which eight years, which ended in 1996, was as a Vice Chairman.

His writing career in Nepal started with a two year stint in 1965/66 as Chief Editor of the Journal of the Nepal Medical Association. He has also been Chief Editor of the Journal of the Institute of Medicine from 1983 to 1992. Besides being an occasional contributor to various newspapers of Kathmandu, he has published more than fifteen books. He writes fiction under the pseudonym Mani Dixit. His published works, with the years of their last edition in paracentesis, are:

Non fiction: Nepal's Quest for Health (2014; 4e); Teen Kitap (2012); A Concise History of Medicine (2010); My 2 Innings Memoirs (2009); 50 Years of NMA (2001)

Fiction: Shatru of Kathmandu (2011); Friend's Colony (2005); Come Tomorrow (2000); Nonsense Verses from Nepal (2000); Happenings in Shangrila (2000); The Avenging Ghost (1999); Conflict in the Himalayas (1998); The Red Temple (1997); The Adventures of Chandra and Damaru (1996); Over the Mountains (1995).

He is also a member of LAN-Nepal.